Strategies for Effective

Balanced Literacy

Word Study

Reading

Writing

Author
Mary Jo Fresch, Ph.D.

Foreword
Michael Opitz, Ph.D.

Publishing Credits

Corinne Burton, M.A.Ed., *Publisher*
Kimberly Stockton, M.S.Ed., *Vice President of Education*
Conni Medina, M.A.Ed., *Managing Editor*
Emily Rossman Smith, M.A.Ed., *Content Director*
Sara Johnson, M.S.Ed., *Content Director*
Kristina Mazaika, M.A.Ed., NBCT, *Senior Editor*
Kyleena Harper, *Assistant Editor*
Robin Erickson, *Multimedia Designer*
Kevin Pham, *Production Artist*

Standards

© 2004 Mid-continent Research for Education and Learning (McREL)
© 2006 Teachers of English to Speakers of Other Languages, Inc. (TESOL)
© Copyright 2010. National Governors Association Center for Best Practices and Council of Chief State School Officers. All rights reserved.

Shell Education

A division of Teacher Created Materials
5301 Oceanus Drive
Huntington Beach, CA 92649-1030
www.tcmpub.com/shell-education
ISBN 978-1-4258-1519-6
© 2016 Shell Educational Publishing, Inc.

Table of Contents

Foreword

I have seen balanced literacy defined in numerous ways over the last forty years, but never before have I seen it defined as it is in this book—and the definition is refreshing. Like others who have written about balanced literacy, Fresch points out that careful assessment and selecting oral or written literacy teaching strategies are important attributes. She extends the definition, however, by including the importance of teaching students how to self-direct learning and, just as important, having fun all the while. Consequently, this book is so much more than a book of literacy teaching strategies. It's about the joy of knowing and using literacy to enrich and broaden learners' and teachers' minds and lives. To that end, the book offers several unique characteristics.

- It is grounded on four key principles:
  - Students are unique individuals with varying strengths and needs.
  - Students need to engage with targeted, applicable instruction.
  - Formative assessment enables teachers to plan instruction.
  - Student-centered classrooms are essential.
- All teaching strategies follow a similar format, which includes instructional steps as well as assessment ideas.
- The teaching strategies are designed to enable teachers to pick and choose those that are most appropriate for their students. In this way, the book is more of a resource that serves teachers rather than a book that teachers serve.
- The teaching strategies extend into middle school, enabling students to receive targeted instruction as they advance in their literacy development.

Taken together, this book brings some continuity to teachers from grades K–8. School district staffs that provide this book as a resource for staff development will equip their teachers with a common language and set of strategies to use.

The new millennium has brought forth several initiatives for novice and practicing teachers alike. Sometimes, managing the initiatives can leave little time for teachers to reflect on why they do what they do. With this book, however, teachers are encouraged to do just that because of the way the activities are designed. The result is empowered teachers who make deliberate, knowing decisions about how to best help their students advance in all areas of literacy—not only to lead more literate lives but, as important, more joyful lives, too.

—Michael F. Opitz, Ph.D.
Professor Emeritus, University of Northern Colorado

Acknowledgments

Many thanks go to Andrea Barton, whose classroom is highlighted in the stories shared in this resource. Without hesitation, you shared your classroom and let me be the "fly on the wall." Together we discovered so much, thanks to the balanced literacy setting you provided every single day for every single child. Now you are preparing the next generation of teachers, and they will learn greatly from you.

Thanks to Jerry Zutell. I benefit from your knowledge and insights into spelling, phonics, and vocabulary. Thank you for mentoring me all those years ago!

Thanks to David L. Harrison, my friend, colleague, and poet extraordinaire. You care about children and teachers—and that is a very good thing.

I must acknowledge two other friends and colleagues: Mike Opitz and Mike Ford. You two have inspired teachers everywhere to have enriched and joy-filled classrooms. You lead by example.

Thanks to Sara Johnson, content director for Shell Education. A few years ago I showed you the developmental continuum chart I created and shared with teachers across the country. You saw the chart as a seed. Thanks for the meetings, emails, calls, and encouragement to make it blossom!

Thanks to Kristina Mazaika, my trusty editor on this project. Your experience as a teacher helped as we worked together to define and refine this resource.

Finally, thanks to my family. Angela and Nate, Mike and Lori, thanks for always encouraging and celebrating my professional accomplishments. You are great parents and my five grandchildren inspire me to ask teachers everywhere to focus on what matters, helping children find joy in learning. Biggest thanks go to my husband, Hank. You have, always, been the wind beneath my wings.

To Nicholas, Vincent, Gavin, Christopher, and Avery—who are the joy of my (and Grandpa's) life. May all your teachers not only teach you to read and write, but show you how to love to read and write.

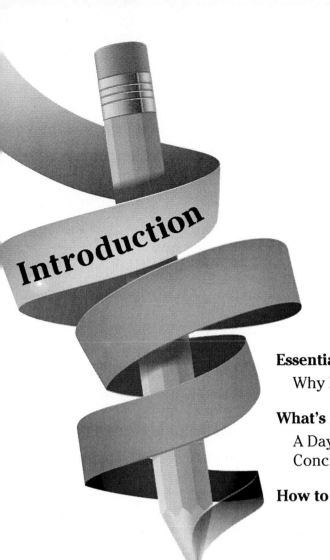

Introduction

Essentials of Literacy Development

One child, one teacher, one book, one pen can change the world.

—Malala Yousafzai

Each and every day a teacher is presented with the opportunity to make a difference in a child's life. For some of our students, coming to school is the best part of the day. What can teachers do to make it memorable, and what can they do to help students move forward with confidence? A teacher's day-to-day life is sometimes like being a juggler keeping all the plates spinning. You've seen it…the juggler starts to spin a plate on a pole, moves to the next plate and pole, then the next, then runs back to the first to keep it going, and so on. Balance is what it is all about—but so are timing, skill, and monitoring of the plates.

Teaching literacy—word study, reading, and writing—is a balancing act. Teachers need to equip themselves with the best strategies for instruction. In word study, teachers must address foundational skills, such as phonics and spelling, as well as vocabulary development across the curriculum. In reading, consider experiences that boost comprehension, using complex texts, requiring close reading, delving into content reading, and examining the author's craft. In writing, have students examine and produce a range of text types and genres. And across all of these areas, plan opportunities for students to develop listening and speaking skills. Keeping students engaged in all of these areas takes careful planning. Some days students need an extra "spin" with reading; other days they seem to be whirling along in writing but need a little "whirl" to try something new or use more complex vocabulary to convey their ideas. How can a teacher accomplish this balance in the classroom? Is it possible to keep the word study, reading, and writing "plates" all spinning at once? Teachers know for students to become literacy proficient they must address all of these areas and recognize that each student has his or her particular strengths and challenges. Selecting the best tools presents the best possibility for engaging learners. Careful assessment, selection of mini-lessons, and teaching students how to self-direct learning are all part of the balancing act.

Why Balanced Literacy?

Ask any adult how to achieve balance in life and you will hear suggestions about work and fun. Balanced literacy is the same. Teachers want students to work but have fun at the same time. Research shows that having students engaged *and* having fun while learning improves memory (Willingham 2008/2009). Choosing how students will work in word study, reading, and writing to advance learning and make them feel successful is the key to a balanced literacy approach. Select a complex text for students to read and consider giving them opportunities to utilize their comprehension skills to engage in a discussion. In that discussion, students may need to return to the text and do another close reading to answer questions or draw conclusions from what was read. Students may also discover unfamiliar vocabulary they must understand to better comprehend what they read. It's important students want to *learn* the skills of literacy so they can *apply* the skills independently.

Becoming a teacher employing a balanced literacy framework is guided by several principles. First, teachers who use the balanced literacy approach believe that the students in their classrooms are individuals with different needs. They understand that some students may need more guidance in learning to read. While students may be able to read, their comprehension may need attention. Reading without drawing meaning is just word calling. The goal is for students to become independent readers, so they can approach any genre with confidence. Other students may need more help in learning to write. Telling students they write for personal reasons as well as for an audience can help students think about how drafts need revision and revisions can become sharable work. And, of course, all students bring different experiences to the classroom. These experiences impact their knowledge of how English works, the depth and breadth of their vocabulary, as well as their ability to translate the many important facets of word knowledge into reading and writing tasks.

Second, teachers who use the balanced literacy approach understand that to improve skills, students must regularly engage in targeted instruction that demands an application of knowledge that challenges but does not frustrate them. Selecting instruction based on an understanding of what students can and cannot do is integral to a balanced literacy approach. One size does not fit all, so planning lessons that are "just right" for our students is pivotal to making them feel successful. Grouping can also guide targeted instruction. Each group of students has reading and writing tasks that build on previous knowledge, while building new connections to literacy skills.

Third, teachers who use balanced literacy see every encounter with a student as an opportunity to inform their instruction through assessment. Formative assessment helps teachers adjust planning based on students' immediate needs. Formative assessment is "an ongoing exchange between a teacher and his or her students designed to help students grow as vigorously as possible and to help teachers contribute to that growth as fully as possible… [it] is—or should be—the bridge or causeway between today's lesson and tomorrow's" (Tomlinson 2014, 11).

These classroom based assessments, created by classroom teachers, not only help guide instruction but research indicates that they also positively influence student performance and motivation (Wiliam and Thompson 2007). Knowing when a student needs more or less challenge, a different guided reading group, or a conference about his or her writing will provide instruction that impacts learning.

Finally, a balanced literacy approach promotes a student-centered classroom. Students are engaged in work that asks them to apply their literacy skills in authentic and measurable ways. Teachers recognize that students need to find joy in their learning as well as feel motivated to participate (Fresch and Harkins 2014). When students feel success, they want to try again and again. That's what promotes learning in a balanced literacy classroom!

What's Ahead: Effective Balanced Literacy

This resource provides a comprehensive approach to teaching the triangle of literacy—word study, reading, and writing—for kindergarten through grade 8. Under each of these areas are the many aspects of being a user of language, a reader, and a writer.

Balanced literacy takes into account both written and oral skills. The explicit instruction of these areas provides models for our students and gives them clear understandings for new, independent learning. Before any instruction begins, assessments must drive our decision-making. Instruction takes place in whole groups, small groups, and in one-on-one encounters. The three sections of this book provide guidance in selecting mini-lessons to address the needs of all students.

Section 1 focuses on word study. *Phonics instruction* gives students a system for attacking new words. The study of letter/sound correspondences provides independence in decoding (for reading) and encoding (for writing) new words. Young students begin with phonological awareness where their initial understanding is situated in phonemic awareness. Once students can hear the phonemes (or sounds) of language, they can begin to connect them to the letter or letter combinations that represent a sound or group of sounds. *Word analysis* helps students in reading and writing, providing balance to their need for identifying new words. Within word study, we also examine *spelling instruction*. How can teachers challenge but not frustrate students while focusing on the spelling patterns of language? As students progress, teachers must address the need to develop their *vocabularies*. Research suggests that students need to learn about 20 new words each day (Graves 2006). That means every opportunity must be taken to point out and have students use and understand new words, as well as how students can work in denotation and connotation during guided reading, content reading, or wherever else students are exploring language with new words.

Section 2 focuses on reading. Consider how to plan and implement *guided reading*. After assessing students, group them for instruction in ways that take advantage of their developing independent skills, without pushing them into frustration. This book examines *modeled and shared reading*. These strategies help develop students' abilities to make predictions while reading, keeping them engaged and improving comprehension. This approach makes the reading process explicit—how does a reader pay attention to print, and how do students check themselves for understanding? It's important to help students be aware of their thinking processes when they read, thus making this somewhat "invisible" step in reading more visible to them (McKeown and Gentilucci 2007). Finally, this book looks at how teachers guide students to select appropriate texts for instructional and independent reading. How do "leveled" textlists assist teachers? Delve into *independent reading* strategies through self-selected reading. During this independent reading, students practice their developing skills in approachable, on-level texts.

Section 3 focuses on writing. *Modeled and shared writing* shape various ways for students to approach writing across the curriculum and across genres. This section moves students into independence during Writer's Workshop through conferencing and mini-lessons, to help students master their skills (Dorn and Soffos 2001). Finding ways to publish student work is often a motivator for reluctant writers. There are many easy, cost-effective ways to bring students' work to final, sharable versions that instill pride in the students. Finally, consider the use of journals as a self-selected writing form.

A Look into the Classroom

K-2

A Day in a Balanced Literacy Classroom

So just how do teachers "keep the plates spinning" in a balanced literacy classroom? Let's take a quick peek at what's in store in this resource by visiting the three grade-level bands used throughout this book: kindergarten through grade 2, grade 3 through grade 5, and grade 6 through grade 8. While these are brief overviews, you will see how word study, reading, and writing are planned to support each other and maximize students' experiences.

Kindergarten through Grade 2

In kindergarten through grade 2 classrooms, teachers are particularly focused on the relationship between formative assessment and instruction. Knowing where students' skills need a "spin" or where they soar is important for challenging but not frustrating young learners. A typical day begins with a *morning meeting* where students gather on a large rug, in chairs grouped together, or on individual carpet squares. Here the community of learners meets to set the day's agenda, talk about classroom goals (and maybe some quick reminders about rules), share any special news, and celebrate class and/or student accomplishments. The teacher uses five or ten minutes to provide an overview of the day's schedule and asks students to think about their personal goals for the day, such as wanting to work on matching the sounds they hear to the print they write. While the teacher has a clear plan for teaching each area of literacy, giving students opportunities to personally connect and take on responsibility for their own learning is important.

Students remain in this morning meeting spot, and the teacher directs their attention to the content of recent word study lessons, such as common features from a word list of long *a* words or sorting hard and soft *g* words. The teacher reminds students to use what they know about word study when they read and write that day, connecting this knowledge to other areas of literacy.

While students are still together, the teacher begins *modeled and shared reading*. The teacher selects a grade-level content appropriate text for this group read-aloud experience that meets a particular purpose, such as a fun read to engage listeners and scaffold their learning; a content text that connects to lessons later in the day; or a text to initiate an important conversation, such as showing kindness. During the modeled reading, the teacher often thinks aloud with comments, such as "Based on this picture, I infer" to let students hear how they should be engaged in reading. During shared reading, the teacher asks students to join in, or individuals may read particular lines of the text. The same text may be read twice for these purposes or the teacher may model reading part of the text aloud

A Look into the Classroom

K-2

and then move into a shared reading. Depending on the difficulty of the text's content or the teacher's intent to revisit the text, this modeled and shared reading takes about 15 to 20 minutes.

A *modeled or shared writing* experience connected to the text typically follows. Perhaps students write a few summary sentences about the content, emphasizing letter/sound connections under the teacher's guidance. If it is a content text, the teacher highlights the important vocabulary in the text. The students assist in writing by interactively writing the sentences, or teachers and students "share the pen" (Pinnell and McCarrier 1994). The level of modeled and shared writing is dependent on the class needs. This takes another 10 minutes.

Next, students move into *guided reading*. The teacher has a clear plan for each guided reading group, depending on their needs and skills. Some groups need skills to be retaught or strengthened. Other groups have lessons that extend and challenge their developing skills. One by one the groups are called to gather where the teacher can guide their reading. The teacher selects appropriate instructional-level texts for each group. While waiting for their group to meet with the teacher, students work in centers or workstations and/or are given individual work, such as *word study* activities. Novice word learners may be matching pictures with letter sounds, while others may be working to sort words according to word families. Students may also have content vocabulary to examine. For example, a previous day's lesson on insects may be revisited by asking students to use a provided list to label an ant's body parts on a graphic. Alternately, students may sit in a special area and set a timer to work for five minutes writing in their journals. They may have a listening station to move to when paper and pencil work is complete. In many classrooms, these activities are set up as literacy centers, so students can move around to complete the agenda presented during the morning meeting. When the work is completed, visiting the library corner or rereading the shared reading text is encouraged. At this level, guided reading groups take about 15 minutes per group.

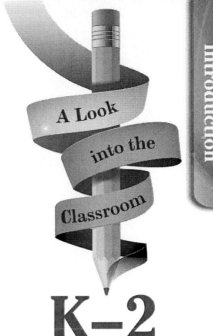

> ***Independent reading** time is used in one of two ways:*
>
> - *an activity option while other guided reading groups meet*
>
> - *a whole-class activity later in the day*
>
> *Either way, each student spends roughly 10 to 15 minutes independently reading self-selected texts. Self-selected texts are texts students choose themselves and can read unassisted. The teacher can utilize the time to hear individual students read aloud from their choices, help students self-select texts, or participate in self-selected reading.*

Following guided reading, students engage in whole-group *word study*. This is a specific lesson the teacher has chosen, which focuses on phonics and spelling. About 10 minutes are spent exploring particular patterns in English, playing with poetry that provides experience in hearing rhymes (Fresch and Harrison 2013), or looking at particular vocabulary, such as high-frequency or content words.

Then, students get their Writer's Workshop folders. The teacher refers back to the shared or modeled writing completed together earlier to remind students of expectations for writing, such as sounding out as best they can and using proper capitals and ending punctuation; or the teacher shares a brief mini-lesson that focuses on a specific aspect of writing, such as adding details or using correct ending punctuation. The teacher takes a quick status of the class to see who needs help developing a story line, finding facts to use for a nonfiction piece, or illustrating a final version. Students move to their individual desks or group tables and begin writing. The teacher then moves around, conferencing as needed, meeting with each student at least once a week. About 30 minutes are spent on Writer's Workshop where each student completes some part of a self-selected written piece. At the end of Writer's Workshop, students gather together, and those who have completed texts can share them with the class.

Grade 3 through Grade 5

In grade 3 through grade 5 classrooms, the teacher's focus is to help students shift from "learning to read" to "reading to learn." That is, teachers want students to *use* the literacy skills learned in the first years of school. The relationship between assessment and instruction is still important. Many students in this grade span still need support in developing skills to keep up with their peers who are ready to tackle more complex texts, particularly in the content areas. A typical day begins with a *morning meeting* where students gather on a large rug, in chairs grouped together, or sit on individual

A Look into the Classroom 3–5

carpet squares. Here, a community of learners meets to set the day's agenda, talk about classroom and individual goals, and share any important news. The teacher uses about 10 minutes to provide the overview of the day's schedule and asks students to think about their day's personal goals in relation to that day's agenda. Do they need to work on utilizing more complex vocabulary in their writing, such as "exclaimed" instead of "said"? Do they have a favorite text they want to do something special with, such as illustrate a new text jacket or make an advertisement to entice other students to read the text? Mapping out the day helps students begin to mentally engage in the work ahead. While the teacher has a clear plan for teaching each area of literacy, giving students opportunities to personally connect and assume responsibility for their own learning is important.

Students remain in this morning meeting spot, and the teacher directs their attention to the content of recent word study lessons, such as doubling a consonant, dropping the *e* before adding a suffix, or reviewing and adding to a content words list. The teacher reminds students to use what they know about word study when they read and write that day, connecting this knowledge to other areas of literacy.

While students are still together, the teacher begins *modeled and shared reading*. The teacher selects an age-appropriate picture or chapter book to read aloud with a particular purpose in mind. It can be a fun read that engages listeners and scaffolds their learning; a content text that connects to studies later in the day, such as a social studies or science topic; a book that initiates an important conversation, such as civil rights; or a book that students individually respond to during work time. Depending on the difficulty of the text's content or the teacher's intent to revisit the text, such as during science for content reading, this shared reading takes about 20 minutes.

A *modeled or shared writing* experience connected to the text typically follows. Perhaps students assist the teacher in writing an outline summary of the content. If it is a content text, the important vocabulary in the text is highlighted and should take another 10 minutes.

Next, students move into *guided reading* groups while completing individual work at their personal workspaces when not with the teacher. The teacher has a clear plan for each guided reading group, depending on students' needs and skills. Some groups need key skills to be retaught or strengthened. Other groups have lessons that extend and challenge their developing skills. One by one the groups are called to gather where the teacher can guide their reading. The teacher selects appropriate instructional-level texts for each group. In the upper elementary grades, students may be self-directing the discussion while the teacher observes and takes notes of individual needs and accomplishments. While waiting for their groups to meet with the teacher, students are given various tasks to complete, such as *word study* activities. Students may have content vocabulary to examine that is connected to the shared reading. They may also have spelling work, such as word sorts or games with classmates. Additionally, students may be asked to sit in a special area to set a timer and work for 10 minutes writing in their journals. They may have a listening station to move to when independent work is complete. In many grade 3 through grade 5 classrooms, these types of activities are set up as literacy centers, so students can move around to complete the agenda presented during the morning meeting. When the work is completed, visiting the library corner or rereading the shared reading text is encouraged. At this level, guided reading groups may take about 20 minutes per group.

> *Independent reading* time is used in one of two ways:
>
> - *an activity option while other guided reading groups meet*
>
> - *whole-class activity later in the day*
>
> *Either way, each student should spend 15 to 20 minutes reading self-selected texts. Self-selected texts are texts students can read independently, so the teacher can utilize this time to hear individual students read aloud from their choices or work with students needing more assistance, such as below-level students or English language learners.*

Following guided reading, students engage in whole-group *word study*. These are specific lessons the teacher has chosen to focus on related to phonics, spelling, and/or vocabulary. About 10 minutes are spent exploring particular patterns in English, hunting for words that connect to the pattern studied for the week, or participating in a discussion about words and their origins.

Then, students get their Writer's Workshop folders. The teacher refers back to the shared writing done earlier to remind students of the expectations for writing; or the teacher presents a short mini-lesson that focuses on a specific aspect of writing, such as the use of figurative language. The teacher takes a quick status of the class to see who needs help developing a story line, finding facts to use for a nonfiction piece, or producing a final version. Students move to their personal spaces and begin writing. The teacher moves around, conferencing as needed. Each student meets with the teacher at least once a week. About 30 minutes are spent on Writer's Workshop, and each student completes some part of a self-selected written piece. At the end of Writer's Workshop, students gather together, and those who have completed pieces can share them with the class.

A Look into the Classroom

6–8

Grade 6 through Grade 8

Many grade 6 through grade 8 classrooms are departmentalized by content area. Therefore, the language arts teacher is primarily responsible for literacy instruction. However, teachers know that there is a need for a shared responsibility for literary development by all teachers regardless of their content area. In these classes, teachers continue to help students hone their word study, reading, and writing skills. However, many schools work in teams. It is ideal for the language arts teacher to work together to map out units of study with the content teachers, creating integrated literacy work for students. For example, a grade 6 science teacher may be teaching about rocks, minerals, and soil, so the language arts teacher might have students read additional informational texts, writing reports utilizing research notes taken in science, and examining content or domain-specific vocabulary. Students may be preparing oral presentations, listening to grade-appropriate picture or chapter books related to the content, and creating graphic representations of their learning. While a range of organizational patterns is evident in middle schools, a typical day for the language arts teacher includes a large block of time, such as 60 to 90 minutes.

The class begins with the teacher giving a quick overview of the upcoming activities. Just as with younger students, middle schoolers need to take responsibility for their own learning and think about their personal goals. The teacher directs their attention to the content of recent *word study* lessons, such as examining Greek and Latin roots or reviewing and adding to a content words list. The teacher reminds students to use this word study analysis when they read and write that day, connecting this knowledge to other areas of literacy. Next, the teacher provides a five to ten minute mini-lesson that ties vocabulary learning to reading and writing. This may then segue into a quick lesson that addresses a reading skill. The students then move into their *guided reading* groups, which often function more as literature circles with reading and discussing. (Note: Some schools have transitioned to the term inquiry circles.) Sometimes the teacher has more control and runs a small or whole-class reading group. Once a week, the teacher meets with each group to discuss its reading, view the group notes, do a comprehension check, and discuss reading goals. This typically spans 20 minutes. The teacher can also use some of this time to meet individually with students still needing skill strengthening.

The teacher then does a *shared reading*. At this level, there is a very specific purpose to the text chosen. The text may connect to the content reading and writing planned for later in the class; it may model a skill in writing the teacher wants to teach; it may facilitate a group lesson on citing evidence through direct or inferential claims;

or it may be used for a group lesson on outlining, close reading, examining complex text, or extracting important vocabulary. This takes about 10 minutes and moves directly into *modeled and shared writing* where the teacher has the students contribute to a written piece they can later use as a guide for their own writing. This modeled and shared writing allows for a multitude of mini-lessons that target specific class needs and standards, lasting around 10 minutes. Students need mini-lessons in many areas, often organized by the three main writing genres of argument, informative/explanatory, and narrative. Argument writing mini-lessons most often focus on how to support claims made with reasoning and evidence, as well as at a higher level, using sources in research of the writing topic. Informative/explanatory writing mini-lessons most often focus on how to organize and develop topics with examples, facts, and details. For narrative texts, students often need guidance on sophisticated transition strategies, how to properly establish context, and sequencing events to orient the reader. About 25 minutes are spent engaged in modeled and shared writing.

Writer's Workshop begins where students may work on writing connected to their content studies, the modeled writing from that day, or their own pieces. The decision for the focus of the workshop changes depending on the instructional and team planning for integrating writing into the curriculum. This workshop time takes about 20 minutes. During this time, the teacher holds individual writing conferences to make notes of needed mini-lessons and assess development.

If any time remains, students can do *self-selected reading*. The teacher can spend some time, on occasion, introducing new texts of a certain genre, author, or topic that is interesting to the age group to students. The teacher has individual conferences with students about the reading they are doing and the appropriateness of their text selections. Additionally, the teacher administers an individual comprehension check or other skill-related assessments.

Conclusion

The remaining sections of this resource are organized into the triangle of literacy—word study, reading, and writing. In each section you will find a wide range of skills addressed. The intent is to think of how to plan across all three areas to bring balance to the work students do. At one time, teachers considered these areas as separate—once finished with reading, teachers moved to writing and so on. But the days of the literacy "silos" are over. It's time to help students see the interrelatedness of these skills. So, roll up those sleeves and start spinning!

How to Use This Book

Strategies for Effective Balanced Literacy is a resource designed to help educators create a comprehensive balanced literacy program or support an existing one. This book is divided into three sections, one for each main component of balanced literacy—word study, reading, and writing. Each section begins with a **classroom vignette** to set the stage. The authentic student/teacher experience is highlighted, helping educators visualize the component covered in that section.

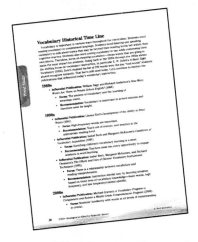

Background information for each component follows each vignette, providing educators with the **research and best practices** they need to feel confident that they are providing their students with the best instruction possible.

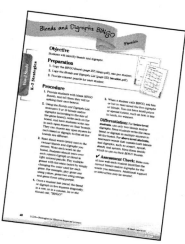

Mini-lessons for each component are provided in each grade-level band (K–2, 3–5, and 6–8) with all student reproducibles for the mini-lessons provided in the appendices, as well as in digital form. A Standards correlation chart can be found in the Digital Resources. Additional mini-lessons can also be found in the Digital Resources.

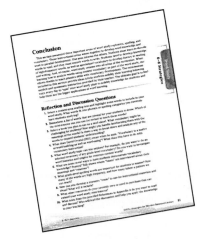

Reflection and discussion questions are offered at the end of each section as self-reflection, collaboration, or professional development tools.

The student reproducibles and extra lessons in this book are available as Adobe® PDFs online. A complete list of the available documents is provided on pages 340–343. Additionally, each mini-lesson includes the file names of the documents needed for the activity. To access the digital resources, go to this website: http://www.tcmpub.com/download-files. Enter this code: **49089964**. Follow the on-screen directions.

ACCESS CODE

49089964

Word Study

Introduction

By words the mind is winged.

—Aristophanes

This section focuses on word study. Word study—phonics, spelling, and vocabulary—instruction provides tools for students to analyze words when reading and writing. Phonics instruction gives students a system for attacking new words. The study of letter/sound correspondences provides independence in decoding (reading) and encoding (writing) new words. Young students begin their initial understanding with phonemic awareness. Once students hear the phonemes (sounds) of our language, they begin connecting the sounds to the letters or letter combinations moving them from phonemic awareness to phonics.

Within word study, we also examine spelling instruction. Effective spelling instruction provides active ways to move learning beyond memorization to develop understanding of the patterns of English words. Memorizing word lists has little carryover to independent written work (Bear and Templeton 1998).

As students progress, address the need to develop their vocabularies. Research suggests that students need to learn about 20 new words per day, which means taking every opportunity to point out and have students use new words during any time they are exploring print. Teachers must also explicitly teach vocabulary. There are a good number of high-frequency words students must learn for reading and writing fluency. It's important to teach the vocabulary that will provide powerful reading comprehension supports. Vocabulary instruction highlights high-frequency words and utilizes robust techniques to expand the depth of knowledge of words across the curriculum. Phonics, spelling, and vocabulary drive word analysis. As students approach an unknown word, analysis enables them to use what they have learned to help them decode or encode. This encourages students to reflect on what they know. *Have I seen this word in print before? What sounds do I hear, and what patterns represent those sounds? What patterns do I see, and what sounds do they make? What larger chunks, such as affixes (prefixes and/or suffixes) or bases, can I take apart and put together to identify or write a word? What other similar words do I know that can help me?*

Prefixes, bases, and suffixes are roots. Each of these roots has a meaning. When joined together, these roots create new words. A word's meaning can be unlocked throuh recognition of its roots (Rasinski et al. 2008).

Teachers must keep all these related plates spinning, helping students see connections among them. For example, a spin on the spelling plate can significantly improve vocabulary when students understand that words related in spelling are often related in meaning. For example, *visual, visor,* and *televise,* which all contain *vis,* meaning to see. This informs us as we spell new words containing *vis.* The continued spin of these three areas of word study undeniably connects to reading and writing, so keeping them all in motion provides important learning opportunities for our students.

Meet Cameron

Mrs. Barton is sitting at the small table at the back of her first-grade classroom. It is week six of the new school year, and Cameron is reading aloud from *Rosie's Walk* (Hutchins 1977). He is struggling with sounding out new words. He carefully draws his finger across the word *yard*, trying to sound out each letter. Earlier, during Writer's Workshop, Cameron had spent considerable time struggling to sound out and write the same word. Suddenly, finger pointing to the word, he looks up with a huge smile. "Hey, that's *yard*!" he exclaims. "I wrote that in my football story." What an "aha" moment for Cameron!

Cameron exemplifies a student bridging multiple areas of sound/letter relationships. His attempts allowed Mrs. Barton to assess his word-attack skills in two settings—writing and reading. When writing he sounded out *yard* several times, hoping to connect the phonemes he heard with graphemes that represent those sounds. When reading, he sounded out and recognized the graphemes and connected the letter/sound combinations until they "clicked" with a word he knew. His spelling attempts during Writer's Workshop required him to think about the sounds of the English language and how those sounds might be represented in print. He connected his earlier writing to his ongoing reading.

A few days earlier, when Cameron struggled with his spelling in the football story, he sought help from Mrs. Barton. She encouraged him to write what he could hear and promised she would help him after that. She wanted Cameron to do the work of listening across the word and then considering what letters or letter combinations would make the sounds. Encouraging students to "do the work" is a common approach in today's classrooms. Asking them to *apply* what they know to what they are trying to decode and/or encode helps show what skills they have and how their teachers might guide their learning.

Word Study Instruction

Phonics Historical Time Line

A brief look at the history of phonics instruction in the United States shows where the US has been as well as where the country is headed. Over time, the US has swung away from and then back to phonics instruction. Research now shows the value in helping students to develop and use knowledge about how the English language works. While this country's phonics instruction history goes back to the early colonial period, the more familiar approaches that linger in current teaching philosophies are from the last century. William S. Gray (1919) was most influential at the beginning of the 20th century with the Look-and-Say Method (repetitive use of high-frequency vocabulary) that inspired his reading series *Fun with Dick and Jane* (Gray and Arbuthnot 1946). He used high-frequency words (*see, look, go*) that provided less strict attention to phonics, offered controlled vocabulary, and encouraged students to answer comprehension questions. Let's take a quick trip from mid-century to today.

1950s

- **Influential Publication:** Rudolph Flesch's *Why Johnny Can't Read and What You Can Do About It* (1955)

  - **Approach:** Criticism of the Look-and-Say Method

  - **Instructional Materials:** Continued use of *Dick and Jane* (and similar Look-and-Say Method basal readers despite Flesch's publication)

  - **Focus:** Flesch challenged the Whole Word method, increasing the pressure to return to phonics instruction. Parent involvement in how their children were taught to read began.

1960s

- **Influential Publication:** Jeanne Chall's *Learning to Read: The Great Debate* (1967)

  - **Approach:** Return to explicit teaching of phonics

  - **Instructional Materials:** Basals and worksheets with repetitive practice

  - **Focus:** Chall's analysis of studies showed that teaching phonics was more effective than Whole Word, and the use of the Whole Word method was gradually discontinued.

1970s

- **Influential Publication:** Continued influence of Chall's *Learning to Read: The Great Debate*

  - **Approach:** Synthetic Phonics

  - **Instructional Materials:** Stories crafted to specifically teach particular sound patterns

  - **Focus:** Patterned word units (*Dan, can, man, fan*) were favored that implemented a sequenced instruction of phonic elements.

1980s

- **Influential Publication:** Kenneth and Yetta Goodman's *Learning to Read is Natural* (1979)
  - **Approach:** Whole language
  - **Instructional Materials:** Children's literature
  - **Focus:** A natural development of skills through reading real texts was used, and the contextualization of literacy skills in books and self-created writing were employed.

1990s

- **Influential Publication:** Marilyn Adams's *Beginning to Read—Thinking and Learning About Print* (1990)
  - **Approach:** Whole language with some instruction shifting to focused phonics
  - **Instructional Materials:** Whole language using children's literature; emergence of phonics-focused materials, such as *Hooked on Phonics*®
  - **Focus:** Known as "The Reading Wars." Publications like *A Nation At Risk* (1983) sparked debate as to whether the decline in the National Assessment of Educational Progress was due to the lack of phonics instruction. The period raised awareness of the need for systematic instruction of phonics, regardless of instructional materials used.

2000s

- **Influential Publication:** *Report of the National Reading Panel* (2000)
  - **Approach**: Recognition by educators of the need for instruction within a framework that includes phonemic awareness, phonics, fluency, vocabulary, and comprehension.
  - **Instructional Materials**: Children's literature supported by systematic phonics instruction
  - **Focus**: Emphasis targeted the utility of phonics to assist a reader and writer. Student-centered instruction was the focus of the time, using a variety of texts to engage students in learning to map the sounds of the language onto the alphabet.

Word Study

Best Practices in Phonics Instruction

Phonics instruction gives students a system for examining new words. The study of letter/sound correspondences provides independence in decoding and encoding new words. Once students can hear the phonemes (sounds) of a language, they can begin to connect them to the graphemes (letters) that represent the sounds.

Phonics is the first step in word analysis, the process that helps students take apart or examine the letter representation of sounds in words. Students begin learning letter/sound relationships by mapping sounds onto letters. They must consider that more than one letter can make the same sound (*c* or *k* can sound like /k/) and that letters can make more than one sound (*g* can sound like /j/ or /g/). Vowels present challenges to students as those five letters (*a, e, i, o, u*) make long sounds, short sounds, and are influenced by the schwa position, *r* controlled, and diphthongs. Of course, *y* can act like a vowel (*cry*) or a consonant (*yellow*). Students begin to understand that letters can combine to make sounds (*sh, th*) and that some combinations include silent letters (*kn, wr*). Learning other combinations, such as blends (*bl, gr, tr*) and digraphs (*wh, ph, ch*), helps students move across words in larger "chunks" rather than letter by letter. Examinations of larger units, such as word families (*-at, -ug, -op*), helps students manipulate letter/sound relationships. Students move into breaking words into morphemes (*smallest units of meaning*). When analyzing a word for morphemes, students identify affixes (*prefixes, such as* re-, un-, anti-, com-, sub-; *and suffixes, such as* -ed, -ing, -ment, -ness, -able) and bases, such as *cred, vis, port*, and *phon*. Therefore, best practices in phonics instruction include the use of the following:

> ***Phonemes*** *are the smallest sounds an individual letter or combination of letters makes.* ***Graphemes*** *are the letters that comprise a writing system.*

- assessments of student knowledge to guide instructional planning
- engaging, age-appropriate strategies for active participation in learning
- differentiated instruction to meet the needs of all learners
- carefully sequenced lessons to build phonics skills over time

Spelling Historical Time Line

This brief overview presents pivotal changes in our understanding about spelling instruction and learning. Spelling instruction in the United States began as a shipment of books to the colonies from England, where students first learned the alphabet, combinations of letters (and their sounds) and *then* learned how to read 180 syllables (Hodges 1977). Time to zoom ahead and review some pivotal influences on spelling instruction since then.

1920s

- **Influential Publication**: Ernest Horn's *A Basic Writing Vocabulary, 10,000 Words Most Commonly Used in Writing* (1926)
  - **Focus**: He designed the "say-cover-write-check" system.
  - **Recommendation**: He advocated that students memorize the list of 10,000 words.

1960s

- **Influential Publications**: Noam Chomsky and Morri Halle's *The Sound of English* (1968) and Richard Venezky's *The Structure of English Orthography* (1970)
  - **Focus**: The English language is not as irregular as previously thought, and memorizing a set of words per week does not provide spelling power.
  - **Recommendation**: Phoneme-grapheme (sound-letter) correspondence using a test-study-test method—still the most common basal spelling method today.

1970s

- **Influential Publication**: Charles Read's *Pre-School Children's Knowledge of English Phonology* (1971)
  - **Focus**: Spelling errors children make are not random. Learning is not passive and is based on a predictable, developmental path.
  - **Recommendation**: Spelling words should be selected to allow students to construct knowledge based on their current understandings.

1980s

- **Influential Publication**: Edmund Henderson's *Learning to Read and Spell: The Child's Knowledge of Words* (1981)
  - **Focus**: Extended Read's work by identifying developmental stages through grade 8.
  - **Recommendation**: Students need systematic instruction to build knowledge of English. Rooting instruction in the developmental needs of the students as seen in their writing, attempts to help students construct knowledge about how the English language "works."

Best Practices in Spelling Instruction

Teachers in balanced literacy classrooms must directly and systematically address students' spelling needs through practice and thoughtful selection of word lists. How do teachers select spelling words? First, they select words students can read. If the word is unknown, the student can only memorize the letter sequence and not master the word for independent recall. Second, they select words that are beneficial. Choosing words because they have immediate content use, such as *pioneer*, but little use in daily writing, does not build students' knowledge network about words. Instead, students should spend time learning spelling words that advance their knowledge of English. ("If I know *identify,* I know *identified, identifies, identifier,* and *identification!*") Third, teachers assess independent writing strategies to determine students' approaches and understandings. This is where balanced literacy shines. By asking students to write, teachers ascertain what students know, what students are working to understand, and what is beyond students' reaches in spelling. They also see what is available to students as readers through viewing their spelling strategies. Now, that's spinning a plate or two!

Vocabulary Historical Time Line

Vocabulary is important in various ways throughout the curriculum. Students need *reading vocabulary* to comprehend language. Students need *listening and speaking vocabulary* to talk about topics that may be beyond their reading levels but within their cognitive reaches. Students also need *writing vocabulary* to use while composing their own pieces. Therefore, focus on *meaning vocabulary*—those words that are going to make the most impact for students. Going back to the 1920s through the 1950s shows the shifting focus on vocabulary instruction, in particular E. W. Dolch's *A Basic Sight Vocabulary* (1936). Dolch claimed his list of 220 words were the key "tool words" students should recognize instantly. That list is still used today. Let's continue to explore the publications that influenced today's vocabulary instruction.

1980s

- **Influential Publication:** William Nagy and Richard Anderson's *How Many Words Are There in Printed School English?* (1984)
  - **Focus:** The amount of vocabulary and the learning of meanings count.
  - **Recommendation:** Vocabulary is important to school success and therefore must be taught.

1990s

- **Influential Publication:** Linnea Ehri's *Development of the Ability to Read Words* (1991)
  - **Focus:** High-frequency words are important.
  - **Recommendation:** Teach out of context, and practice at the appropriate reading level.
- **Influential Publication:** Isabel Beck and Margaret McKeown's *Conditions of Vocabulary Acquisition* (1991)
  - **Focus:** Enriching children's vocabulary learning is a must.
  - **Recommendation:** Teachers must use every opportunity to engage students in word learning.
- **Influential Publication:** Isabel Beck, Margaret McKeown, and Richard Omanson's *The Effects and Uses of Diverse Vocabulary Instructional Techniques* (1991)
  - **Focus:** There is a relationship between vocabulary and reading comprehension.
  - **Recommendation:** Instruction should vary by learning situation based on three tiers of vocabulary knowledge—basic words, high frequency, and low frequency/context specific.

2000s

- **Influential Publication:** Michael Graves's *A Vocabulary Program to Complement and Bolster a Middle-Grade Comprehension Program* (2000)
  - **Focus:** Students' familiarity with words at all levels of understanding is crucial.

- **Recommendation:** Students must not just be introduced to vocabulary, but they must know the meanings, examine the relationships between words and roots, learn multiple meanings, explore content words and other complexities, and develop word consciousness.

- **Influential Publication:** *Report of the National Reading Panel* (2000)
  - **Focus:** Research studies that support best practices are to be utilized.
  - **Recommendation:** Direct instruction in rich contexts, repetition, and multiple exposures to words likely to appear across a variety of contexts and active engagement of the learner are to be employed.

- **Influential Publication:** Isabel Beck, Margaret McKeown, and Linda Kucan's *Bringing Words to Life: Robust Vocabulary Instruction* (2003)
  - **Focus:** Provide ways of choosing words and strategies for teaching vocabulary.

- **Recommendation:** Implement a three-tier framework for approaching vocabulary instruction, including everyday words usually not "taught" in school, academic words students need to know, and specialized words related to specific content studies and other uncommon words.

- **Influential Publication:** Michael Coyne et al.'s *Teaching Vocabulary During Shared Storybook Readings: An Examination of Differential Effects* (2004).
  - **Focus:** Explicit vocabulary instruction is the most effective.
  - **Recommendation:** Early intervention with explicit vocabulary instruction shows the greatest gains in word knowledge.

- **Influential Publication:** Michael Graves's *The Vocabulary Book: Learning and Instruction* (2006)
  - **Focus:** Effective instruction is addressed.
  - **Recommendation:** Four essential components must be included in vocabulary instruction—encourage wide reading, explicitly teach individual words, teach word strategies, and foster word consciousness.

2010s

- **Influential Publication:** Andrew Biemiller's *Size and Sequence in Vocabulary Development* (2010)
  - **Focus:** Studies show the sequence of vocabulary acquisition is similar across different populations, such as English language learners, above-level learners, and the "normative-English speaking" (241).
  - **Recommendation:** Word acquisition can be accelerated for those students who lag if gaps in vocabulary are targeted. Use of grade-level vocabulary lists provides guidance in both accelerating and extending students' word knowledge.

Best Practices in Vocabulary Instruction

While the home environment is important to the beginning of vocabulary development, teachers must plan ways to engage students in reading, writing, listening, and speaking that will increase their knowledge of words. Hart and Risley's research (1995) indicates that students who come to school with smaller vocabularies are at risk for learning gaps. They discovered that these at-risk students heard fewer words at home than many preschool peers. Swanborn and de Glopper (1999) found that without instruction, students will "learn [only] about 15 percent of the unknown words they encounter" (261). At the same time, remember that students need to be learning 20 new words each day (Graves 2006).

Time and again, research has found that teachers need to *explicitly* discuss words and their meanings, use them in teaching, and encourage students to explore them further in their reading and writing. Continuing to find ways to scaffold new words onto known vocabulary increases the success of retention. Like spelling, the use of memorized word lists has little long-term use. Mini-lessons that show students how to deeply analyze words for their meaning and construction will provide memorable experiences and learning.

*Graves (2006) analyzed a large number of research studies. He observed the following **benchmarks regarding vocabulary learning**:*

- *School-aged children learn roughly 3,000 words each year.*

- *The difference between linguistically advantaged students and linguistically disadvantaged students' vocabularies is approximately 50 percent.*

- *By the time students graduate from high school, they need a reading vocabulary of at least 50,000 words.*

One way to pick appropriate vocabulary words is to take opportunities to point out and review high-frequency words for the grade level. Another way is to "deconstruct" grade-level words—what is the base, prefix, and/or suffix as well as what other words do we know like these?—choosing content vocabulary that students will use immediately and in the coming years. Words that students will use across the years have the most benefit to long-term learning. Teachers should immerse students in words every chance they get. Voicing interest in a word may spark attention in students. Multiple exposures and different approaches—visual, auditory, tactile—will also help students learn and retain new words.

Setting Up the Word Study Classroom

While thinking about word study in the balanced literacy classroom, consider how to organize students in phonics, spelling, and vocabulary instruction. Planning engaging lessons helps students solidify and develop new understanding about how English works. Also, students need to learn how to independently use classroom resources for self-selected reading and writing. Additionally, classrooms need to be organized around a variety of learners. Teachers need resources and planning to meet the needs of below-level learners, on-level learners, above-level learners, and English language learners. Finally, plans and resources should show that learning is fun. Joyful engagement "capitalizes on what we know about how to best motivate students" (Fresch 2014, 6). The strategies presented here within the mini-lessons have been purposefully selected to engage and motivate *all* students. While the mini-lessons are grouped in grade-level bands (K–2, 3–5, 6–8), looking back or looking ahead will help to adjust instruction to meet the needs of both below-level and advanced learners, as well as English language learners.

Balanced literacy creates well-rounded readers and writers by utilizing best practices in the areas below as well as by providing opportunities for students to read quality texts at instructional and independent levels.

- *Word Study (phonics, spelling, and vocabulary)*
- *Reading (modeled, shared, guided, and independent)*
- *Writing (modeled, shared, guided, and independent)*
- *Content-Area Literacy (reading, writing, and vocabulary)*

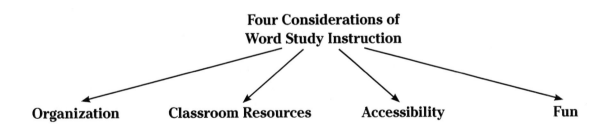

Four Considerations of Word Study Instruction

Organization   Classroom Resources   Accessibility   Fun

Word Study in Kindergarten through Grade 2

The primary grades are a time of discovering language. Students need hands-on materials to help them learn the alphabet and develop both phonological and phonemic awareness. It is important to scaffold learning early as "Correlational studies have identified [phonemic awareness] and letter knowledge as the two best school-entry predictors of how well children will learn to read during the first two years of school" (National Reading Panel 2000, 1–2). Opportunities to assess what students know and then use those assessment results to plan explicit instruction to guide their learning are needed. Providing opportunities to play with and manipulate the sounds of our language builds a solid foundation for reading instruction (Ehri et al. 2001). Therefore, the following kindergarten through grade 2 resources are recommended and will help you to implement these strategies:

1. **Sets of alphabet letters in both lowercase and uppercase**—Initially, having these as magnetic, cardboard, or foam letters enables students to physically manipulate them. Later, having printed sheets displaying the letters serves as a reference for students as they do paper-and-pencil work.

2. **A hanging pocket chart and individual file folder pockets**—The pocket chart is used to sort words that belong together for particular instruction, such as comparing long and short vowels or taking a set of individual letters and challenging students to create words. The individual pockets are easily created. See *File Folder Pocket Instructions* (page 251; folderpocket.pdf) for directions. Students are given letters (*single letters*, *word families*) written on slips of paper to place in the pockets in the correct order.

3. **A collection of age-appropriate alphabet and rhyming books**—Alphabet books that align with content studies, such as an ocean unit in science or a community unit in social studies, will double as a place for word study and content vocabulary development.

4. **A collection of children's dictionaries**—These can be purchased or class created with a collection of words the students are learning and use often.

5. **A word wall placed at student eye level**—Students can easily use word wall collections by placing their papers next to words they want to copy. Word walls are generally organized alphabetically. Be sure to clearly mark each section by letter or word families to further help students locate words.

6. **A collection of pictures for sorting**—Think about the sound patterns students use. Pictures can be simple clip art figures or images cut from magazines. For example, a picture of a cow can help sort the hard and soft sound of *c*, as an exemplar for the /ow/ sound, or for word and picture matching. One way to organize the pictures is to place them in folders marked with the corresponding sound patterns (*e* marker, long *a*, short *o*). For pictures with more than one use, such as *cow*, keep a list at the front of each folder noting their locations.

7. **A large area of white space for writing**—This can be a stand with chart paper, a whiteboard, a bulletin board, or other places where words can be written and discussed during whole-group meetings.

8. **A collection of checklists for assessment purposes**—Observational checklists are ideal for quick "on-the-run" assessments for teachers, while students need checklists for self-assessment and goal setting.

9. **A designated area for small-group word work**—This is usually an area with a table and chairs but can take other forms depending on space availability.

10. **A designated area/learning center for independent word work**—Keeping all the resources in one easy-to-access place in your classroom allows students to independently attempt resolutions to their own word-related challenges. For example, they might remember a book that contained the word they want to write, so being able to pull that off a shelf builds independence.

Word Study in Grade 3 through Grade 5

Grade 3 through grade 5 finds students refining their knowledge of phonics and spelling. Because they can read using the spelling patterns of language, such as word families and affixes, they can also use similar strategies in their writing. For example, a student may see *ick* in the word *brick* and be able to visually separate the onset (the first consonants of the word) from the rime (word family) of *–ick*. The student can more efficiently sound out the word when seeing larger units or "chunks" of the word. That same information may later assist the student in writing "stick" because the onset *st* is familiar and all that needs to be added is *–ick*. Systematic instruction in word recognition assists learners as they encounter more specialized vocabulary (Chall and Jacobs 1990). Finding ways to scaffold the learning of new words into known vocabulary structures increases the success of retention (Bruner 1986). While many of the items described in kindergarten through grade 2 classrooms are useful at these grade levels for continued support for below-level learners or English language learners, grade 3 through grade 5 classrooms need the following more-complex resources:

1. **Three kinds of readily available dictionaries**—These should include one set of children's dictionaries, a class-created dictionary composed of words students are learning and use often, and personal dictionaries filled with words individual students are struggling to remember or find interesting and want to keep for use in their writing.

2. **A word wall placed at student eye level**—At this level, students are encouraged to contribute to the posted words.

3. **A set of labeled file folders, one per student**—Hanging folders in a crate helps to centralize this tool. These folders can be used for ongoing writing, spelling activities, and personal dictionaries.

4. **A collection of age-appropriate children's literature**—These books span the genres: nonfiction/informational texts, literature (historical and realistic), more complex alphabet books, and poetry. All of the texts provide resources for new words.

Word Study in Grade 6 through Grade 8

In grade 6 through grade 8, students add to their content vocabulary and knowledge of multisyllabic words. They have firmly shifted from "learning to read" to "reading to learn," so new encounters with reading and writing words continue to expand their knowledge of the language. Focusing on instruction in Greek and Latin bases allows these students to make connections in word learning during their content studies. For example, an examination of the Greek base *therm* (heat) helps students read and retain science words, such as *thermal, thermometer, thermostat, thermodynamics, thermos,* and *hypothermic.* Understanding prefixes and suffixes, such as *inter-* (between), *ignis-* (fire), *bene-* (good), and *–ward* (direction of), can unlock content vocabulary. This is also a time for teachers to assess their students' knowledge of academic language. Coxhead (2000) suggests direct and explicit instruction of vocabulary. Her list of 2,000 academic words provides guidance in the words students (both native and second language users) should be mastering.

Thus, grade 6 through grade 8 classrooms need many of the same resources previously outlined, plus the following resources:

1. **Content-area resources**—These may be content-specific dictionaries, trade books, posters, maps, or any print material students use as references for writing.

2. **Thesauri**—These provide students with resources to revise their writing.

3. **Word origin books**—Examining the history of words can be an engaging way to learn and understand new vocabulary.

4. **Internet workstations**—Students need access to not only research topics, but they also need access to quickly use online dictionaries and thesauri.

5. **Literature by genre**—Students often search for the genre they read for enjoyment, so organizing books by genre in a classroom library helps students quickly find independent reading books.

6. **Stations for reading**—Adolescent learners love their own spaces and being comfortable there. Providing comfortable chairs or space away from their desk mirrors where they sit outside of school to read, providing authentic reading experiences.

7. **Word walls**—These walls are created by students, for students. These are words that come up authentically in shared reading or read-aloud experiences where students encounter certain words.

Academic Vocabulary

When you craft written pieces for students to work with, such as in the following mini-lessons, go to http://www.nottingham.ac.uk/alzsh3/acvocab/awlhighlighter.htm.

Type in your text, and it will highlight the academic words you have used. In this way, you can utilize vocabulary students should be familiar with while teaching other skills, such as editing.

Differentiation

No two learners are alike. In today's classrooms, teachers are acutely aware of the need to provide support for below-level learners provide linguistic scaffolds for English langauge learners, continue to engage on-grade learners, and challenge advanced learners. A student who is an excellent reader may struggle with spelling. A student who loves to write may avoid reading whenever and however possible. There is no exact description for what a first grader or seventh grader can do. We have "targets" provided by standards, but where students are on a continuum of learning varies. Teachers understand that one-size-fits-all instruction does not exist (Fresch and Wheaton 2002). "Differentiated Instruction offers a framework for addressing learner variance as a critical component of instructional planning" (Tomlinson and McTighe 2006, 1–2). Instruction can be differentiated in content (what a student learns), process (how a student learns), and/or product (how a student shows learning) (Tomlinson and McTighe 2006).

Word study can be differentiated to meet the unique needs of each learner. Specific suggestions for differentiation can be found in the following mini-lessons. However, the following general ideas may help you as well:

1. **Look back**—If a third grader is struggling, looking back to strategies and mini-lessons that are designed for second grade can help meet that student's needs and the development of any necessary foundational skills. Picture and sound matching may help an English language learner finally "get" or unlock sound patterns. An eighth grader struggling with content vocabulary might benefit from an examination of bases and affixes that on-level peers already understand.

2. **Reuse mini-lessons by changing the focus**—Students can focus more quickly on the words since they are familiar with the strategy. For example, the *Slam Dunk* mini-lesson requires students to sort as they compare and contrast words. Any number of different phonic patterns can be used for the strategy. Students will immediately know what they need to do and can spend time really focused on the words for the sorting instead of focusing on learning the procedure of a new strategy. The embedded related exposure is effectively beneficial to use with English language learners.

3. **Pick words for word lists that students can read**—Knowing words helps students "dig in" and analyze phonic or spelling patterns. If they are comfortable reading the words, they can spend time more efficiently when asked them to take words apart for analysis.

4. **Pair up students**—Allowing below-level students to work together gives them opportunities to collaborate with peers in addition to interacting with the teacher.

5. **Adjust the number of words**—Give below-level students fewer words and/or fewer patterns to master. Give above-level students more words and/or patterns to master.

6. **Challenge above-level students to find their own words to fit the focus of the word study**—Above-level learners students are often underserved (VanTassel-Baska and Stambaugh 2005). Differentiation means meeting the needs of *all* students, so be sure to engage advanced learners. For example, have students use content books, books they are reading, or words from websites they are using for inquiry projects to find words for their spelling or vocabulary studies. Glossaries are great resources. Once students understand how phonics works, regardless of grade level, automaticity of reading (or, quick word identification) results (Ehri 2004). Rather than increasing the number of words on their word lists, find more appropriate words that challenge them.

7. **Model, model, model**—English language learners may not know how to approach sounding out a word for writing. Explicitly model your thinking aloud: *How do I think this word is spelled? What sounds do I hear and how might those be written? Let me write it and then check to see if it looks right. What other words do I know that might help me spell this word?* In particular, when working with small groups, this "think aloud" can be valuable as learners listen to you work across a word with them.

8. **Examples**—Have above-level students explore the depth and complexity of words, such as through multiple-meaning words, idioms, cognates, and analogies. Have English language learners gain confidence and mastery, using words that appear frequently in literature and informational texts.

Integrating Technology

Immersing students in a variety of experiences with words, spelling patterns, and sounds of the English language provides learning experiences for all learners. Think about the different learners within the classroom. Here are a few ideas for incorporating technology into their learning experiences.

1. **Find word games online**—Many sites provide free resources for playing with words. *Reading Is Fundamental* (www.rif.org) and PBS's *Between the Lions* (pbskids.org) are student-friendly sites that provide wonderful and engaging experiences.

2. **Use a digital notes program**—You can create a field of words, one per note. Students can drag notes together as they sort them by the selected word features.

3. **Provide a word document with a blank two-column table with as many rows as needed to sort words**—Label the top of the column with the chosen compare and contrast features, such as *Long A/Short A*. Give students a list of words and ask them to click on the box under the correct heading to type in each word. Have students print their documents when they are done.

4. **Create a word web using a digital graphic organizer**—Many organizers are readily available online. Students can type directly into the organizers or print them to write on. Most sites will provide a variety of organizers so the requirements can be differentiated.

5. **Create your own organizers in a word processing program**—Use the drawing tools to create boxes or circles connected by lines to enable students to fill in related words. These can be as simple base words with affixes (*hooked, hooking, rehook, unhook*), or more complex bases (*volv*) tied to related words (*evolve, revolve, revolt, volume, involve*).

6. **Use Web resources**—Bookmark sites that provide quick resources for students. Online dictionaries and thesauri offer quick references. Introduce word histories as a way to encourage curiosity about words. Sites, such as www.etymonline.com, provide information that can be shared with classmates. Google also maintains a search engine that is safe for students to use: http://www.safesearchkids.com/.

Overview of Skills and Strategies
Kindergarten through Grade 2

This section includes basic small-group mini-lessons for simple practice of the following skills for kindergarten through grade 2. Details regarding each strategy can be found on the subsequent pages. For additional lessons, download the Digital Resources. (See page 20 for the website address and access code.)

Mini-Lessons

Phonics

Lesson	Skill
Blends and Digraphs BINGO (page 40)	consonant blends and digraphs
Rhyme Time (page 41)	phonemic/phonological awareness
Slam Dunk (pages 42–43)	preconsonant nasals
Stash the Syllable (page 44)	syllables
Who Belongs Together? (page 45)	long vowels

Spelling

Lesson	Skill
Alpha-Books (page 46)	alphabet; consonants
Hop to It! The Magic of E (page 47)	*e* marker
Presto Chango! (page 48)	short vowels

Vocabulary

Lesson	Skill
Build a Word (page 49)	inflectional endings (–ing, –ed, –s, –es); common prefixes and suffixes
Mix and Match (page 50)	compound words
Scavenger Hunt (page 51)	irregularly spelled words; high-frequency words

Some websites that serve to enhance instruction and provide additional opportunities for students to explore word study topics are:

- www.wordle.net
- www.studyladder.com
- www.starfall.com
- www.pbskids.org/lions
- www.sightwords.com

Some apps that serve to enhance instruction and provide additional opportunities for students to explore these various topics are:

- Sight Words: Kids Learn (Teacher Created Materials)
- Sight Words List—Learn to Read Flash Cards & Games (Innovative Mobile Apps)
- Spelling Magic 3 (Preschool University)

Word Study

Additional Lessons—Digital Resources

Listed below are additional lessons available as digital downloads to help students develop their word study skills. See page 20 for the website and access code to download these files.

Phonics

Lesson	Skill
Monkeys in the Trees (monkeytree.pdf)	short vowels; long vowels; consonant blends and digraphs
What If? (whatif.pdf)	phonemic/phonological awareness; short vowels

Spelling

Lesson	Skill
All Together Now (alltogether.pdf)	short vowels; consonant blends and digraphs; inflectional endings (–ing, –ed, –s, –es); common prefixes and suffixes
Go Team! (goteam.pdf)	long vowels
Under Construction (construction.pdf)	high-frequency words

Word Study

Objective

Students will identify blends and digraphs.

Preparation

1. Copy the *BINGO Board* (page 252; bingo.pdf), one per student.
2. Copy the *Blends and Digraphs List* (page 253; blendlist.pdf).
3. Provide colored pencils for each student.

Word Study

K–2 Strategies

Procedure

1. Provide students with blank *BINGO Boards*, and tell them they will be making their own boards.

2. Using the *Blends and Digraphs List*, announce 9 or 16 blends and/or digraphs (according to the size of the game board), write each on the board, and have students write one in each open square on their boards. They can choose any open square for each blend or digraph so that all the boards are different.

3. Read aloud words listed next to the various blends and digraphs you named. Write each word on the board. Students should trace over each related digraph or blend in light colored pencils. Play multiple games with the same board by simply changing the color used for each game. For example, play game one using yellow, game two using orange, and game three using purple.

4. Once a student has traced the blend or digraph in five squares diagonally, in a row, or in a column, he or she should call, "BINGO!"

5. When a student calls BINGO, ask him or her to read aloud the five digraphs or blends. You can have small prizes or special tickets, such as first in line to lunch, for winners.

Differentiation: For **below-level students**, use only two blends and/or digraphs. Have students write the same blend or digraph in multiple squares to fill the board. For **above-level students,** announce words that contain both blends and digraphs, such as *scratch, squash, sketch,* and *splotch.* Have them decide which to use on their *BINGO Boards.*

✔ **Assessment Check:** Make note of how well each student identifies the correct blends and/or digraphs for the words you announce. Additional support or instruction may be needed.

Rhyme Time

Phonics

Objective

Students will develop phonemic and phonological awareness through rhyme to bridge to phonics.

Preparation

1. Choose a simple rhyming poem or nursery rhyme. You can also choose a poem that connects to a content area your class is studying. For example, if you are doing an animal unit in science, find a poem about an elephant or hippo.

2. Display a copy of the poem for students.

Procedure

1. Read the poem aloud to students.

2. Read the poem aloud a second time, emphasizing the words that rhyme. For example, if you read "Twinkle, Twinkle Little Star," emphasize words *star/are* and *high/sky.*

3. Point to words that rhyme and have students listen. Ask them if they can hear the rhyming sounds the words make. Have students help you identify the parts of the words that rhyme, such as the long *i* in *high* and *sky.*

4. Have students think of more words that rhyme with the ones from the poem. You may wish to write words students suggest on the board. Encourage students to add to the list throughout the day.

Differentiation: For **below-level students**, use simple, short rhymes. For **English language learners**, select poems that have vocabulary words that students are familiar with so they are more likely to hear the rhyming sounds. Provide **above-level students** with longer texts to locate rhyming words. Discuss the idea that words can rhyme but not be part of the same rime family, such as *high* and *sky* versus *bat* and *cat.*

✔ **Assessment Check:** Before you move to your next activity, have each student tell you a pair of rhyming words. If students choose words that do not rhyme, revisit this activity to give students more practice and instruction.

Word Study

K–2 Strategies

Objective

Students will distinguish preconsonantal nasal endings.

Preparation

1. Copy *Basketball Hoops* (page 254; hoops.pdf).

2. Choose and write preconsonantal nasals on each basketball hoop (*mp*, *nch*, *nd*, *ng*, *nk*, or *nt*).

3. Glue each hoop on top of a 12" x 18" sheet of paper, labeling each paper *Slam Dunk*.

4. Post the hoops at student eye level, creating a word sort area and temporary word wall.

5. Copy *Basketballs* (page 255; basketballs.pdf), including extras to use later.

6. On the basketballs, write any words ending with preconsonantal nasals, such as *jump*, *bump*, *champ*, *blimp*, *branch*, *lunch*, *pinch*, *bench*, *friend*, *ground*, *sand*, *bend*, *bring*, *rang*, *king*, *lung*, *think*, *thank*, *dunk*, *sank*, *want*, *went*, *mint*, and *runt*.

7. Provide tape so students can put the basketballs underneath the basketball hoops.

> ***Preconsonantal nasals*** *(mp, nch, nd, ng, nk, nt) appear at the ends of words and make subtle letter/sound consonant combinations. The sound comes from air going through the nose into the mouth. The second consonant dominates, absorbing the first as in* bump *or* sink.

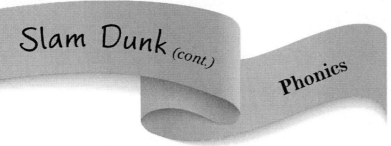

Procedure

1. Post the basketball hoops with the preconsonantal nasals. For beginning readers or below-level students, focus on only two at a time. For above-level students, add additional preconsonantal nasal basketballs to the activity.

2. Gather students in front of the basketball hoops and show one of the basketballs. Read the word aloud. For example, show the basketball with the word *friend* written on it. Model how you hear the ending *nd*.

3. Have students find the basketball hoop with *nd*, and tape the word *friend* under the *nd* basketball hoop. Continue with the remaining words.

4. Have extra blank "basketballs" in a container. Tell students to take "basketballs" whenever they find words that can be added to the basketball hoops. They should write the words on the basketballs and tape them in the right locations.

Differentiation: For **below-level students**, have a small-group meeting in front of the "basketball hoops" and play *What word am I thinking of?* Give a hint about a word. (For example, *We eat this meal in the middle of the day at school.*) After students guess the word, ask one student to come up and point to the "basketball" with that word printed on it. This will model looking directly at the text as a resource.

✔ **Assessment Check:** Keep track of any students who have difficulty sorting the words or who have difficulty associating the ending sounds in the printed words. Additional practice may be needed.

K-2 Strategies

Word Study

Stash the Syllable

Phonics

Objective

Students will differentiate words by syllables.

Preparation

1. Select 10–12 words that range from one to three syllables, based on students' reading abilities. You may want to choose words from content area studies to integrate word study into science, social studies, and mathematics.

2. Write each word on a note card. Make enough sets of the words for multiple small groups to each have one.

3. Gather small, empty containers. For each group, mark three containers as 1, 2, and 3. The containers can be lunch-size paper bags, small boxes, or small plastic bins. Be creative! For example, you can print the words on strawberry shapes and use small plastic strawberry baskets.

4. Create a self-checking answer sheet, and provide it to each group.

Procedure

1. Model to students how you can read a word aloud as you listen for the number of syllables. Once you know the number of syllables in the word, place the word card in the correct container: 1, 2, or 3 syllables.

2. Have students work in small groups, taking turns reading words aloud. Have students decide together into which container each word should be placed.

3. Each group can use the self-checking answer sheet to affirm or adjust its answers.

Differentiation: **English language learners** can be given cards that have words and pictures for context support (*snake*, *shoe*, and *basketball*). Have **below-level students** work with only one- and two-syllable words before adding in three-syllable words. Have **above-level students** make suggestions of other words that would fit in the 1, 2, or 3 syllable containers.

✔ **Assessment Check:** Make notes as students read and place the words in the correct containers. Students who do not accurately read a word will have problems hearing the syllables. If they drop sounds or endings, you may have to change the words they work with so students have practice hearing syllables in familiar words.

Objective

Students will compare and contrast sounds.

Preparation

1. Copy *Who Belongs Together?* cards (page 256; belongs.pdf) and *Who Belongs Together? Answer Key* (page 257; belongans.pdf).

2. Cut the answer key in half horizontally. Cut apart the individual pictures and place all the pictures in a container, keeping the *baby* and *pig* pictures to use as models.

3. In one corner of the room, post the letter *b*. In another corner, post the letter *p*. Have a shelf, desk, or other space available near each letter. On this surface, place the *p* or *b* answer key picture page facedown. This enables students to self-check.

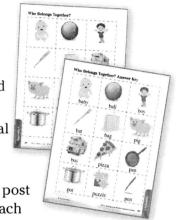

K-2 Strategies

Word Study

Procedure

1. Show students the picture of the *baby*. Model saying the word *baby* and demonstrate how to listen for the first sound (/b/). Write the letter *b* under the picture or the card.

2. Walk to the corner marked *b*, and place the image on the table in that corner. Repeat with the *pig* picture card, placing it under the *p*.

3. Have students select pictures from the container.

4. Have each student show their card, say the word, say the first sound in the word, say the letter for that sound (*p* or *b*) and write the letter on the card.

5. Students go to the corners in the room where their pictures belong. When students are where they think their pictures go, tell them to turn the answer keys over to verify that they're right.

6. Collect the pictures, shuffle them, and repeat the activity.

Differentiation: For **English language learners**, preteach the /p/ and /b/ sounds before the activity. Explain that the /p/ is voiceless (hand on throat—no vibration) and /b/ is voiced (place hand on throat—vibration). For **above-level students**, have them focus on ending sounds instead of beginning sounds. Or, bring in old magazines and have students search for pictures of items that begin with /p/ or /b/. The pictures can also be varied to focus on vowels.

✔ **Assessment Check:** After students go to their designated corners, make note of any students who misheard the sounds for sorting. This may indicate additional practice in listening to beginning sounds is needed.

Alpha-Books

Spelling

Objective

Students will identify and differentiate the 26 letters of the alphabet.

Preparation

1. Using 26 large sheets of paper, such as 12" x 18", label each individual page with a letter of the alphabet in upper and lowercase—*Aa, Bb, Cc.*

2. Place the papers along with a variety of markers around the room so there is space for students to work. A good way to organize this is to place the papers on worktables and student desks while the students are out of the room.

Procedure

1. Ask students to stand by the papers that have the same letters as the beginnings of their names.

2. Using markers, students should write their names on the correct papers.

3. Have students also write other words that begin with the same letters as their names. For example, Stephanie can write *start* or *salad.*

4. Provide time for students to move to other papers where they know words that begin with the letters and record those words. Encourage students to look around the room for words. Do they see words they can use in particular areas in the room?

5. Have students help put the pages in proper sequence and staple them together to create a class alphabet book.

6. Invite students to add to the alphabet book throughout the day.

Differentiation: Have **below-level students** draw pictures of items that fit the letters and write at least the first letter of the word, such as a dog on the *Dd* paper. Have **above-level students** write multisyllabic words or words from the content areas.

✔ **Assessment Check:** Move among the papers to observe and note who is actively contributing to the activity. If a student does not participate, use the sheets during guided reading to encourage him or her in a one-on-one setting.

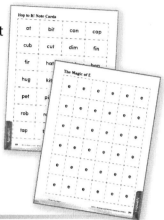

Hop to It! The Magic of E

K–2 Strategies

Word Study

Objective

Students will use long consonant *e* spelling patterns to change short vowel sounds to long vowel sounds.

Preparation

1. Copy and cut apart the *Hop to It! Note Cards* (page 258; hoptoit.pdf), at least one per student.

2. Copy *The Magic of E* (page 259; magice.pdf) and cut out one square per student. Don't forget one for yourself.

3. Tape a letter *e* card to the toe of your shoe.

Procedure

1. Place the *Hop to It! Note Cards* on the floor of the classroom, spreading them out so students can move around easily.

2. Find the card with the word *hop* on it. Have students gather around the card. Place the toe of your shoe so the *e* is next to *hop*.

3. Ask students if anyone knows what the new word is now that you "hopped to it" with the letter *e*. (*hope*)

4. Tape an *e* to the toe of each student's shoe, and ask students to "hop" from word to word, adding the *e* to make new words. Tell them to say the words on the cards and then the new words they make by adding *e*.

5. Gather students together and take a "walk" past each card, so you can be certain they understand the concept that adding *e* to a word makes the vowel long. Extend the lesson by putting the cards and letter *e*'s at a learning center for additional practice.

Differentiation: Have **English language learners** select a "magic *e*" word pair to illustrate. For **above-level students**, use words that challenge them such as *lob/lobe, crud/crude, dot/dote, fad/fade, glad/glade, glob/globe, grim/grime, grip/gripe, plum/plume, prim/prime, twin/twine,* and *slop/slope.*

✔ **Assessment Check:** Observe students as they make new words. Are they able to properly pronounce the new words with long vowels? If not, it may indicate additional practice or support is needed.

> *The reason* e *does not work with words such as* have, glove, *or* love *is that at one time in English, those words did not have the* e *at the ends. Then, scribes added the* e *at the ends of words with* v—*even though the pronunciation did not change.*

Objective

Students will change the vowel in CVC (consonant-vowel-consonant) words to spell new words.

Preparation

1. Copy *Presto Wands* (page 260; presto.pdf) onto cardstock, one wand per student.

2. Cut apart the wands. If cardstock is not available, tape a drinking straw to the back of each wand to make it sturdy.

3. Write the following words on the board: *bed, tip, cup, pot,* and *ten*. Write them approximately the same size as the vowels on the wands.

Procedure

1. Read the words on the board together. Point out the CVC pattern and how the vowels all have short sounds.

2. Tell students they are going to be magicians and make the words magically change. Model how to hold up a wand with a vowel different from the one on the board. For example, you might hold up the *a* wand over the *e* in *bed* and ask students what word you magically changed bed to. (*bad*)

3. Have students volunteer to use their wands to change other words.

4. Extend this activity by having students search for other CVC words in the classroom or in other locations within the school. If they find any, challenge them to "magically" create new words using one of the five vowel wands.

Differentiation: Have **above-level students** use wands to create CCVCC words, such as *plump, sport, blast, shell,* and *think*.

✔ **Assessment Check:** Repeat the activity in small groups to assess how well each student can hear and substitute the short vowels. Additional support or practice may be needed.

Build a Word

Objective

Students will read and manipulate base words and inflectional endings.

Preparation

1. Copy *Build a Word Sample List* (page 261; buildword.pdf), one per student. If you prefer, you can create and copy your own master list of words and suffixes you want students to examine.

2. Cut apart the words along the dashed lines.

3. Provide scissors for each student.

Procedure

1. Choose one word card. Ask students to cut the base word apart from its suffix.

2. Ask what word remains when they remove the suffix. Repeat for all the words in the set.

3. Have students create two piles of cards—base words and suffixes. Ask students to match the suffixes to various words, such as *wishing*, *looks*, and *mixed*. What new words do they make? Have students write their new words on the board. You can also model this using a pocket chart by showing students how suffixes change the words.

4. Discuss how the suffixes change the word meanings, such as *–ed* means something that already happened, while *–ing* means something currently happening.

Differentiation: For **below-level students**, use all base words with only *–ed* or *–ing* attached to focus the task on these two suffixes. For **above-level students**, include additional suffixes, such as *–er*, *–ful*, and *–less*. Provide blank strips for students to create more words.

✔ **Assessment Check:** Walk around and observe students as they make new words using the base words and suffixes. Offer guidance where needed, and extend learning with new base words (*jump*, *fall*, and *dash*) where needed.

Mix and Match

Vocabulary

Objective

Students will determine and clarify meanings of compound words.

Preparation

1. Copy *Mix and Match Compound Pairs* (pages 262–263; mixcompound.pdf) and *Mix and Match Vocabulary* (page 264; mixvocab.pdf).
2. Cut apart the pictures cards and words cards.
3. Put everything in a bag from which the students can draw.
4. Copy *Compound Pairs* (page 265; compoundpair.pdf), one per student.

Procedure

1. Mix up the cards and distribute them to students facedown.
2. On your signal, have students look at their cards. Those who have word cards will find and sit with students who have the matching picture cards.
3. Have each picture/word pair figure out compound words that can be made with their picture/word. For example, *bird* could become *birdhouse* or *birdbath*.
4. Tell students to walk around the room in pairs and find another pair of students with cards that they can use to create a compound word. For example, the *basket* pair might join with the *ball* pair to create *basketball*.
5. Have foursomes share their compound words. As a class, find the words on the *Compound Pairs* page. Talk about what each word means by itself and then what the compound words mean.
6. Post the words, pictures, and pairs on a bulletin board for students to use for future reference.
7. Post the words, pictures, and pairs on a bulletin board for students to use for future reference. The *Compound Pairs* can be left out for students to use as guides for matches.

Differentiation: Give **below-level students** their corresponding *Compound Pairs* card to support them as they make their picture/word compound matches. Place the picture and word cards in a learning center for students to revisit for additional practice. Have **above-level students** create their own compound pictures/words.

✔ **Assessment Check:** Circulate as students match picture and word cards. Listen in as they discuss the possible compound words that their words can become. Look for students who might benefit from additional practice either in small groups or at a learning center.

Objective

Students will identify and recognize high-frequency words.

Preparation

1. Select a page of text with a large number of high-frequency words. (For a list of these words, see the *Top 100 High-Frequency Words* [page 266; hfwords.pdf].) This can be a children's literature book, a text you are using in a content area (science, mathematics, or social studies), a young reader's magazine, or the newspaper.
   Note: Vary the difficulty of the text based on the reading levels of the students. Students can use different texts but still look for the same words.

2. Make copies of the text(s), one per student.

3. Make a list of the high-frequency words found in the text(s).

4. Provide each student with a whiteboard marker and a sheet protector.

Procedure

1. Give each student a text, a marker, and a sheet protector.

2. Explain that a scavenger hunt is a search for something in particular. As an example, you might hide something in the room, such as a book, and have students hunt for it. What did they need to do? Point out that they had to look carefully. Explain that they now need to look carefully for certain words.

3. List on the board the words you want students to look for, such as *the*, *about*, *with*, *down*, *I*, and *was*.

4. Show students how to insert the copies of the text(s) into the sheet protectors, hunt for the words, and circle them using the whiteboard marker.

> This strategy can also be changed to require students to hunt for words with particular sound patterns, such as words with long a, words with specific consonant blends, and words with short e.

Differentiation: Give **below-level students** individual copies of the list of high-frequency words they need to find so they have the words in close proximity to their texts.

✔ **Assessment Check:** After students are finished, collect the sheet protectors and record how many of the words they found. Additional exposure to finding words within texts may be needed for some students.

Overview of Standards and Strategies
Grade 3 through Grade 5

This section includes basic small-group mini-lessons for simple practice of the following skills for grade 3 through grade 5. Details regarding each strategy can be found on the subsequent pages. For additional lessons, download the Digital Resources. (See page 20 for the website address and access code.)

Mini-Lessons

Phonics

Lesson	Skill
Build a Vowel House (page 54)	vowel alternations
Circus Circles (page 55)	r-controlled vowels
Crafty, Quiet Letters (page 56)	silent letter long vowels
Syllable Teams March Down the Field (page 57)	syllables

Spelling

Lesson	Skill
Awesome Automobile (page 58)	complex vowel patterns
Cutting on the Double (page 59)	doubling before adding ending
Delicious Super Supper (page 60)	doubling before adding ending
Doubled or Dropped? (page 61)	consonant patterns, blends, and digraphs

Vocabulary

Lesson	Skill
Ant Re-Attach-Ment (page 62)	Greek and Latin affixes and roots
Flipping for Compound Words (page 63)	compound words
Line Up! (page 64)	comparatives and superlatives
Pears for Pairs (page 65)	homophones, antonyms, synonyms

Some websites that serve to enhance instruction and provide additional opportunities for students to explore these various topics are:

- www.flashcardstash.com
- www.vocabulary.co.il
- www.spellingcity.com
- www.sadlierconnect.com
- www.kubbu.com

Some apps that serve to enhance instruction and provide additional opportunities for students to explore these various topics are:

- Long Vowel Word Study (Thomas Wilson)
- Abby Phonics (Arch Square)
- My Spelling Test (Mathan Education)

Additional Lessons—Digital Resources

Listed below are additional lessons available as digital downloads to help students develop their word study skills. See page 20 for the website and access code to download these files.

Phonics

Lesson	Skill
Digging In (digging.pdf)	consonant patterns, blends, and digraphs

Spelling

Lesson	Skill
Dear Deer (deardeer.pdf)	homophones, antonyms, synonyms
Hanging Out Together (hangingtogether.pdf)	diphthongs
Hey! Let's Play in the Hay (hayplay.pdf)	vowel sound of *y*
Shhhh! Fishing in Progress (fishprogress.pdf)	silent letter long vowels
Uh...How Is That Spelled? (uhspelled.pdf)	schwa

Vocabulary

Lesson	Skill
Cube It (cubeit.pdf)	compound words
Family Tree (familytree.pdf)	Greek and Latin affixes and bases

Word Study

Build a Vowel House

Objective

Students will identify vowel alternations.

Preparation

1. Copy the *Vowel House Template* (page 267; vowelhouse.pdf) for each small group. The two-dimensional house will be two strips placed at an angle for the roof and two upright strips for walls.

2. Use the *Vowel Alternations List* (page 268; vowelalt.pdf) for the activity.

> *Vowel alternations* are vowel sounds that are altered or eliminated from words.

Procedure

1. Divide the class into small groups.

2. Write a word from the *Vowel Alternations List* on the board, such as *deal*, and have students read it.

3. Then, write the vowel alternation word, such as *dealt*. Have students identify which vowel sound changed. Point out the spelling similarities and how the vowel sound changed.

4. Have each group build a house as they identify which vowels changed in each pair. For example, with *dealt* students can use the *e* roof or the *e* wall. Each house can only use each vowel once. Thus, if students pick the *e* roof, they cannot use the *e* wall. As a group, students must decide which strip to use—the vowel roof or the vowel wall. If another word is read that has a vowel alternation the group has already used, it cannot add to the house unless it opts to use a wild card. The first group to build a house wins. Continue reading words and their vowel alternation forms. Be sure students listen to how the vowels are changing so they can decide how to build their houses.

Extend the lesson by putting the pairs of words on cards at a learning center. Students can use these to compete against each other as they build homes. One student picks a card, reads the word, and tells the vowel alternation. Then, each student adds to his or her own vowel house to see who can build one the fastest.

Differentiation: For **below-level students**, limit how many word pairs you use and make the word cards visible to students as visual cues of what has changed. For **above-level students**, use more difficult words such as *proclaim/proclamation* and *oppose/opposition*.

✔ **Assessment Check:** As small groups decide which vowels changed sounds, keep track of students who contribute to the discussion. One-on-one work may be needed to clear up any misconceptions.

Circus Circles

Phonics

Objective

Students will distinguish among *r*-controlled vowels.

Preparation

1. Copy *Circus Rings* (page 269; circusring.pdf), *Circus Animals* (page 270; circusani.pdf), and *Circus Performers* (page 271; circperform.pdf).

2. On the animals and beneath the performers write *ar*, *er*, *ir*, *or*, and *ur* words from *Circus Words* (page 272; circword.pdf). Create one with *fern* to use as an example.

3. Provide tape or glue sticks.

Procedure

1. Gather students by the circus rings. Review the *r*-controlled vowel sounds (/ar/, /or/, and /er/) by showing students the letter combinations on the rings. Remind them that a vowel followed by an *r* makes neither a long nor short sound. Instead, the vowel sound is "controlled" by the *r*, such as with *fern*.

2. Tell students the circus is in town, and they need to put the animals and performers in the right circles.

3. Show the picture with *fern* written on it. Ask students which vowel sound they hear in the word *fern*. (/er/) Attach that picture with glue or tape to the *er/ir/or* circus ring.
   Note: This strategy is done with students reading the words to help them match the sounds and spellings. The *r*-controlled vowel spellings *ir*, *er*, and *ur* produce the same *r*-controlled vowel sound, /er/, so using the print makes the point that students must also look at a word when they write so

they can make certain we have chosen the correct vowel spelling.

4. Continue with the remaining words, having students connect the animals to the correct rings.

   Extend the mini-lesson by providing blank animals and performers and inviting students to add to the rings with other words they find throughout the day.

Differentiation: Have **below-level students** begin by comparing two circus rings, such as *ar* words with *or* words. After they feel comfortable with those two sounds, introduce other *r*-controlled vowels.

✔ **Assessment Check:** Observe which students contribute to the sound sorting. This strategy can be repeated in small groups for one-on-one assessment. Ask students to initial any new words they contribute so you can keep track of who participates and can encourage others individually.

Word Study

3–5 Strategies

✔ Objective

Students will identify silent long vowel patterns.

Preparation

1. Write the silent long vowel patterns (*ai, ea, ei, igh, oa, ow,* and *ue*) on craft sticks or strips of paper. Make multiple sets of these to distribute for small-group work.

2. Copy and cut apart *Quiet Letters Cards* (pages 273–274; quietlet.pdf).

Procedure

1. Show a *Quiet Letters Card* with a missing vowel pattern, such as *copyr__t*.

2. Hold up each craft stick (or strip of paper) with a silent long vowel pattern on it until the students see a pattern that makes a word, such as *copyright*.

3. Discuss the pattern and how the *gh* is silent. Point out how our "reader's eye" needs to check that we have correctly spelled words where we do not hear all the sounds. Continue with other words from the list.

4. Have students work in small groups to make lists of the words they create using the *Quiet Letters Cards* and silent long vowel patterns.

Differentiation: Have **below-level students** focus on fewer vowel patterns, such as <u>*ea*</u>, <u>*ai*</u>, and <u>*igh*</u> to learn them very well before expanding to other patterns. Have **English language learners** share an example sentence for each word they create so that the words have more context.

✔ Assessment Check:
Keep a checklist of students who successfully participate in creating the words using the silent letter patterns. Some students may need more instruction and practice with the long vowel patterns and word cards.

Syllable Teams March Down the Field

Objective

Students will decode syllables.

Preparation

1. Copy *Football Jersey* (page 275; jersey.pdf), one per student pair.

2. Create a list of words that have one to four syllables. You can easily integrate this strategy across content-areas by using content-area vocabulary words that students are studying.

3. Write each word on a note card.

4. Copy the *Football Field* (page 276; football.pdf), one for every four students.

5. Provide gameboard markers, such as dried beans or paper clips, one per pair.

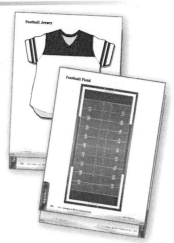

Procedure

1. Give each student pair a *Football Jersey*. Have them name their teams and color the jerseys. This will help you differentiate the jerseys.

2. Place the pairs together in groups of four. Distribute one *Football Field* per group. Have each student pair select a gameboard marker.

3. Each student pair then randomly draws one note card. They are to decide how many syllables the word on the card has and move from one end zone to the other end zone by going 10 yards for each syllable. For example, students pick *recycle*. The word *recycle* has three syllables, so they would move 30 yards or three 10-yard marks. Each game continues until one team reaches the end zone. As they play, students must keep lists of the words they pick (and their syllable values) on the backs of their *Football Jerseys*.

4. Leave the activity out for students to continue to play alone or in small groups during independent work time.

Extend the lesson by revisiting the game in reading groups using vocabulary words students are learning. This reinforces reading the new words and allows for variation in the difficulty of words chosen.

Differentiation: For **English language learners**, focus on context-rich one- or two-syllable words. Have **above-level students** work with more abstract four- or five-syllable words, such as *personality*, *unidentified*, *abdominable*, *imagination*, and *electricity*.

✔ **Assessment Check:** Make note of students who struggle with correctly counting the syllables. Additional support, practice, or instruction may be needed.

Objective

Students will discriminate among complex vowel patterns.

Preparation

1. Make as many copies of *Automobiles* (page 277; automobiles.pdf) as number of words you will have the students work with. For a list of suggested words, see *Awesome Automobile Words* (page 278; awesome.pdf). Consider also using content-area words, such as *fauna*.

2. Use a long sheet of black or brown paper with yellow lines drawn on it to simulate a road. Or, if the weather permits, draw a "road" with chalk on an outside area, such as the playground.

3. Have an automobile card prepared with *aw* to use as a model.

Procedure

1. Show students the three automobiles and remind them that those letter combinations all say /aw/.

2. Tell them you want to write the word "fawn," a young deer. Which sound automobile should you use? Take an *aw* automobile and write *f* and *n* on the vehicle where they belong to make the word.

3. Place the auto on the road. A fun way to organize this is to let students "drive" the autos into "parking lots" that are drawn and labeled with the three vowel patterns.

4. Give student pairs or small groups several automobiles of each vowel pattern.

5. Read a word aloud, and have students decide which spelling of the pattern looks right. Provide blank paper for them to "try out" the spellings and proofread for the correct answer.

6. Have each pair or group hold up the automobile they think is correct. Do a quick check for accuracy.

7. Have students decide how to spell the rest of the word. Check for accuracy before allowing the final version to be added to the road.

8. Make blank copies of *Automobiles* available for the rest of the day or week for students to write on when they find new words that fit these patterns.

Differentiation: Have **above-level students** work with words such as *sought, squawk, scrawl, trauma,* and *nausea.* Have **below-level students** work with words such as *haul, sauce, draw, raw,* and *bought.*

✔ **Assessment Check:** Make note of any pairs or small groups that incorrectly identify the vowel patterns. Additional guidance, practice, or instruction may be needed.

Objective

Students will use ending patterns.

Preparation

1. Copy *Double Consonant Cards* (page 279; consonant.pdf), one per student.

2. Cut apart the individual word cards.

3. Provide one pair of scissors for each student.

Procedure

1. Distribute the word card *flipping* and a pair of scissors to each student.

2. Have students cut off the *–ing*. Ask what word they have. (*flipp*) Ask if this is the way to spell *flip*. Ask what they need to do to spell it correctly. (*Cut the final* p *off.*)

3. Ask if anyone knows why the extra letter is there. Discuss how we double a consonant at the end of a word with a short vowel to keep the vowel short.

4. Distribute the remaining word cards.

5. Have students cut off the endings and any additional final consonants. Do this one word at a time or have students work independently.

6. Have students mix up the words, doubled consonants, and endings on their desks.

7. Invite students to combine words with doubled consonants and endings to make new words, such as *babysit-t-er* to make *babysit-t-ing*; *zip-p-ing* to make *zip-p-er* or *zip-p-ed*.

8. Have students create lists of the new words they create.

9. Guide students to talk about the words and why the consonants were doubled.

Differentiation: Below-level students may also need help identifying the short vowels. For above-level students, ask students to search for words in books that fit with the spelling pattern of doubling the consonant, such as *cropping*.

✔ **Assessment Check:** Circulate as students create new words with the cut-apart pieces. Keep track of who can combine words and endings. Give some additional base words (*hop*), and ask students how the words should be spelled. This will indicate who needs additional practice, guidance, or instruction.

Delicious Super Supper

Spelling

Word Study · **3–5 Strategies**

Objective

Students will use syllable patterns.

Preparation

1. Use paper plates to make VCV and VCCV signs. Provide two plates per student or per small group of students.

2. Copy the *Meatballs Template* (page 280; meatballs.pdf), one per student. Cut apart the "meatballs."

3. Select words to use for this activity, or use the words provided on *VCV and VCCV Word Suggestions* (page 281; vccv.pdf). The first three words in each category are strong examples. Students can see the change and how the syllables are divided. Additional words are also included for students to sort.

4. On one meatball, write *super* (VCV); on a second, write *supper* (VCCV).

Procedure

1. Show students the VCV plate, and explain that VCV means vowel-consonant-vowel. Show the word *super*, and point out the VCV (*upe*).

2. Ask students to listen to the vowel *i*. Explain that in VCV words a new syllable *usually* starts right after the vowel. This makes the first syllable on open syllable (ends with a vowel) and the vowel sound is *usually* long. Place the *super* meatball on the VCV plate.

3. Show students the VCCV plate, and explain vowel-consonant-consonant-vowel. Show the word *supper* and point out the VCCV (*uppe*). Place the *supper* meatball on the VCCV plate.

4. Ask students to use the blank meatballs to write the words as you say them. Tell students to listen to the vowels and determine how many consonants there are in each word.

After they write each word, they should put the meatball on the right plate: VCV or VCCV.

Differentiation: For **English language learners,** have the words already written on meatballs. Work with them to read the words, and have students practice sorting them to the correct plates.

✔ Assessment Check: Circulate as students write the words to see who may need more support or who may need more challenging words.

> In VCCV words, the first syllable ends between the two consonants. The first syllable is closed (ends with a consonant), and the vowel sound is short.

51519—Strategies for Effective Balanced Literacy · © Shell Education · 60

Doubled or Dropped?

Objective

Students use ending rule patterns.

Preparation

1. Use the *Doubled or Dropped Word List* (page 282; doubled.pdf) to select words for this strategy. Write these words on note cards. Keep two cards as models—one with a double consonant (*hopping*) and one without (*hoping*).

2. Copy and cut apart the *Arrow Template* (page 283; arrow.pdf).

3. Have a supply of blank note cards.

4. On a pocket chart or wall, place two signs—*Doubled* and *Dropped*.

Procedure

1. Have students gather in front of the *Doubled* and *Dropped* signs.

2. Show students the *hopping* card. Ask them what they notice about the letter *p*. (*There are two of them.*)

3. Ask them what the word was before –*ing* was added, and have them spell it. Write *hop* on a blank note card. Explain how the *p* was doubled to keep the short *o* vowel sound. Place *hop* under the *Doubled* sign. Post an arrow next to it pointing to the right. Then, post the card *hopping* next to the arrow.

4. Show students the *hoping* card. Ask them what the word was before the –*ing* was added, and have them spell it. Write *hope* on a blank note card. Explain how the *e* was dropped to keep the long *o* vowel sound. Place *hope* under the *Dropped* sign. Place an arrow next to it pointing to the right. Then, post the card *hoping* next to the arrow.

5. Distribute the cards to students, and provide blank note cards.

6. Ask students to decide what each base word was before the suffix was added and write it on a blank card. They can then put the cards and arrows under the correct sign.

7. Leave the word cards displayed for a few days, inviting students to add any dropped or doubled words (along with the base word cards) they find in their reading.

8. Vary this activity by using –*ed* or –*er*.

Differentiation: For **below-level students**, teach the base word for each word on the list before beginning the activity. Give **above-level students** three- or four-syllable words, such as *forgetting, submitting, amazing, operating,* and *deciding*.

✔ **Assessment Check:** Make note of students struggling to understand the concept of doubled letters or dropped silent *e* before adding endings. Additional guidance, practice, or instruction may be needed.

Objective

Students will use affixes and bases.

Preparation

1. Make 10 copies of *Ant Template* (page 284; anttemp.pdf).

2. Select 10 words from current content-area studies. Glossaries in resource books can be helpful. Each word should have a prefix (*un–*, *re–*, *pre–*, *sub–*, *semi–*, *hemi–*, *mis–*, *dis–*), a base (*appear, agree, cover, attach*), and a suffix (*–less, –ful, –ness, –ship, –able/–ible, –ed, –ing, –ly, –ment*). *Disagreement, disappearance, nonreturnable, nonrefundable, recovered, redoing, impossible, exception, predicted, containment, inedible,* and *unfriendly* are some examples.

3. For each word selected, write the prefix above the ant's head on the *Ant Template*, the base above the ant's thorax, and the suffix above the ant's abdomen.

4. Make one copy of the ant using the word *reattachment*, with *re–* written above the head, *attach* written above the thorax, and *–ment* written above the abdomen.

5. Cut apart the ants so all the prefixes, base words, and suffixes are separated.

Procedure

1. Gather together a small group of students and show them the three body parts for *reattachment* and how, when you put the ant together, you create a word with a prefix, a base, and a suffix.

2. Distribute only the ant parts with prefixes and suffixes. Ask students to locate thoraxes that they can attach to the heads or abdomens. What words can they make? Some of the parts can be joined with more than one base word.

3. Discuss what each prefix means and how it changes the base. Repeat this discussion with each suffix.

4. Continue until all students have reattached their prefixes or suffixes. Provide blank ant parts and encourage students to add to the ant colony with other words they find.

Differentiation: For **English language learners**, work together to create symbols that represent the prefixes. For example, a red circle with a line through it could represent *non–*. These symbols can be posted in the room as visual reminders for students.

✔ **Assessment Check:** Note which students quickly match body parts. This may indicate who is ready for more challenging words or new affixes and base words.

Flipping for Compound Words

Objective

Students will identify compound words.

Preparation

1. Copy *Pancake Compounds* on cardstock (pages 285–286; pancake.pdf).
2. Have a small spatula or pie server ready.

Procedure

1. Place the *Pancake Compounds* cards facedown on a table in a grid pattern. Gather students around so they can see. Have a student use the spatula to flip two pancakes, and have the rest of the group decide if the words make a compound word. If not, turn the pancakes back over.

2. Have students take turns flipping pancake pairs over. On each turn, a player will flip two pancakes over, hoping to make a single compound word. If a compound word is made, the player keeps the pancake pair. If not, the pancakes are turned back over and the next student flips two pancakes. Continue until all pancakes are matched. If a match was made that leaves an unmatched pair of pancakes, ask students to look over the words and see which ones might need to be switched.

3. Leave the activity out for students to revisit during independent work time. You can also have students create new pancakes to extend the game. Have students use current reading or content-area materials to find words.

Differentiation: For **below-level students**, have a list of the compound words from the game available for students to reference. For **above-level students**, have them stop after they flip the first pancake each time. Ask them to name possible compound words that contain that word.

✔ **Assessment Check:** As students work, make note of any nonsense words made, indicating a misunderstanding of meaning. Clarification or additional instruction may be needed.

Word Study

3–5 Strategies

Objective

Students will use comparatives and superlatives.

Preparation

1. Copy *Comparatives and Superlatives List* (page 287; comparative.pdf).
2. Place students into groups of three.

Procedure

1. Explain that you are going to describe an order and each group must order themselves in that way. Refrain from using words that might embarrass students or make them uncomfortable. For example, "I'm looking at your heights. One of you is tall, one is taller, and one is the tallest. Please stand in that order."

2. Continue with *Comparatives and Superlatives List*, having students rearrange themselves each time according to the words. Contextualize the set of words each time, such as, "I see someone in your group has a *long* shoe, one has a *longer* shoe, and the third person has the *longest* shoe." Alternatively, instead of giving three words to students, tell them what you are looking at ("I'm looking at your hair."), and let them decide how to order and describe themselves.

3. Have each group come up with their own comparisons. For example, they might arrange themselves according to clothing color. Encourage students to correctly use –*er* and –*est* to end their comparatives and superlatives.

Differentiation: For **below-level students**, give additional practice using words they know, such as *soon/sooner/soonest* or *wise/wiser/wisest*. For **English language learners**, write the three words on the board during the activity to let students visually connect the print to the words. In small groups, give **above-level students** the first word of irregular comparatives, such as *good*, and ask them what would come next (*better, best*). Other irregular comparatives are *bad/worse/worst*, *many/more/most*, and *little/less/least*.

✔ **Assessment Check:** Listen in as students discuss the sets of descriptive words. Note any students who struggle and provide focused additional guidance and practice.

Pears for Pairs

Vocabulary

3–5 Strategies · **Word Study**

Objective

Students will distinguish homophones, antonyms, or synonyms.

Preparation

1. Copy *Pear Template* (page 288; pear.pdf), one per student.
2. Write homophone pairs on each pear. For a list of suggested pairs, see *Word Pairs* (page 289; wordpairs.pdf). Create one with *tale/tail* to use as your example.

Procedure

1. Tell students you have a pair of homophones written on your pear. Say, "One of us means a story; the other means something a dog wags. Who are we?" (*tale/tail*)

2. Discuss how homophones sound alike but are spelled differently. Tell students to use the spelling and/or context clues to understand the meaning of an individual homophone word.

3. Distribute a *Pear Template* card to each student. Explain that each pear shows a homophone pair. Have students write clues for their words. Allow them to work with partners if needed.

4. Have students read their clues to the class. Ask students to guess each word pair. Create a bulletin board that displays the pears and their matching clues.

    Provide blank pears so that students can add to the display when they find new homophone pairs.

Differentiation: Have **English language learners** create quick visuals next to each word in the homophone pair to add context to the words. Give **above-level students** more abstract homophone pairs, such as *symbol/cymbal*, *sweet/suite*, *manner/manor*, *who's/whose*, *straight/strait*, *Greece/grease*, *pray/prey*, *medal/meddle*, *cord/chord*, and *flare/flair*.

✔ **Assessment Check:** Circulate as students create clues. Listen for conversations that show their understanding (or misunderstanding) of the words. Follow up with clarification or guidance as needed.

This activity can be changed to antonym pairs or synonym pairs. Write antonym or synonym pairs on the pears instead of homophones. The Word Pairs list includes suggested words for this extension. This can also be used as a learning center activity.

Overview of Standards and Strategies
Grade 6 through Grade 8

This section includes basic small-group strategy lessons for simple practice of the following skills for grade 6 through grade 8. Details regarding each strategy can be found on the subsequent pages. For additional lessons, download the Digital Resources. (See page 20 for the website address and access code.)

Mini-Lessons

Phonics

Lesson	Skill
The Great Wordini (page 68)	multisyllabic words

Spelling

Lesson	Skill
Four-Corners Spelling (page 69)	spelling commonly misspelled words
Hit or Miss (page 70)	spelling commonly misspelled words
Sentence-Strip Editing (page 71)	spelling commonly misspelled words

Vocabulary

Lesson	Skill
Fix Up a Word (page 72)	Greek and Latin affixes and bases
Make-a-Word (page 73)	Greek and Latin affixes and bases
Match Me (pages 74–75)	suffixes (-*tion*, -*sion*)
On a Bases and Affixes Stroll (page 76)	Greek and Latin affixes and bases
Say What? (page 77)	word nuances and connotations
Unlock the Word (page 78)	Greek and Latin affixes and bases
Word Hunt (page 79)	homonyms, antonyms, synonyms
What's My Base? (page 80)	Greek and Latin affixes and bases

Some websites that serve to enhance instruction and provide additional opportunities for students to explore these various topics are:

- www.quizlet.com
- www.classzone.com
- www.wisc-online.com
- www.webenglishteacher.com

Some apps that serve to enhance instruction and provide additional opportunities for students to explore these various topics are:

- WordTree 3D Free (Apple Learning)
- Middle School Vocabulary Prep (Peekaboo Studios LLC)
- SpellingCity (SpellingCity)
- Homophones Free—English Language Arts Grammar App (Abitalk Incorporated)

Additional Lessons—Digital Resources

Listed below are additional lessons available as digital downloads to help students develop their word study skills. See page 20 for the website and access code to download these files.

Phonics

Lesson	Skill
Play Ball! (playball.pdf)	consonant alternations
Soak it Up! (soakup.pdf)	assimilated prefixes

Vocabulary

Lesson	Skill
Meet the Relatives (meetrel.pdf)	Greek and Latin affixes and bases

Objective

Students will determine multisyllabic words.

Preparation

1. Cut strips of paper (4.5" × 7"), one per student pair.

2. Write the numbers 3–5 on craft sticks or strips of paper to use for random drawings.

3. Copy *Top Hat Template* (page 290; tophat.pdf), one per student pair.

Procedure

1. Each student pair becomes The Great Wordini and his or her Brilliant Assistant.

2. The Great Wordini draws a number (3–5). He or she must find 10 words with that number of syllables. Direct students to look around the room for posters, signs, or books to find words. To extend this and/or make it more complex, encourage students to look for words with particular spelling patterns, such as words with *r*-controlled vowels, or to find particular content-area words as they search.

3. As each Great Wordini finds his or her 10 words, the Brilliant Assistant writes the words on the strips of paper that fit into the *Top Hat Template*.

4. To finish the magic word encounter, each Brilliant Assistant should cut a slit in the *Top Hat Template* and feed the word strip through as The Great Wordini reads each word.

5. Students switch roles and repeat the activity using the blank backside of the word strip.

   Extend the lesson by having students look up their words in the dictionary for proper syllable breaks and annotate the words on the word strips.

Differentiation: Have **below-level students** find one-syllable words, while **above-level students** find four-syllable words.

✔ **Assessment Check:** Keep a checklist of the words made by students during the activity, seeing who may need additional support or who may need more complex words.

Word Study

6–8 Strategies

Objective

Students will correctly spell commonly misspelled words.

Preparation

1. Prepare four signs—*A*, *B*, *C*, and *D*—and place one each in four distinct corners or areas of the room.

2. Select a list of words students commonly misspell and prepare three common misspellings for each word and one correct spelling. Put the four spellings of each word on a large sheet of paper or project them for students to analyze.

Procedure

1. Have students stand at their desks.

2. Read a word from the chosen list aloud, use it in a sentence, and show the four ways of spelling it (three incorrect and one correct), labeled *A*, *B*, *C*, and *D*. For example, *A: knawlege*, *B: knowledge*, *C: knowlege*, and *D: knawledge*.

3. Ask students to study the four versions and then walk to the letter corner with the spelling that they think is correct.

4. Reveal the answer, pointing out the features of the word, such as *knowledge* has the word *know*. Ask if they hear *ledge* as the last syllable.

5. Have students return to their desks, and continue with the other words you have selected.

Differentiation: Have **English language learners** complete the activity in pairs so they can discuss before they go to one of the corners. Have **above-level students** create additional cards for a future four-corners game.

✔ **Assessment Check:** Keep track of students who seem unsure of which corner to go to. Those who wait and watch the other students may be struggling with the words and may need individual practice with the correct spellings in context to solidify their knowledge.

Hit or Miss

Spelling

Objective

Students will use current content-area vocabulary.

Preparation

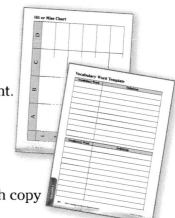

1. Copy *Hit or Miss Chart* (page 291; hitmiss.pdf), one per student.

2. Select 10 content-area vocabulary words students need to spell correctly. Write them, along with their definitions, in both tables on the *Vocabulary Word Template* (page 292; vocabtemp.pdf).

3. Copy your completed *Vocabulary Word Template* and cut each copy in half horizontally so that each student has one chart.

Procedure

1. Tell students to write vocabulary words from the list on their *Hit or Miss Charts*. They should put one word per square. There are more boxes than words, so blank boxes are acceptable.

2. Arrange students so they are facing each other. Stand a book or other screen between the students so their papers are hidden.

3. Have students decide who starts the game, or they can do it depending on whose first name begins with a letter closest to *A*.

4. Instruct the first student to give a coordinate, such as C4. If the partner has a vocabulary word in that box he or she says, "Hit," and reads the word aloud. The first student scores one point. Then, the first student must write the word spelled correctly in the indicated box on his or her own *Hit or Miss Chart*. Once the word is written, he/she checks the spelling and scores an extra point if it's correct.

   If the square (for example, C4) is empty, the partner says, "Miss."

5. Both students mark their respective sheets to record the hits and misses. If it's a miss, play returns to the second student.

6. Play continues until all the words on one of the charts have been hit.

Differentiation: Be sure to choose words that are on level for all students. This may mean that **below-level students** use slightly less complex words. Have **above-level students** spell and define each word when they get a hit.

✔ **Assessment Check:** Collect the *Hit or Miss Charts* after the game. A quick check will indicate how well they are learning the words. If it's clear that some students are still struggling, then additional contextualized experiences might be needed.

Sentence-Strip Editing

Objective

Students will edit spelling in sentences.

Preparation

1. Write sentences on sentence strips. In each sentence, have one word spelled incorrectly. Have one sentence strip per student.

2. Number and tape up the sentence strips around the room in random order.

3. Provide lined paper, one sheet per student.

Procedure

1. Have students number a sheet of lined paper to match the number of sentence strips placed around the room.

2. Have all students get up and start at a different number so they are spread out around the room evenly.

3. Tell each student to begin by reading the sentence in front of him or her and to figure out which word is spelled incorrectly. Then, they have to write the word, spelled correctly, next to the corresponding number on their lined paper.

4. Have students circle the room until all sentences have been edited by all the students. As students finish, they can return to their seats.

5. Share the answers and have students grade their papers for accuracy.

Differentiation: Allow **below-level students** time after they have circled to all the sentence strips. Give them access to dictionaries and encourage them to check the spellings of the words they wrote. Assist them as necessary. Have **above-level students** also choose at least one word in each sentence to edit. Their goal is to make the sentences have more imagery or description.

✔ **Assessment Check:** Circulate as students work. Notice any students referring to their peers for help. Note which students have difficulty with the correct spellings. Collect the papers. Look for any patterns to the words that were challenging for students. Additional support or practice may be needed.

Objective

Students will define and use affixes accurately.

Preparation

1. Prepare affix/words cards, one set per group of two to four students. Each note card needs an affix at the top. Under that, list (in random order) five words that combine with the affix to make real words and five words that do not. Example words for the prefix *pre-* could be: *cook, act, fix, cross, heat, game, approve, dry, phone,* and *try.*

Procedure

1. Arrange students into small groups of two to four, giving each group a set of affix/words cards.

2. Have each group define the first affix and study the list of 10 words.

3. Students should determine which five words combine with the affix to make real words and which five do not. Suggest to students that they say each word aloud to hear if the words are familiar or not. Each group should then record its lists of real words and not real words. (In the example, these are real words: *precook, prefix, preapprove, preheat,* and *pregame.* These are not real words: *predry, preact, precross, prephone,* and *pretry.*)

4. Have students repeat these steps for each affix/words card.

5. Conduct a whole-class discussion once the groups are finished. Ask groups to suggest other words for the affixes. Encourage students to use glossaries or dictionaries to find additional words.

Differentiation: For **below-level students**, allow them to use dictionaries as they work to look up the words. For **above-level students**, have them create their own cards.

✔ **Assessment Check:** Note who struggles to identify real words. As students work in groups, also note who contributes to the discussions. Misconceptions may need to be addressed in a future lesson or additional practice may be needed.

Make-a-Word

Objective

Students will use bases and affixes.

Preparation

1. Copy *Make-a-Word Cards* (page 293; makeword.pdf), one per student.

2. Prepare an answer key (*injection, understanding, relaxation, construction, incredible, transportation,* and *proceeding*).

3. Provide each student with a pair of scissors.

Procedure

1. Have students cut apart the *Make-a-Word Cards.*

2. Ask students to sort the word cards into three categories—prefixes, bases, and suffixes.

3. Have students work to combine bases and affixes to create seven real words.

4. Once all the students have created the seven words, reveal answers or provide the answer key.

Differentiation: Have **below-level students** work in small groups to determine the seven words from the cards. Provide **English language learners** sentences that use each of the real words. Have **above-level students** create their own cards to challenge one another.

✔ **Assessment Check:** Make note of who correctly matches the word parts and who struggles. Follow up with further practice as needed.

Match Me

Vocabulary

Objective

Students will add *–tion* and *–sion* to words and consider the meanings of the new words.

Preparation

1. Copy *Word Cards* (page 294; wordcard.pdf). Copy enough to have one individual word card per student.

2. Copy *Explanation Signs* (page 295; explanation.pdf). Cut the page in half and post the *–tion* and *–sion* signs on opposite walls of your classroom. Add a large blank sheet of chart paper next to each sign to record the words created during the activity.

Procedure

1. Give students time to read the *Explanation Signs*.

2. Show students the *direct* word card. Read the word and orally add the ending sound /shun/.

3. Ask students which ending correctly finishes the word based on the rules posted. (*–tion*) Walk to the *–tion Explanation Sign,* and write the word *direction* on the chart paper. Ask if that looks right. Review how the ending was added. *Direct* ends in *–t*, so *–ion* was added.

4. Ask students what the new word means. (*Direct* is a verb that means to cause someone to go in a particular way; *direction* is a noun that means the course or path on which something is moving or pointing.)

5. Show students the *examine* card. Ask them which ending it should have and what the word would sound like with the /shun/ ending. Guide them to listen across the word and notice that an *a* must also be added. Write the new word on the blank paper by the *–tion Explanation Sign*.

6. Ask students what the word now means. (*Examine* is a verb that means to look at something closely and carefully; *examination* is a noun that means the act of looking at something closely and carefully.)

7. Distribute the rest of the cards to students. For each word card, have a student look at the card and decide what ending to walk to. Remind students to listen and look at their words. Guide students to carefully look at their words in relation to the rules.

8. Have students correctly write and double-check their words and endings on the chart paper once they have arrived at the correct sign.

9. Invite students to share and define their words. Have them circle the room to examine the words made on both pieces of chart paper.

10. Have students discuss in groups how the words follow the posted rules and affect the words' meanings.

11. Ask students to pick independent reading books, glossaries of resource texts, or dictionaries, and hunt for additional words to add to the lists.

Differentiation: Have **English language learners** use resources, such as dictionaries, to verify their answers before going to the posted signs. For **above-level students**, add –*cian* to the sort. Some options for words include *magic, music, beauty, optic, electric, politics,* and *mathematics,* which are all jobs. Have students decide the rules for adding this ending.

✔ **Assessment:** Watch as students add their words to the lists. This will help determine who needs additional practice and who needs more challenging words.

6–8 Strategies

Word Study

Objective

Students will use Greek and Latin bases and affixes to create words and determine the meaning of bases..

Preparation

1. Copy *Bases and Affixes* (page 296; baseaffix.pdf) on cardstock. On the page, each base is first. There are six affixes for each base.

2. Spread the five root cards on the floor, far enough apart that small groups can stand around each base. Use *vert* for the example.

3. Spread affixes around the base cards. (Use *con*, *ible*, *intro*, *re*, *ical*, and *di* for the example.)

4. Place blank paper and small blank paper squares near each base card.

Procedure

1. Show students how to stand next to or on the base (*vert*) and walk to an affix that can be added to make a word (*ical* = *vertical*). Tell them they may walk to more than one affix each time (*convertible*) to make a word.

2. Divide students into groups.

3. Ask students to use the blank papers to record and define their group's words as each student takes a turn walking from the base to its affixes.

4. Ask students to use the blank squares to write any other affixes they can think of to make new words.

5. Rotate the groups around to the different sets of bases.

6. With all the groups, return to each base and discuss the common meaning that the base brings to the related words.

Differentiation: For **below-level students**, group them homogeneously for this activity and spend extra time supporting this group of learners.

✔ **Assessment Check:** Collect the papers and check which groups were able to make words by combining the base and affixes. Additional support or instruction may be needed.

The study of bases can significantly increase a student's vocabulary. Knowing the meaning and spelling relationship between words is essential to independence in reading and writing, especially as students approach more complex texts. Making sure to point out such relationships is a vital part of vocabulary instruction.

Say What?

Vocabulary

Objective

Students will replace words based on nuance and connotation.

Preparation

1. Create sentences that combine multiple parts of speech in complex ways. You might want to select words that the students use in their own writing, such as *beautiful, develops,* or *enjoyed.* Example sentences may include the following: *It is his junior year in high school, and he has learned a lot. Not enough, however, to make the varsity team. He is older, <u>faster</u>, and bigger than all his JV teammates. He's the only one who <u>throws</u> a perfect pass. It's going to be a <u>terrible</u> season.*

2. Write individual sentences on slips of paper. When writing the sentences, underline words you want students to consider replacing as shown above. Choose words that have strong synonyms. Place all the slips in a container.

Procedure

1. Have each student pair choose a sentence from the container. Provide time for them to read and consider the underlined words.

2. Ask each pair to compile a list of about five descriptive words to replace each underlined word. Then, ask them to rewrite the sentence to make it more powerful or meaningful.

3. Have student pairs share their new sentences. Discuss how each sentence has a different connotation due to the better descriptive words. Additionally, student pairs can pantomime their sentences, such as how *throws* looks compared to *tossed* or *spiraled.* Discuss the nuances of the changes made through the more descriptive words.

4. Discuss with the whole group how word choices need to be very descriptive. This important vocabulary skill can be applied to any writing project.

Differentiation: Have **above-level students** choose their own words in the sentences to change.

✔ **Assessment Check:** Ask students to search their own writing for sentences to change. They can write their old sentences on strips and list possible descriptive words to replace the original words. This will be a quick check on how they apply the lesson's idea to their personal writing and will help you determine who needs additional support.

Objective

Students will use common Greek and Latin bases.

Preparation

1. Choose four to six bases to teach from *Greek and Latin Bases* (page 297; greek.pdf).

2. Write each base and its meaning on a note card. For example, *acro—height*.

3. Create word cards with words that contain the bases. Make enough note cards for each student pair to have at least one word. Some example words are included on *Greek and Latin Bases*.

4. Have one highlighter for each student pair.

Procedure

1. Read aloud one base to students, asking if anyone knows its meaning. Show the base card to students. Share the other base cards as well. Leave the cards on display.

2. Distribute word cards to student pairs, and have students highlight the bases in the words.

3. Have each student pair examine the other parts of its word to unlock its meaning.

4. Have students write the meanings of the words on the cards. Then, have students share their words and meanings with the class. Students can repeat the process for the other cards or have them turn the cards over and think of other words that contain that base.

Differentiation: Have **English language learners** work together to write sample sentences on their cards to give the words context. Have **above-level students** use an unabridged dictionary to find even more words that contain the bases taught.

✔ Assessment Check:

Circulate as students work to listen to their conversations as they unlock the meanings. Additional practice opportunities or more challenging bases may be needed.

Word Hunt

Vocabulary

Objective

Students will use synonyms and/or antonyms.

Preparation

1. Copy *Word Hunt Cards* (pages 298–299; hunt.pdf), one card per student and one for yourself.

2. Write a word on the first *Word Hunt Card*. See *Synonyms and Antonyms* (page 300; synant.pdf) for word suggestions. As an option, use content-area words, such as *democracy* or *solidify*. Write the same word on the bottom line of that card. Follow this pattern so that the second word on each card is the first word of the next, such as I *found <u>blunt</u>. We're going on a word hunt for a synonym for <u>quarrel</u>. I found <u>quarrel</u>. The hunt is over!*

3. Cut the word cards apart.

Procedure

1. Review the definitions of synonyms or antonyms, depending on the lesson's focus.

2. Distribute the filled in *Word Hunt Cards*. Ask the student with the starting card to begin the game, "We're going on a word hunt for a synonym for _____." The answer card will be held by one of the students who will read it aloud when he or she recognizes that his or her word answers the hunt.

3. Have students read their individual cards to see if they found the word hunted for in the card read before them. This continues until the word on the last card is found. If time permits, shuffle the cards and play again.

4. Repeat the activity with antonyms or a mix of antonyms and synonyms. Leave the *Word Hunt Cards* out during independent work time and ask students to create other cards to add to the set.

Differentiation: For **below-level students**, provide a list of the synonyms and/or antonyms being used in the lesson at the onset of the hunt. For **English language learners**, provide a list of example sentences for the synonyms and/or antonyms being used in the lesson at the onset of the hunt.

✔ **Assessment Check:** Ask students to initial any cards they add to the set to assess their understanding of synonyms and/or antonyms. During the game, note any students who need assistance. This is a good listening and problem-solving activity. Note who quickly answers and who needs more support.

Word Study

6–8 Strategies

Objective

Students will recognize common Greek and Latin bases.

Preparation

1. Copy *Base Template* (page 301; basetemp.pdf), one card per student, plus an extra to serve as a model.

2. At the top of each card, write a Greek or Latin base, such as *vid/vis*. Underneath, write four words with the base, such as *video*, *visual*, *visible*, and *visor*. For examples see *Base Examples* (pages 302–303; baseexamp.pdf).

3. You can place students in small groups so that each group has a unique set of cards, allowing cards to be repeated for large classes.

Procedure

1. Show the model card. Explain that students are to give each other clues to the words on the list without saying the word, such as *This is a sort of hat that shades your eyes. Some golfers wear it.* (*visor*)

2. Practice with all four words. Highlight the base in each word. Ask what other words students know that have *vid/vis* in them.

3. Place students in small groups. Distribute blank note cards and tape one *Base Template* card on the back of each student, but do not allow him or her to see the card. Only other group members may see it.

4. Tell students to take turns showing their backs to group members and asking for clues about their four words. On their note card, students should write the words they figure out and then study them for one common base. Once they figure out their base, they can guess it. If they are correct,they can add more words related to that base and take the *Base Template* card off their back.

5. Post the cards for students to read on subsequent days. Invite them to add more words to the cards.

Differentiation: For **below-level students**, include mostly familiar words as the examples for each base. For **above-level students**, select newly acquired or unfamiliar words.

✔ **Assessment Check:** Listen as students give clues to each other. Make note of their command of definitions and their ability to describe the words. Additional practice with these bases or new bases may be needed to further develop their vocabulary skills.

Conclusion

This section presented three important areas of word study—phonics, spelling, and vocabulary. These instructional areas weave together to develop word knowledge and work in parallel development. One area informs the others. Students must learn to decode words to read, and they must encode words to write. Students need to develop knowledge of high-frequency words, as well as specialized vocabulary to develop fluency in reading and writing. And, of course, word study crosses into all areas of the curriculum. When learning how to analyze words using content vocabulary as part of the word study, our efforts double to teach phonics skills with vocabulary development. The mini-lessons included in this section provide ideas tohelp students solidify their learning following explicit and systematic instruction provided by their teacher. The ultimate goal is to find ways every day to "spin" your word study plate to solidify knowledge for students and help them see the bigger applications of word learning.

Reflection and Discussion Questions

1. Select a content-area reading text and highlight some words to include in your word study. What words fit into phonics or spelling categories you currently have students studying?

2. Brainstorm a list of words that are pivotal for your students to know. Which of the mini-lessons can you use (or revise) to teach these words?

3. Select a book you plan to use as a read aloud. What vocabulary might be challenging for students? How might you handle familiarizing them with the meanings of the words? Is there a way to break down and analyze any of the words to expand students' understanding?

4. What does David Crystal (2011) mean when he says, "Vocabulary is a matter of word-building as well as word-using"? What does this have to do with vocabulary instruction?

5. What word study topic can you explore? For example, do you want to do an informal inventory of key grade-level vocabulary? Do you want to investigate word histories and origins for common content words?

6. What are some novel ways to have students demonstrate vocabulary knowledge? Posters? Talk shows where "bases" are interviewed about their meanings and "relatives"?

7. What grade-level spelling words are important for students to master? How many of the words are high frequency, and how many follow a pattern we can teach?

8. How can you develop a resource "room" to use for instructional materials and ideas? What will it include?

9. What other resources do you currently own or need to purchase that can extend your word study mini-lessons?

10. What texts from the provided References in Appendix A do you want to read and discuss? Who will lead the discussion and help you apply the knowledge to your teaching?

Reading

Introduction

To learn to read is to light a fire; every
syllable spelled out sparkles.

—Victor Hugo

This section focuses on reading instruction for balanced literacy classrooms. Reading has many "spinning plates." Several plates are instructional because teachers have multiple ways to show students the how and why of reading. The planned instruction of reading can spin into small- and whole-group instruction, shared and modeled read alouds, as well as independent reading. This is one area of literacy where your students can help you spin the plates. By having students choose books for independent reading, they direct the excitement of the application of growing reading skills. Turning over some of the responsibility to your students to participate in the magic of reading develops important independent skills that will last a lifetime. Additionally, they can help organize the classroom to be a place of literacy learning all day long.

Organizing the reading classroom helps students and teachers to work efficiently and as a community of learners. Lev Vygotsky (1978) long ago argued that learning is a social act. You must establish a place of learning where students support each other, learn from each other, and learn through active engagement. "Creating a safe community in which peers and teachers are viewed as allies is essential for greater engagement and academic achievement" (Vygotsky 1978, 1). This chapter presents how to plan and implement guided reading in kindergarten through grade 5 and literature circles in grade 6 through grade 8. Once students have been assessed, you can group them for instruction in ways to take advantage of their developing independent skills without pushing them into frustration. Teachers can also examine modeled and shared read alouds across all grade levels. Students need modeled strategies to help develop their abilities at making predictions while reading, keeping them engaged, and improving comprehension. Additionally, this section examines how to craft comprehension questions that help students to not only better understand what they read, but also to think deeply about how engaged they are with the text. Teachers must make the reading process explicit. How does a reader pay attention to print? How do students check themselves for understanding? Teachers must help students to think about their thinking when they read, thus making this somewhat invisible process more visible (McKeown and Gentilucci 2007). Finally, this section examines ways to guide students to select appropriate books for instructional and independent reading, and also delves into the importance of independent reading. During this independent reading, students practice their developing skills in approachable, readable texts.

Meet Isabella

Mr. Loomis carries a basket of books into his fourth-grade classroom. At the same time, Isabella is coming in from the bus. She sees Mr. Loomis and dashes to walk in beside him. "Did you get my book? Did you get my book?" Laughing, Mr. Loomis replies, "Yes, Isabella, I sure did." Isabella grins widely and asks if she can have it as they enter the classroom. Mr. Loomis digs through the basket and hands Isabella a book.

Hugging the book tightly to her chest, Isabella exclaims, "Oh, my book, my book!"

To the casual observer there is nothing really special about the book. But for Isabella, this is no ordinary book. Isabella came to fourth grade still struggling with reading. Many words caused her difficulty. Mr. Loomis realized quickly that Isabella would need additional phonics instruction, intense guided reading, and strategies to give her independence. One day, Isabella pulled a book that Mr. Loomis had borrowed from the library from the shelf. Word by word Isabella plodded along, reading independently. Over the next several days Isabella pulled out that same book, again reading word by word and each time gaining fluency. Finally one day, she declared to Mr. Loomis, "I love this book! I can read it! This is MY book!"

Of course, the time came when Mr. Loomis had to return the book to the library. But, surely, he thought, Isabella would find another book in which to anchor her growing reading skills. But, when Isabella tore through the library corner looking for "her book," he realized it meant more than just print on a page. It confirmed to Isabella that she *was* a reader, something she had not felt in previous years. She knew she could read *that* book and her confidence needed the boost. Her tearful expression told Mr. Loomis he needed to get back to the library for the book.

Anchor texts *are texts students self-select and reread because they are familiar with them and feel confident reading them. These repeated readings allow students to practice their developing skills with relative ease and confidence. Like a boat's anchor that keeps us from drifting, anchor texts help students maintain the skills they have well in hand.*

Knowing our students' strengths and needs are the keys to successful reading instruction. We need to know what they can do and in what ways they still need to grow. While assessment of skills guides our instructional planning, knowing our students' interests and confidence levels is equally important. Isabella is a good example of a student needing an "anchor book" (Fresch 1995). This anchor book can provide familiarity. As they develop as readers, our students may seek repetition as it helps them "gain control of reading strategies by drawing on what they already know" (Fresch 1995, 221). This self-selection, of course, is only one piece of the reading instruction that every classroom must have. By providing targeted instruction during guided reading, engaging students in read alouds, and providing time for independent reading, we can offer a well-rounded experience to our developing readers.

Setting Up the Reading Classroom

Like any profession, teachers need the tools of their trade. They need ready access to materials and students need to know they can self-direct their learning. Having students know exactly where they can find what they need to direct their word study, reading, and writing reduces the number of procedural questions and lets teachers spend their time teaching to meet their conceptual needs. For example, let's return to Mr. Loomis's classroom. Organized to make word study, reading, and writing priorities all day long, Mr. Loomis not only makes lots of materials available to students, but he also has a professional corner filled with resources to assist in his teaching. The environment in his classroom loudly proclaims, "We are all about literacy here!" So, let's examine how classroom materials can enhance and support learning.

In the Word Study section, word-focused materials are suggested. In addition to those materials, your classrooms should have a library, reading zone, and listening area.

The Library

This section of the classroom is filled with a wide assortment of books used for read alouds and independent reading. It is also an inviting space for students to sit and read. Choose to organize your library in a way that meets the learning needs of your students as well as your teaching needs. Some classrooms group books by reading levels, such as Lexile® levels. Some classrooms group books according to guided reading groups. While such organization signals how easy (or not) a book may be to read, research shows that providing students with access to all books encourages them to stretch their developing skills (Fresch 1995). Organizing by genres is particularly important for grade 3 through grade 8. Teachers often put books together by current and past thematic units. In any of the grade levels, a section can be devoted to an author study, which may mix genre and topic.

Organization for a classroom library can change over the school year. For example, a section of nonfiction/informational books can include topics covered in social studies and science. These books might also be used for read alouds and to model how to pay attention to new vocabulary. These books can be left together after a topic is covered for students to revisit during independent reading. One section might be specifically designated for alphabet books that cross over into the content areas, such as oceans or ecology for science, or communities or the Civil War for social studies. Sophisticated alphabet books for older readers provide a great resource for studying content-related vocabulary. A section can be specifically marked as "Featured Books"—those books used in read alouds—which are often returned to for independent reading. Student-authored books can also be available in a special section for other students to select.

The books should offer various levels of difficulty, ranging from wordless picture books, which are highly supportive for young or second language learners, to chapter books. If multiple copies are available of single titles, students can readily use them for literature circles or research.

Some teachers like to organize books in baskets according to reading level difficulty. Evaluating the level of a text is important to the selection of books to use during guided reading. However, research has demonstrated that when left to their own choosing for

Have students each complete a bookmark for texts they recommend and place the bookmarked texts in designated spots in the classroom library. A Bookmark Template *can be found on page 304. The bookmark should stick out of the text for easy viewing. Students can provide one reason they would recommend the text. Alternatively, have students create an "ad" for the text on the bookmark to entice a reader without spoiling the contents.*

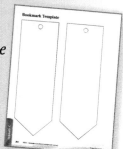

independent reading, students will more often pick books much more difficult than their reading "level" might suggest (Fresch 2005). A peer's recommendation of a "really good book" might be enough to encourage a student to pick a book they would normally not choose. A title, cover, illustration, or unusual book topic can all be reasons for a student to pick up a book. Many public libraries have a special area called "Staff Picks," so similarly, an area in the classroom library labeled "Our Favorites" or "You Just HAVE to Read This!" may entice a reluctant reader to give a book a try.

For independent reading, students should feel comfortable in their choices, yet able to read for meaning. Teaching students how to select books to read is an essential strategy to ensure that the wide range of texts offered in the classroom library are utilized thoughtfully and purposefully by your students. The process below helps students navigate these waters.

To practice this, have students each pick a book. Ask them to place the books on their desks, a table, or the floor and open to any page. Then, ask them to each hold one hand out and make a fist. Have them each begin reading. Tell students to put up one finger each time they see a word they do not know. (Alternatively, they can write the words on *The Five-Finger Rule* [page 305] graphic.) At the end of the page they should use the following to help decide if they should try to read the book:

0 fingers up = too easy

1 finger up = too easy, but good practice

2 fingers up = you can pick this, but next time try one a little harder

3 fingers up = just right

4 fingers up = give it a try

5 fingers up = may be too hard; try it, but feel free to stop reading if you have trouble

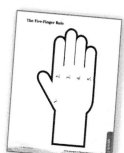

The Reading Zone

While this area may be near the classroom's library, a designated space where students know reading is *the* activity is a sure fire way to send the message that reading is a very important part of your classroom. Regardless of the reading material—books, magazines, or content materials—students know they can "retreat" to engage in undisturbed reading. Lots of other things might be going on in the room, such as guided reading groups or literacy centers/workstations, but this area is designed to empower students to take charge of their own reading and learning. Ideally, this space is somewhat away from the bookshelves or crates, so students are not stepping over others to make book selections. Large decorated "privacy" cardboard boxes, beanbag chairs, or even a small area rug work well to create private spaces for reading. If space permits, buddies can meet here to read together, too. In classrooms short on space, having a visual "signal" that someone is "in the reading zone" also works. For seat work, tape or hot glue red and green plastic cups together (bottom to bottom) and place one on each student's desk. Have students flip the red cup up to indicate "Do Not Disturb," indicating they are deep into reading at their own workspace. If the green cup is up, the student is doing other work that can be interrupted for a peer utilizing the "ask three, then me" (Frey 2010, 81) strategy, where students are encouraged to request help from three peers to answer academic questions rather than interrupt the teacher engaged in small-group instruction.

The Listening Area

Studies show that students listen at least 50 percent of the day, yet rarely do students receive instruction in how to do so (Opitz and Zbaracki 2004). Listening is not simply "hearing." It is an important skill that enables students to learn and comprehend aurally. It provides opportunities to tap into background experiences and develop new oral language skills. By setting a purpose for listening, you provide guidance in how to listen. One way to encourage listening is to provide audio versions of books. The public and school libraries often have popular children's books with accompanying CDs. Alternatively, you can make your own by recording books using your computer's software, such as *GarageBand*, or a free program on the Internet. You can burn CDs or create MP3s and students can use computers or CD players with headphones to listen. For young readers, you can add a sound, such as a bell ringing, to signal turning a page.

For an assessment opportunity, provide a listening guide for students. For kindergarten through grade 2, create simple instructions that ask them to draw or write something about the book after they listen, such as, "Draw your favorite part of the story," or "List five things you learned after listening to this book." For grade 3 through grade 5, give them a few comprehension questions to answer. Aim for questions that take some thought and are not simple recall. For grade 6 through grade 8, provide a menu of "after listening" options, such as, "Write about a connection you made to another text while listening to this book," "What fact(s) surprised you the most?," and "What more do you want to know about the character/information learned/topic in general?"

Students can also record their own readings of books and add these to the

Websites with Recordings of Books

Just Books Read-Aloud *is a well-organized site of video read alouds of a variety of children's books. The site offers readings in six languages. It is child-safe. They cannot navigate away from a video to something unrelated or inappropriate.*
http://www.justbooksreadaloud.com

Storyline Online *is sponsored by the Entertainment Industry Foundation and the Screen Actors' Guild. Hear actors read well-known children's books. Videos of the illustrations accompany each read aloud.*
http://www.storylineonline.net

Lit2Go *uses the Flesch-Kincaid Readability Formula to level books. PDFs of the texts are downloadable.*
http://etc.usf.edu/lit2go/readability/flesch_kincaid_grade_level

Storynory *has a large collection of stories, ranging across grade levels. From nursery rhymes, to fairy tales, classic stories, and even Greek myths, a wide age range of students can enjoy these audio stories with accompanying texts.*
http://www.storynory.com

listening—area. Students love to hear their classmates read and will often listen simply because a friend recorded it. Additionally, these recordings are a great way for students to hear their progress over the year. Ask them in the springtime to rerecord books they read in the fall. After recording, have them listen to their first versions and reflect on the changes in their fluency and cadence when reading. These student-made recordings are a good way to revisit books several times before actually making CDs, thus providing vital practice in fluency. The recordings can be sent home at the end of the school year as gifts to the families to show how students grew in fluency.

For an assessment opportunity, ask students to tell you (kindergarten through grade 2) or write (grade 3 through grade 8) about what they notice about the differences in how they read at the beginning of the year and then again at the end of the year. What changed? What goals do they have in the coming months based on listening to themselves?

Assessing Students in the Reading Classroom

Assessment is integral to instruction. The origin of the word explains its purpose. "Assess" comes from the Latin meaning *to sit beside* (Fresch and Wheaton 2002). In each of these assessments, teachers "sit beside" and observe how well students are progressing. "Assessment is today's means of understanding how to modify tomorrow's instruction" (Tomlinson 2014, 18). Assessment is for all students from those who struggle to those at grade level to those who are above-level learners. Assessment allows every student to be taught with respect to his or her unique needs and continued development. In planning the reading classroom, three types of assessment should be used to guide instruction:

- diagnostic assessment
- formative assessment
- summative assessment

First, with *diagnostic assessment*, teachers assess before beginning teaching to give them an indication of the competence students have in the skills needed for the reading lessons. Teachers seek information that allows them to view where students lie along a continuum of development expected at any given grade level. If there is a gap in the expected development of a student's skills, then that must be addressed with appropriate instruction to introduce or reteach the skill. If a student is beyond the expected grade-level standards, then the teacher must think of ways to challenge, refine, and expand his or her abilities. Diagnostic assessments provide information to help guide the formation of reading groups as well as the mini-lessons selected.

Second, during teaching, teachers are continuing this *formative assessment* constantly, where they monitor students as they work to identify their strengths and instructional needs. Formative assessment helps teachers gather information as students are engaged in learning. This type of assessment is ongoing during the teaching of a lesson or when a student is working independently, so teachers can observe him or her.

Finally, after a lesson or unit, teachers may do a *summative assessment*. A summative assessment evaluates how well students learned or performed tasks. A summative assessment can also show where reteaching of a skill or lesson may be needed. Teachers may even need to choose a different way to teach it. For example, if the teacher initially taught it visually, he or she may need to reteach it using an auditory or tactile approach.

Early Literacy Assessment

Planning for reading groups begins with diagnostic assessments. For example, in kindergarten, an early literacy assessment can highlight a student's emergent literacy skills. It can also be used in grade 1 to identify gaps in development and inform the introduction of or reteach a needed skill. Such an assessment is also helpful in showcasing how English language learners are transferring literacy knowledge from their native languages to English. Two useful reading diagnostic assessments are oral reading records and the Qualitative Reading Inventory (QRI). These assessments enable the teacher to view students in "real time"—how are students using their reading strategies as they approach texts? Additionally, oral reading records can be utilized during instruction to provide "on the run" assessments of any student.

Early literacy assessments generally evaluate how students are mastering several areas that are beneficial to developing reading skills. Once these areas are assessed, you can do the following:

- Find students with similar strengths and needs to group for guided reading.
- Make note of the skills the group members need.
- Select texts fitting their needs.
- Select mini-lessons to target skill development.

Five areas of emergent literacy skills are generally observed for development. These are described in the sections that follow. A class checklist (*Early Literacy Skills Class Checklist*, page 327) can help with grouping students based on common skills and needs. After each observation, make note of who seems to still be working on a skill and who has mastered it to help as you organize guided reading groups and choose mini-lessons.

Auditory Discrimination

Auditory discrimination is the ability to hear differences and similarities in sounds. This first step toward phonological awareness is important to assess, as lack of auditory discrimination may be an early indicator of later reading problems (Truch 1994). Auditory discrimination "skills have long been correlated with reading ability. Some specialists believe that [auditory discrimination tests] should be a component of all reading programs and that poor auditory discrimination can be a major factor in children's failure to reach reading targets" (Encyclopedia of Children's Health 2015, para. 1). You need to observe a student's ability to listen carefully and to tune into the differences in the sounds of the English language.

Phonological awareness is the ability to identify and manipulate sound units in spoken words.

Phonemic Awareness

Phonemic awareness is the ability to break spoken words into individual sounds. It is becoming more apparent in reading comprehension research that "the importance of the ability to hear the sounds of our language was best stated by Keith Stanovich (1993) when he observed that phonemic awareness is one of the best predictors of reading acquisition, even more so than IQ" (Fresch and Harrison 2013, 5). Having phonemic awareness plays an important role in the ability to segment words. Children who enter kindergarten with this skill "make faster progress in learning to read in the first two years of instruction than children who lack these capabilities" (Ehri and Roberts 2006, 114).

Alphabet Knowledge

We need to assess students' knowledge of the letters of the alphabet and whether they are beginning to connect letters to sounds. Research shows "letters and corresponding sounds are the basic building blocks of alphabetic languages, such as English. Children who understand the 'alphabetic principle,' or insight that printed words consist of letters that can be mapped to sounds, have achieved an important first step in learning to read and write" (Piasta 2014, 203). Indeed, correlational studies have identified that both phonemic awareness and letter knowledge are the best predictors of how well children will learn to read during their first two years of school (Fresch and Harrison 2013). Adams (1990) argues that not only must students quickly identify letters, but they must be able to do so out of sequence. In this way, teachers have an accurate picture of students' knowledge of the letters as well as the sounds they make. Assessing and teaching the alphabet, then, has important implications for planning instruction for young readers. The presentation of the letters and words for matching sounds should intentionally not be presented in alphabetical order. Research studies have shown there is a progression of easier to harder letter naming and letter sounding acquisition (Piasta 2014). The *Letters and Sounds of the Alphabet* lesson (pages 118–119) provides a clear option for teaching.

Statistics on the Consonant Sounds for C, Q, and X *(Adapted from Eldredge 2004)*

The letter c represents the /k/ sound about 76 percent and /s/ 23 percent of the time. The remaining 1 percent is other sounds, such as /sh/ in ocean. The letter q is generally represented by /kw/ at the beginning of a syllable or word. In all English words, q is followed by u. The letter x appears in only 95 of the 5,000 most frequently used English words. In those 95 words, x sounds like /ks/ 86 percent of the time. The remaining 14 percentage sounds like /z/ (xylophone) and /gz/ (exact).

Concepts of Print

Concepts about how print and books "work" are important to early reading success. Children who struggle with these concepts are at risk of having difficulties learning to read (Clay 2006). The important concepts students must develop about print and books are the following:

- directionality, left to right and top to bottom
- print, rather than picture, carries the message
- matching oral and written text (voice pointing)
- word recognition in context
- technical language—*word, letter and sentence, first and last, period*
- word recognition in isolation

Word Construction

Word construction is the ability to connect letters to the sound(s) they make. Connecting alphabet letters and their sounds enhances students' ability to learn words (Ehri 2005). Word construction activities allow teachers to directly observe students' abilities to manipulate letters to demonstrate their understanding of the sounds needed to create whole words. Asking students to use letter cards to construct simple words demonstrates how they are hearing across sounds. For example, "What letters are needed to make *hat*?"

Oral Reading Record

With practice, oral reading records can be quick and easy to complete. Having a student read a text aloud enables a teacher to listen in as the student uses his or her strategy "on the run." Watch as he or she uses the three cueing systems to navigate the text.

The Three Cueing Systems

Graphophonic
(visual)
Does it look right?

Semantic
(meaning)
Does it make sense?

Syntactic
(structure)
Does it sound right?

(Adapted from Adams 1998)

Graphophonic (visual) cues are the letter/sound connections. Knowledge of the sound/symbol relationships in the English language goes to work when you try to sound out words. If a student sees *c*, he or she must determine if it will sound like /s/ or /k/.

Semantic (meaning) cues are used to guide meaning. Background knowledge may help with this, as having prior experiences can assist in learning as students encounter new words. Being familiar with the concepts (everything from how a story line works to presentation of facts in nonfiction) can be useful as you read.

Syntactic (structure) cues relate to the acceptable structure of a text. Awareness of how words are ordered in a sentence guides you as you make meaning. Parts of speech, such as nouns, verbs, and adjectives, help verify that what you read is grammatically correct.

The format for oral reading records is to ask a student to read aloud from a text they have not read before that contains 100–200 words. Choose a text that you think a student can read reasonably well but will offer some challenge, so you can note what strategies he or she uses. To begin, use a narrative story. Later, an oral reading record can be taken using a nonfiction text to evaluate how the student approaches reading that genre, along with decoding new vocabulary. Jot down a few questions you will ask the student after the reading to ascertain comprehension. Try for a little variation—a few "in the book" and a few "in my head" questions will give you an idea of how the student paid attention to meaning. Keep these brief so as to make giving the oral reading record manageable.

Find a quiet spot where you can sit beside students and make notations of their readings. You do not need a separate copy of the text; a blank piece of paper will work, or use the *Oral Reading Record Form* (page 307). Be sure you are able to see the text to record errors.

1. Tell the student you want to hear him or her read an unfamiliar book aloud. Encourage the student to do his or her best reading of the book.

2. As the student reads, make a checkmark for every correct word read and record any misread words. The marking system for an oral reading record is shown in Figure 3.1.

Figure 3.1 Oral Reading Annotations

Type of Annotation	Annotation Note	Example
Substitution: Word from the text is written with the substituted word written above.	substituted word text word	pony horse
Omission: Word from the text is written and crossed out.	~~text word~~	~~mane~~
Insertion: Words from the text on either side of the insertion are written. The insertion is noted with a caret (^).	inserted word text ^ text	boy A ^ rant
Repetition: Repeated word is noted as "R" with checks to denote number of repeats. Or for a phrase, write words from the text with an arrow above to denote repeat. Can add a number if a phrase is repeated more than once.	√√√√R (denotes 4 repeats) ⟵ words in text reread	√√R ⟵ Then, he said,
Self-Correction: Any errors noted above have a slash followed by "SC."	wrong word / SC text word	deg / SC dog
Teacher Given: Sometimes you'll need to provide words to assist the student. Wait time here is crucial. Only supply a word when it is obvious the student will not or cannot go on. The word is written and noted "TG."	TG text word	TG house

Record the errors you hear to analyze what strategies the student did or did not use. While looking at the errors, try to discover what print information students are or are not using. Teachers can never be absolutely sure of what, but they can make a professional judgment based on observations. You are looking for windows into the student's strategies that are still in need of development to guide mini-lessons planned for groups or individuals.

Comprehension Check

Follow the read aloud with the comprehension questions. Remember to keep these brief. They will give you an idea of the amount of concentration and "energy" it took the student to read. If the student can only provide low-level responses, he or she may have needed to concentrate on decoding too much and could not attend to comprehension. One option is to allow the student to reread the text silently and then try to answer the questions. As a rule of thumb, comprehension levels are generally 90 percent correct for independent reading level, at least 75 percent for instructional reading level, and below 50 percent comprehension is considered frustrational reading level (Betts 1946). Instructional attention regarding comprehension may take priority over the errors the student made while reading the text. You will need to carefully consider if the student simply struggled with this one text (even after allowing a silent rereading) or if a lack of comprehension is the bigger issue. Also, with a short text, only a few questions may have been asked, so missing one question can impact the percentage score.

Analyzing the Oral Reading Record

Next, analyze what the student's reading errors show you. Figure 3.2 outlines common errors and what they mean for instruction.

Figure 3.2 Oral Reading Record Analysis

Error	What It Means	Questions to Ask
Substitution— replaced words in the text	• Student reads for meaning not utilizing graphophonic cues. • Student may not know a word so uses a different word that maintains meaning. • Student is not using semantics if the substituted word changes the meaning.	• Is the student relying on prior knowledge to "fill in" where he or she is uncertain of the word? • Does the word maintain syntax? • Is there any visual similarity between the text word and the substituted word? • Is the student using illustrations or photographs to guess the unknown word? • Does the student use his or her oral language to make the text sound right but different from the author's intention?
Omissions—words skipped over and not read aloud	• One-to-one matching of words in the text to the words read do not correspond. • Student is not using graphophonic cues to follow print. • Student may not be attending to meaning or not listening to himself or herself read.	• Does the student understand "reading for meaning"? • Does the student have knowledge of all letter/sound relationships? • Does the student lack knowledge of one or more phonic elements? • If an entire line is skipped, is there a visual issue? • Does the student rush through reading?
Insertions—words added that are not in the text	• One-to-one matching of words in the text to the words read do not correspond. • Student is using semantics to create additions to the text. • Student is not using graphophonic cues to follow print.	• Is the student "semantically centered" so that creating a story becomes more important than attending to the print? • Is the student using personal language skills, such as slang, to "fill in" the story? • Is the student using illustrations or photographs to guess the story line?
Repetition—words that are repeated	• Student is unsure of a word so stalls for time to decode the unfamiliar word in the text by repeating the preceding word(s). • Student needs a "running start" to connect back to the meaning.	• Is the student overly concerned with word-for-word accuracy? • Is the student lacking in confidence as a reader? • Are there too many unknown words in the text, making this text fall into their frustrational range?
Self-Corrections— words that are misread, but corrected by the student	• Student is reading for meaning and corrects words omitted, inserted, or substituted. • Student may notice a graphophonic mismatch and make a correction.	• Does student make comments, such as "that doesn't make sense" or "that doesn't sound right"?

Error	What It Means	Questions to Ask
Teacher Given— words you must provide to assist the student	• Student is unable to use any of the three cueing systems to decode a word. • Student is afraid to make an attempt to decode the word.	• Does the student have enough word-attack strategies, such as using semantics, to attempt the word? • Is the student lacking in confidence as a reader? • Does the student understand the carryover of phonics instruction to reading? • Does the student normally work independently, or is he or she "adult dependent" to complete literacy work? • Is the text selected too difficult for the student? If so, stop the assessment and select an easier text.

After annotating the oral reading record, look at each error. Decide what cues the student used. For example, the text reads, "The horse ran across the field." The student sees an illustration of a horse and reads the word *pony* instead of *horse*. In this substitution the student is using semantics and syntax. The error did not change the meaning. The student, however, did not use graphophonic cues. If the student read *house* for *horse*, the student used partial graphophonic cues, without using semantics. The meaning was changed and is of more concern than substituting *pony* for *horse*.

If you want a more detailed analysis, fill in the *Record of Analysis of Oral Reading* (page 309). Self-corrections and repetitions do not count as errors. In fact, self-corrections are important to note since they indicate the student is monitoring his or her own reading. Errors on proper names are only counted once. For example, the student reads *Mr. Pepper* instead of *Mr. Popper*. If the student says *Mr. Pepper* multiple times, it is only considered one error over the entire reading and not the number of times the name is mentioned. Speech problems (*w* for *r*) or dialect are also not counted as errors. Contractions count as one error (*I'll* for *I will* or vice versa). If a line is skipped, count every word as an omission. *Sample Record of Analysis of Oral Reading* (page 310) provides an example of an the analysis of an annotated text.

Knowing the three cueing systems (graphophonic, semantic, and syntactic) helps us see how students attempt to read unknown text (Adams 1998). What system do they use most often and which seems to be lacking? You see that these cueing systems overlap. The cues work together to help us achieve meaning from our reading. Sometimes we rely heavily on one more than another, depending on the demands of the text. Knowing what students continually use, such as an over-reliance on sounding out, can help direct the selection of mini-lessons.

Qualitative Reading Inventory

In grade 3 through grade 8, the QRI is an appropriate way to assess how well students use word-attack skills and comprehend what they are reading. This assessment presents a student with a leveled reading text. The assessment is *qualitative* because it is more than just obtaining a score for a student's reading performance. Like oral reading records, you need to analyze why a student makes particular errors. By looking closely, you can better match their reading instruction to their strengths and needs. Each level of the QRI has its own graded texts, questions, and percentages for instructional, independent, and frustration levels in both word recognition and comprehension. Many levels also provide measures for fluency.

On a QRI, a student is given a graded passage to read aloud, retell, and answer comprehension questions about. A QRI generally begins with a text a student can read successfully and then move on to more difficult texts. Like oral reading records, you want to observe a student's strategies "on the run." After reading the text aloud, the student is asked to retell it. Questions that are literal, inferential, and evaluative are then asked. The purpose is to find a student's instructional level. After evaluating a student's performance, a teacher can organize small groups for reading and for targeted mini-lessons.

Fluency is the "freedom from word identification problems that might hinder comprehension in silent reading or the expression of ideas in oral reading" (Harris and Hodges 1995, 85).

The assessment can be used to document growth. Passages read at the beginning of the school year can be reused about mid-year. A comparison of reading accuracy, fluency, retelling, and comprehension can all be compared. The teacher can then determine the next instructional steps and show progress so far.

Questions to Guide Comprehension

Whether you read a book aloud to our students or ask them to read independently, in the end comprehension is what reading is all about. Comprehension is "the process of simultaneously extracting and constructing meaning through interaction and involvement with written language" (Snow 2002, 11). Without understanding what they have read, students have only let their eyes pass over the print. Comprehension connects reading to previous experiences, expands knowledge, and provides verification that the cueing systems are working. Comprehension is an active seeking of meaning. The findings of the National Reading Panel (2000) suggest that comprehension can and should be explicitly taught. Developing quality questions is needed to ensure that students are not simply asked for one-word answers that take little thought and engagement. The application of comprehension outside classroom reading is evident in the National Assessment of Educational Progress. In defining the proficient reader, the National Assessment Governing Board states that "students will be expected to read comfortably across genres within fiction, nonfiction, procedural texts, and poetry...successfully answer[ing] questions, 70 percent to 80 percent of which call for the integration, interpretation, critique, and evaluation of texts read independently" (Raphael and Au 2005, 206–207). Thus, comprehension must be checked throughout the guided reading and literature circle lessons.

Before Reading

Begin a new text by helping students set goals for reading. Before reading questions generally fall into the following five categories:

1. **Accessing Prior Knowledge**—What do I know about this book/topic from the title/topic/cover illustration?

2. **Analyzing Text Structure and What it Means as Readers**—How should I use the illustrations/speech bubbles/tables/charts I see in the text?

3. **Making Predictions**—What do I think this text is going to be about?

4. **Brainstorming**—What vocabulary do I think I will see in this reading?

5. **Generating Questions**—What questions do I want to keep in mind as I read? What information should I look for? (Dymock and Nicholson 2010)

Any or all of these might be explored before the new text is read. Think of these as the "road map" to the upcoming reading experience. You provide students with a way to stay engaged, look for meaning, and meet reading goals. Ask these in a small group before reading, or request that students respond to the questions in writing.

During Reading

Questions generated before reading help students approach the text with intention. Then, as they read they should continue to ask questions, such as the following:

- Does this make sense?
- Is that what I thought was going to happen?
- What surprised me here?
- How can I figure out this word?
- What does this story remind me of?

Studies show "the strongest scientific evidence was found for the effectiveness of asking readers to generate questions during reading" (NICHHD 2000, 4–5). Helping students develop questions takes modeling by the teacher. While reading with students, talk through your thinking aloud so students can hear how a fluent reader asks questions. For example, you might say, "As I was reading, I was wondering what would happen next. I got stumped on the word *paralegal*. I decoded the word by thinking about what *legal* means. Then, I thought of the word *paramedic*. Paramedics help doctors, so maybe paralegals help lawyers. That makes sense in context. What does the lawyer think the defendant should do? I wonder about how the court case will end up. The defendant looks really sad in the picture, so I ask myself why that might be."

After Reading

Having specific reasons to return to a text provides experiences in skimming, retelling, summarizing, and inferring. This provides opportunities for close reading (NGA and CCSSO 2010). *Close reading* is "a careful and purposeful rereading of a text" (Fisher 2015, 2). Returning to the before-reading questions enables students to evaluate how well they predicted, what unanticipated content they encountered, and what details they need to answer. Constructing questions ahead of time ensures students are engaged in the close-reading activity.

*When you ask students to **retell** something they read, you evaluate how much detail they are able to remember. It is "one of the best devices for developing both comprehension and awareness of text structure…[particularly] for average and struggling learners" (Gunning 2013, 363). **Summarizing** requires students to determine the main idea and supporting details. Students must comprehend the text and then analyze it for the "big ideas." It is a "complex skill that takes years to develop" but has big payoff in helping develop comprehension skills (Gunning 2013, 327).*

Question-Answer Relationship

A useful framework for writing questions to use while teaching is the Question-Answer Relationship (QAR) strategy. It has been shown to have "practical value [and is useful] across a variety of settings" (Raphael and Au 2005, 208). The questions move from literal to higher-level thinking. The questions rely on two sources: the text itself (*in the book*) and the reader's background knowledge and experiences (*in my head*). Using familiar terms, students know where to find the answers to questions posed by the teacher.

QAR—In the Book

In QAR, most text-dependent questions fall into two categories: right there and thinking and searching. *Right there questions* are answered by going directly back into the text. These are typically questions that ask *who, what, where,* and *when.* Students are encouraged to point to the place in the text (or repeat the words from the text) that contains the answer. For example, the teacher may ask when something happened, and students can point to the specific date in the book. While there is a place for response to literal questions, teachers must be sure these do not take the largest part of any discussion. Ruddell (2009) found that 70 percent of questions asked by teachers are considered literal. Therefore, we should quickly cover information-seeking responses and move on to more engaging questioning.

Thinking and searching questions ask readers to go back and pull information together from several parts of the text to create their responses. A sequence of events may need to be reviewed to decide on the answer. For example, the teacher may ask how some event happened, and students need to recall a series of events that led up to the resolution. The teacher might also ask for the description of something from a story, and students need to recall several sentences or paragraphs. An explanation may be required, so students again recall a series of events or facts that are combined to explain something. Students are encouraged to provide the "clues" that helped them construct their answers.

QAR—In My Head

QAR questions using the reader's background knowledge and experiences also fall into two categories: the author and me and on my own. *The author and me* questions utilize what was read to tap into background knowledge and experiences. For example, a teacher might ask, "If you had the same experience as the person (fictional or real) in the text, how would you react?" Students need to make inferences and text-based predictions and to visualize to answer these types of questions.

On my own questions require readers to use some of their own ideas to answer the questions. For example, before reading, a teacher might ask what students already know about the topic or what they think the story may be about based on illustrations, title, author, or topic covered. After reading, the teacher may ask what other knowledge students have that connects to the book (perhaps a personal story or another book read). Today's college- and career-readiness standards place more emphasis on the other three types of questions since they require more direct evidence from the text.

The most consistent finding of Taylor et al.'s (2003) study "was that teachers who emphasized higher-order thinking, either through the questions they asked or the tasks they assigned, promoted greater reading growth" (3). Thus, by varying the types of questions asked, students are more likely to read for deeper meaning. They will think about and search for answers guided by the types of questions they are asked. During guided reading, you can model how to find the answers to both *in the book* and *in my head* questions. Through this modeling, you help students develop questions to ask themselves as they read independently. You want to emphasize the need to be aware while reading, knowing that passive encounters with text do not assist students in learning to read *and* comprehend.

Reading

Guided Reading in Kindergarten through Grade 5

In guided reading, "teachers can show children how to read and can support [them] as they read" (Fountas and Pinnell 1996, 1). During this time, students have direct support from the teacher as they learn and practice strategies for reading. This support allows for the gradual release of responsibility of reading from teachers to students. Rehearsed under the teacher's guidance, the strategies are carried over when students read independently. Cunningham and Allington point out that "the goal of guided reading is to assist readers in developing independent control in selecting and using appropriate strategies when reading" (1999, 56). During this time, teachers model, demonstrate, explain, brainstorm, and anticipate to initiate discussions about the text read and the strategies used to guide comprehension. Under the guidance of explicit instruction, students can have enjoyable, successful experiences as they read for meaning.

While guided reading is the heart of reading instruction in a classroom, such instruction should also take place throughout the school day and across subject matter areas. Many of the suggestions provided here, especially for mini-lessons, can be utilized in the content areas where students are also required to read and comprehend material.

Guided reading is essential in every classroom (Fountas and Pinnel 1996). It has the following benefits:

- allows students to develop as independent readers while participating in supported activities
- provides teachers with opportunities to observe student readers as they process text
- gives students opportunities to develop new strategies they can use when reading independently
- offers students an enjoyable, successful experience as they read for meaning
- helps students understand how to approach new texts

Reading levels provide benchmarks for how well a student can recognize the words in a particular text. According to Armbruster, Lehr, and Osborn (2001), these levels are Independent (student can read/identify words with 95–100 percent accuracy), Instructional (student can read/identify words with 90–94 percent accuracy), and Frustrational (student reads/identifies words with less than 90 percent accuracy).

Best Practices in Guided Reading

It is essential to use assessments to guide the formation of guided reading groups. Many teachers use beginning-of-the-year assessments to initially form groups. At some grade levels, information provided by the previous year's teacher might be used. However, some students may decline in reading development over the summer since they are not in formal programs, are not receiving home support, or have limited access to reading materials (Allington and McGill-Franzen 2003). At the same time, there is growing evidence that having students participate in summer programs connected to community activities (day camp, library offerings, recreation programs) can slow the decline in skills and actually boost learning (Miller 2007). Therefore, assessing each student is important for beginning appropriate instruction.

Periodic assessment and observations also inform grouping and regrouping. A quick oral reading record can be done as each student reads aloud. Observing the problem-solving strategies a student uses helps understanding of how students are growing in competency and where they need more instruction. Note what strategies students use to read, such as sounding out, searching the illustration or other parts of the text, or relying on meaning. Make note of words they struggle to read aloud, even though they are familiar with the text. If some words repeatedly come up as troublesome for a student, additional one-on-one instruction and practice may be needed.

Once assessments are completed, small groups of students with similar needs for learning to read are formed. By homogenously grouping students according to strengths and needs, teachers can have significant impact on their reading development (Fountas and Pinnell 1996). These groups of five to six students should remain flexible. Students will learn and develop new skills at different rates. If a student advances more quickly than his or her group, he or she can be moved to a group with more demanding texts. At the same time, a student who is struggling may need to move to a group with less challenging texts.

Classroom Management for Guided Reading

1. *Post a list created during the morning message or morning group time that tells students what independent activities need to be completed during guided reading.*

2. *Review what students must complete and what activities are optional.*

3. *Make students accountable for the time they are not in guided reading groups. A checklist of completed activities or a finished project is handed in at the end of each guided reading time.*

4. *Remind students how to handle questions they might have while you are with another group. (Write their name on an "I need help" list; ask a peer; or reread directions.)*

Establishing such routines early in the year creates a productive work environment for all students.

Guided Reading Lessons

Depending on grade and skill levels of students, guided reading groups typically meet three to five times per week for 10–30 minutes. Students are given texts at their instructional levels and, under the teacher's guidance, learn strategies to carry over to independent reading. A *Lesson Plan Template for Guided Reading* (page 319) is provided if you want to create your own guided reading plans. There are also suggested lessons provided in this resource starting on page 112.

The group gathers at a small table where the teacher can sit across from students to assist in and direct reading. The reading lesson begins by having students reread a familiar text. This is a text introduced in a previous lesson. Students are familiar with the text and vocabulary. As they read (in a whisper or silently), the teacher asks each student to read a portion of the text aloud. In this way, the teacher can employ a quick check on fluency and use of reading strategies. A quick review can be completed with a focus on word work skills, such as rhymes, blends, vocabulary, and punctuation, or comprehension skills, such as summarizing.

Then, a new text is introduced and the book title and author are shown. Depending on the reading level of the student and the text selected, a picture walk through the book is conducted (Cunningham, Hall and Defee 1998, 653). A *picture walk* is a quick flip through the text's images to have students familiarize themselves with the possible story line or facts to be read. Less-experienced readers may need more time during this guided walk through the book. Students are asked to make text-based predictions. Difficult vocabulary is pointed out, such as an unusual name, if the use of decoding strategies may not assist the reader, and reading strategies are discussed, such as utilizing the three cueing systems for decoding. Possible discussions might include: modeling how to problem solve an unknown word; demonstrating how to sound out or use base word information; brainstorming the text's content; predicting what facts might be encountered; and previewing what they may read by studying illustrations, the title, and headings.

The teacher may read a portion of the text aloud to less-experienced readers to model the use of strategies, while more-experienced readers can begin reading independently immediately after the book is previewed. Watching for self-monitoring, the teacher may ask students to read a portion aloud so "on the run" assessments can be done. What strategies is the student using *while* encountering a new text?

After reading, the story or topic is discussed and questions are posed. This allows students know that while they are working on their strategies for decoding, they are always thinking about comprehension—what was the story about or what facts did they learn?

Finally, a mini-lesson may be taught. Select a strategy you want students to specifically focus on to gain additional experiences. This is a time for explicit instruction. As the lesson is brought to close, perhaps ask a quick question or two to assess students' learning, such as *What was your favorite part of the new book?* or *What do you think you are getting better at when you read? Give me evidence.* The lesson should also include an explanation of the independent work students need to do when they leave the group. As soon as students leave the table, the teacher should jot notes to record improvements observed or remediation needed. Later, these notes can be transferred to individual checklists.

Creating Guided Reading Groups

Diagnostic assessments can help determine the reading levels of students and strengthen the formation of your guided reading groups. Organizing by instructional reading level is the most useful way to group students. It is important to remember that assessment is ongoing, so students can change groups depending on need. Keeping groups stagnant penalizes students who are progressing faster than peers needing more continued support. Conversely, students who feel frustrated by instruction in a particular group need to work with peers who are working at paces similar to them. Shifting guided reading groups to meet the needs of students provides important flexibility to the balanced literacy classroom.

Once groups are formed, your next tasks include selecting texts for instruction, developing comprehension questions, selecting vocabulary to focus on, selecting mini-lessons, and determining independent work.

Selecting Texts

Selection of texts is key to successful guided reading instruction. Selecting books students can read with success, yet stretch them in terms of skill development, is the guiding factor in choices made by the teacher. No matter what grade level, skills and strategies are addressed in explicit ways during guided reading.

Choosing an appropriate text for each group is important in engaging each student in guided practice, as "leveled text is a useful teaching tool for guided reading, as long as it is used in the classroom as one part of a balanced reading program that includes shared reading and read-aloud experiences" (Dzaldov and Peterson 2005, 228). It is also important to remember that the groups remain flexible, based on how well students are working with the selected instructional texts. Rog and Burton explain "as students progress in their ability to decode and comprehend increasingly difficult text, the groups are adjusted" (2002, 356) throughout the year.

Guided reading is the most appropriate time to intentionally choose a book for a student to develop needed skills. During other times of the day, you want students to freely pick books for reasons other than what reading level they are on using *The Five Finger Rule*. When thinking about the type of books used for guided reading, consider a variety of genres (literature or informational texts). Opitz and Erekson remind us that "we are teaching children to be readers rather than just merely teaching them to read" (2015, 109), so we want to give students scaffolded experiences to approach different types of texts. Because the "essentials of guided reading are that the teacher explains and/or demonstrates for children the important things to be done while we read" (Cunningham and Allington 1999, 54), text choices are virtually limitless. With a greater emphasis on nonfiction texts at all grade levels (NGA and CCSSO 2010) along with research that demonstrates a "scarcity" of informational texts in primary grades (Duke 2000), teachers must find ways to integrate the curriculum when selecting texts to provide additional experiences for learning content as well as reading. Camp (2000) suggests that having students first read narratives and then use nonfiction texts about the topic supports development in both reading and content knowledge. Doing a unit on the ocean? Find literature and informational texts related to ocean animals. Not only will you guide students' reading development, but you will teach important grade-level content and skills in how to approach reading different genres.

Important Strategies Developed in Guided Reading

- *Recalling relevant background knowledge*
- *Predicting what will be learned and what might happen*
- *Making mental pictures or "seeing it in your mind"*
- *Self-monitoring and self-correction*
- *Using fix-up strategies, such as rereading, pictures, and asking for help when you cannot make sense of what you read*
- *Determining the most important ideas and events and seeing how they are related*
- *Drawing conclusions and inferences based on what is read*
- *Offering opinions—Do you like it? Do you agree? Do you think it is funny? Can this really happen?*
- *Comparing and contrasting what you read to what you already know*
- *Deciphering unknown words—what strategies do you use?*
- *Summarizing what has been read*

Many criteria are applied to text leveling, including difficulty of words, length of sentences, support from illustrations, and instructional support (Cunningham et al. 2005). Fry (2002) reminds us that some lists of grade-appropriate texts are based on **readability** and others on **reading level**. Readability formulas measure syntactic (grammatical) and semantic (meaning) difficulties. They are fairly objective because texts can be entered into computer software programs for the readability to be determined. Reading levels take more text features into consideration, such as those elements that provide support for the reader (content, illustrations, length, language structure, and format). Thus, knowing how a suggested list of texts was developed is important. A text that has a low readability but stilted language does not necessarily support a young reader (Fry 2002). When selecting books, choose texts that provide reasonable challenges while allowing for some independence. Ideally, students should be able to identify at least 90 percent of the words and comprehend at least 75 percent of the text or higher (Betts 1946).

A Comparison of Word Recognition and Comprehension Levels

Independent Level:
Word recognition 95–100 percent; Comprehension 90 percent

Instructional Level:
Word recognition 90–94 percent; Comprehension at least 75 percent

Frustrational Level:
Word recognition below 90 percent; Comprehension less than 50 percent

(Word recognition according to Armbruster, et al. 2001; comprehension according to Betts 1946)

The comprehension skills demanded of a reader may be as important (or maybe *more* important) than the reading level. If a student's comprehension falls into the frustrational range with a particular text, then moving to an easier level would be well advised. Comprehension remains an important factor throughout the grades. If a student does not understand what is being read, then he or she is only "word calling" and not truly reading. If students struggle with sight words, then selecting texts that include plenty of sight words is a prudent choice. If students are ready to dive into multisyllabic words and more complex texts, then finding books that engage readers in good stories (or interesting informational text) compels them to pay attention to longer words and decode accordingly.

Books that intentionally guide student learning are key to instruction. "In guided reading, scaffolding becomes the metaphor for teaching and learning. Scaffolding enables teachers not only to determine where the learners are developmentally but also where they need to be, so teachers can plan sensitive, responsive instruction that provides a bridge between these two points" (Ford and Opitz 2008, 74).

Teachers also must be aware of the three cueing systems, mentioned earlier, in which students need additional practice (graphophonic, semantic, and syntactic). *Graphophonic cues* are those used visually—the sound/letter combinations, prefixes, suffixes, and bases. *Semantic* and *syntactic cues* address meaning and structure. These three cueing systems act as a check and balance as students read. For example, a page may say, "The pony ran across the field." A student reads, "A potato ran across the field." You know the student uses graphophonic cues (the *po* made them guess based on the first letters), but semantically it does not make sense. You would then ask the student if a potato can run across a field. Structurally, *potato* and *pony* are nouns, but semantics tell the reader he or she needs to go back and try again.

The books teachers choose for guided reading can provide opportunities for teachers to point out these cueing systems and help students develop their own independence in reading complex texts. No matter the grade level, there will always be new vocabulary, text structures, and content to be read. Helping students become independent in word attack and comprehension will provide lifelong skills.

According to Rasinski et al. (2008), prefixes, bases, and suffixes are all types of roots. The base is found in the middle of the word, providing the basic meaning of the word. For example, the root mot means "move" and provides the base for motor and movement.

Focus on Vocabulary

Focusing on vocabulary occurs in the following places in guided reading lessons:

- After reading a familiar text, teachers can turn students' attention to words of particular interest for the lesson focus. For example, students might compare how endings were added to words or which words have common phonetic elements.

- Before reading a new text, the teacher may want to point out and discuss any words that might be challenging for students. When previewing a text to use for a guided reading lesson, decisions must be made if pre-teaching some words is necessary. However, rather than pre-teaching the vocabulary you *think* will stump students, you want to encourage students to use their decoding strategies.

- Under teacher guidance during small groups, students verbalize the strategies they might use when they encounter unknown words while independently reading. Doing this helps develop skills that will carry them through a variety of settings.

The vocabulary students encounter when they read can be extended into their word study for the day. For example, students may have read a story about a dog that was *unable* to find his home. Conversations about the prefix *un–*, meaning not, can lead students to participate in word hunts through independent reading books, looking for other words that start with the prefix *un–*. These can be shared in the next guided reading group meeting. Because teachers try to make connections across the day and the curriculum, extending vocabulary development beyond guided reading groups provides additional experiences for students.

Guided reading provides a perfect opportunity to assess students' skills for reading new vocabulary. As they read aloud, you can hear the application of their word-attack skills. For young readers, you can hear them connect letters and sounds, working their way across words. For older students, observe if they are using strategies to break words into prefixes, bases, base words, and/or suffixes. When you hear a student working across a word, make note of his or her strategies. After the reading, you can revisit the word or words by asking students to share what the word means. You can encourage them to use context clues to solve for meaning. You can also deconstruct the word with the student. Which part of the word is a prefix? What does that prefix mean? Does knowing the prefix help to figure out the word's meaning?

Guided Reading in Kindergarten through Grade 2

In kindergarten through grade 2, groups work in texts that are highly supportive, using illustrations and moving from easily decodable texts to more complex reading as skills develop. Some students may be working to understand basic concepts about books, while others may be dipping into texts using common sight words. Still others may be mastering the use of phonics to help them decode multisyllabic words. Once guided reading groups are formed, mini-lessons that target specific needs of each group can be selected. Teachers should use their state-adopted standards for the appropriate benchmarks.

Assessing Students

Teachers of kindergarten through grade 2 must assess students with emergent skills as well as those who are already reading. Observation helps teachers determine emerging literacy skills, while oral reading records can provide accurate pictures of how they read texts. Teachers need to know which foundational skills kindergarten through grade 2 students have control over and which still need development. If a student in grade 1 or grade 2 shows gaps in understanding any of the foundational skills, a quick check using an appropriate observation is suggested. For example, if a grade 1 student seems to have difficulty with word construction when he or she is writing, you might have the student sound words out loud so you can assess his or her phonemic awareness and phonics knowledge. This formative assessment allows teachers to adjust mini-lessons as needed. While a teacher may have one lesson planned, instruction may take another direction after the observation. This is at the heart of formative assessment, observing students as they work and then responding with real-time adjustments to meet their current needs. Once kindergarten through grade 2 students are reading, or at least beginning to try to work across words in texts, they should be assessed using oral reading records.

Planning Guided Reading Groups

Following your assessments, look for common needs to create small groups of five to six students. Different color checkmarks can be a helpful way to mark the areas of most concern for each student, emphasizing specific needs for each group. For example, marking the alphabet cell on the *Early Literacy Skills Class Checklist* (page 327) with a yellow checkmark will allow you to see which students still need to work on learning their letters. An orange checkmark means students are approximating this skill (draws sometimes, but generally writing words). A green checkmark means students show consistent use of the skill. For students who complete an oral reading record, use the *Oral Reading Record* (page 309) to record their performances. Remember that the groups should be flexible with students moving as often as needed.

Develop a list of skills and mini-lessons with which you want each group to work. Organize these in order of instruction. Figure 3.3 shows an example of this for a second-grade classroom. The charts at the beginning of the Reading mini-lesson section (page 111), the correlation to the standards (standards.pdf), and the *Developmental Continuum Chart* (pages 337–339; continuum.pdf) provide guidance in selecting appropriate skills and mini-lessons. By creating an ordered list of strategies, you can plan across several days and weeks for each group.

Figure 3.3 Example Guided Reading Group Skill Lessons—Second Grade

Group 1

Skill: Understands onset and rime Aids in word reading (chunks)	**Lesson**: Practice exchanging onsets with familiar word families.
Skill: Word-by-word reading	**Lesson**: Practice reading into PVC phones.
Skill: Self-monitors/self-corrects based on one or more cues (graphophonic, semantic, syntactic)	**Lesson**: Create a cloze passage to practice using cues to fill in the blanks.
Skill: Phrase-by-phrase reading (some fluency)	**Lesson**: Reread the same passage to provide familiarity and increase fluency.

Group 2

Skill: Self-monitors/self-corrects based on one or more cues (semantic, graphophonic, syntactic)	**Lesson**: Create a cloze passage to practice using cues to fill in the blanks.
Skill: Phrase-by-phrase reading (some fluency)	**Lesson**: Students select books to perform as reader's theater presentations.
Skill: Automatic word recognition	**Lesson**: Students skim and scan for new vocabulary learned.
Skill: Variety of reading styles	**Lesson**: Students search the classroom library for two books on the same topic from different genres.

Group 3

Skill: Automatic word recognition	**Lesson**: Students skim and scan for vocabulary from similar word families.
Skill: Variety of reading styles	**Lesson**: Students discuss comprehension when hearing a story versus reading a story.
Skill: Reads faster silently	**Lesson**: Students read passages aloud, and then reread silently with timers to compare.
Skill: Self-monitors for comprehension	**Lesson**: Students pose their own questions at the end of the reading.

Next, select a text for each group to read. With younger readers, adequate copies are needed so that each student can have an individual copy. This is important as young readers often need to finger point and whisper read, or they read at different paces. As students are able to read the print without finger pointing, texts can be shared by student pairs. The text should give opportunities for students to work on the skills they need to practice under your guidance. So, for students needing to work on text features, such as moving from left to right, using context to help unlock new words, or reading sight vocabulary, be certain the text provides opportunity to address these skills.

Lesson plans are an essential way to keep track of what skills students have worked on, what notes you have made on individual readers, and which texts have already been read. The notes from your lesson plans and the plan of the sequence of skills and strategies a particular group needs provide a useful "road map" to instruction.

Having a plan that guides your lesson is important to keep track of all the strategies you cover. The lesson plans are also evidence of how you are meeting students' individual needs. The plans can be adjusted as needed and repeated if you feel the group needs more experiences with similar work. Store plans for handy referral when you are teaching. A quick look back to a previous lesson lets you remind students of past books or strategies, helping to tie together ongoing work.

The ebb and flow of teaching and assessment is a natural outcome of this arrangement. A good organizational tip is to keep each group's lesson plans in a three-ring binder. Keep these near the table where you hold guided reading groups. Find notebooks with front vinyl pockets into which you can slip a list of the students in each group. As a general hint, by simply calling the names of students you want to come back to the table, you eliminate the idea of permanent groups. The days of the "crows" and "bluebirds" are long gone. You want students to feel welcome in each group of peers you place them with by not labeling the group in some way.

After reviewing the notes from previous lessons, you can decide what the next lesson might be. Mini-lessons can even be repeated with different books. Or subsequent book choices may need reconsideration, depending on the skill and strategies of the members of the various guided reading groups. Also, be aware of students needing to move to different groups, either to provide more supportive reading or more challenging work.

Suggested K–2 Mini-Lessons

This section includes basic small-group strategy lessons for simple practice of the following skills for kindergarten through grade 2. Details regarding each strategy can be found on the subsequent pages. For additional lessons, download the Digital Resources. (See page 20 for the website address and access code.)

These guided reading mini-lessons are meant to provide specific experiences with print. Teachers want opportunities to explicitly teach skills and strategies young learners need to become independent readers. Teachers can easily connect any of the activities suggested for kindergarten through grade 2 in the Word Study section to specific words read during guided reading and/or any of the writing approaches presented in the Writing section. The mini-lessons are brief explanations for teaching concepts. However, many of these lessons are most effective when repeated or divided over several days. While these are a sampling of mini-lessons, your own ongoing assessment is the best directive for picking strategies to teach.

Mini-Lessons

Lesson
Compare and Contrast (page 112)
Create an Events Time Line (page 113)
Draw What You Visualize (page 114)
Echo Reading (page 115)
Key Ideas and Details (page 116)
Letter/Sound Combinations (page 117)
Letters and Sounds of the Alphabet (page 118)
Punctuation (page 120)
Reading the News (page 121)
Tracing Character Development (page 122)
Sight Words (page 123)
Words with Common Features (page 124)

Digital Resources Lessons

Lesson
Analyzing Images for Details (analyzephoto.pdf)
Concepts About Print (conprint.pdf)
Connecting to Writing (connectwrite.pdf)
Circle the Pattern (circlepat.pdf)
Cloze Procedure (cloze.pdf)
Create a Graphic Representation (graphicrep.pdf)
Identifying Author and Illustrator (authorillus.pdf)
Look Around the Room (lookroom.pdf)
Retell the Story (retellstory.pdf)
Rhyme with Text Words (rhymewords.pdf)

Some websites that serve to enhance instruction and provide additional opportunities for students to explore these various topics are:

- www.primarygames.com
- www.starfall.com
- www.funenglishgames.com
- www.pbskids.org
- www.storynory.com

Some apps that serve to enhance instruction and provide additional opportunities for students to explore these various topics are:

- Mee Genius Children's Books (Houghton Mifflin Harcourt)
- Pango FREE (Studio Pango)
- SparkleFish (Whosagoodboy Partners)

Compare and Contrast

Objective

Students will compare and contrast two texts.

Preparation

1. Select a text for the guided reading group that is similar to a previously read text. This can be a literature piece with a similar story line or an informational text on the same topic.

2. Make a list of how the books are the same and how they are different.

3. Copy *Compare and Contrast Template* (page 312; comparetemp.pdf).

Procedure

1. Show students the two texts.

2. Review the content of the familiar text. Ask students for the main idea and some key details. Make a list on the board.

3. Give students the *Compare and Contrast Template*. Have students label each circle with the book titles and fill in the circle with what you've listed for the familiar text.

4. Present the new text, and have students read it. Instruct students to talk about what is the same and what is different about the two texts. Provide a classroom example first, such as *Sara has brown hair and so does Akeelah. But Sara's hair is long, and Akeelah's hair is short.*

5. Complete the *Compare and Contrast Template*, using student suggestions. Refer to your previously prepared list to be sure everything is either mentioned by students or prompted by you.

Extend the mini-lesson into independent work by having students complete the *Compare and Contrast Template* with two books or topics of their choosing, such as two seasons or a literature text with an informational text on the same topic.

Differentiation: For **English language learners**, scaffold the assignment by reading one of the items on your list aloud and having students suggest where it should be placed on the diagram. For **above-level students**, add a third circle to the *Compare and Contrast Template* and have students complete the additional circle using other texts of their choosing.

✔ **Assessment Check:** Listen as students suggest ideas to include in the circles. Note students who seem to struggle with picking out key details. These students may need additional practice under your guidance. Being able to compare and contrast is an important aspect of understanding text structure.

Create an Events Time Line

Objective

Students will identify events from an informational text.

Preparation

1. Make a list of time-ordered events from a familiar or new text, such as the life stages of a butterfly. Use four to six events for kindergarten and six to eight events for grades 1–2.

2. Write the events on note cards and shuffle them.

Procedure

1. Tell students you have chosen events from the text they read during their guided reading time.

2. Place the cards on a table, face up.

3. Read two of the note cards, and ask students to order them as they occur in the text.

4. Read the next card, and have the group determine where it should be placed in the existing sequence. Repeat until all events are correctly placed in the order that they occur.

Extend the mini-lesson into independent work by having additional sets of event cards for students to place in order. Students can also be asked to illustrate the events.

Differentiation: For **above-level students**, ask them to create the cards for this activity. This will require them to individually revisit the text to consider possible time line events.

✔ **Assessment Check:** Use the independent work to assess how well students can independently create time lines. Note which students need help ordering the events. Additional practice opportunities or reteaching may be needed. Time lines help students improve their comprehension of nonfiction.

Draw What You Visualize

Objective

Students will visualize the words they hear in a narrative text.

Preparation

1. Select an unfamiliar narrative text, either without images or with the images covered.
2. Provide a large piece of drawing paper and pencils/crayons/markers for each student.

Procedure

1. Explain that as we read, we picture what is going on. *Seeing the story* happens because the author uses words to help us visualize the events as they unfold.

2. Read the unfamiliar narrative aloud, having students visualize the various events they hear as you read.

3. Ask students to discuss the text's events. You can tie this to the mini-lesson on *Key Ideas and Details* (page 116). Ask students to think about and draw what they are *seeing* in their minds while listening to the story.

4. Extend the mini-lesson into independent work by having students finish their drawings.

Differentiation: Have **English language learners** discuss their drawings and sequence them as they occurred in the text. For **above-level students**, have them add labels or sentences to their drawings to describe details and sequence.

✔ **Assessment Check:** Note how engaged students are during the listening and if they are able to picture events in the text. The drawings give us windows into our students' thinking processes during reading. The details in their drawings can indicate their level of auditory comprehension.

Echo Reading

Objective

Students will practice their reading fluency.

Preparation

1. Select a text. Display it for the group or give students individual copies. It is important for students to see the text to reinforce concepts about print.

2. Decide how you will break up the echo reading, such as one line at a time or one page at a time.

Procedure

1. Explain that an echo is similar to going through a tunnel or being in a cave where our voice "bounces" back to us. Tell them that they will be your echo as you read.

2. Give the text to students, or have them sit so they can all see the text.

3. Read the preselected line or page.

4. Have students repeat the line or page. Continue until you have read the whole text.

> Echo reading is when the teacher reads a portion of text and the students repeat it.

Differentiation: Ask **above-level students** to take turns being the "first" voice in an echo reading of a text. Lead **below-level students** to read orally with dramatic hand gestures.

✔ **Assessment Check:** If students struggle with the echo reading, there may be issues with memory. Make note of these students as you may need to follow up with additional work that utilizes memory, such as giving them three tasks to do (get a red crayon, bring it to me, then sit by the window).

K–2 Strategies

Reading

Objective

Students will identify the key ideas and details in both text and illustrations/photographs.

Preparation

1. Choose a familiar text.

2. Make a list of the key ideas and details that support the main idea. For literature, these ideas and details often relate to the setting, character, and plot. For informational texts, these are the facts that provide important information. Keep this list on hand during the discussion.

Procedure

1. Review the main idea of the text. Write it on the board or chart paper.

2. Ask students what details help readers understand the main idea and why.

3. Write these details with the main idea on the board or chart paper. Guide students to choose only key ideas and details that are pertinent to the main idea.

   Extend the mini-lesson into independent work by having students complete graphic outlines of the main idea, followed by the key points recorded on the board or chart.

Differentiation: For **English language learners**, provide strips of paper with the events, ideas, details, and images from the text. Have them sort the strips to make piles representing the key details and main idea from the text.

✔ **Assessment Check:** Note which students do not seem to understand the concept of key ideas. They may need assistance rereading a text under your guidance and then returning to the text for a close reading of the details. Choosing details can be tricky for some students. They need to develop this skill so they can understand and support main idea discussions.

Reading

K–2 Strategies

Letter/Sound Combinations

Objective

Students will identify specific letter/sound combinations to help them decode words.

Preparation

1. Select five to eight words from a text read during a guided reading lesson that have similar letter/sound patterns, so students can analyze the similarities, such as *pig*, *dig*, and *big* and *chain*, *bait*, *paint*, and *paid*.

2. Write each word on a note card.

3. Set aside a space on a whiteboard or post a sheet of blank chart paper.

Procedure

1. Spread the word cards out on the table so students can see all the words.

2. Read the cards aloud together.

3. Ask students what similar sounds they hear. Encourage them to look at the words and tell you what letters might make the sounds they hear.

4. Use a highlighter to highlight the letter patterns. Write the patterns on the whiteboard or posted paper.

5. Have students suggest other words that have the pattern. Record these on the display.

6. Discuss how we can use what patterns we know in a word, such as *pig*, to help us read another word, such as *big*.

   If time permits, have students return to the text the words came from and skim the text until they find the selected words. This helps contextualize the words and reminds students they are learning these patterns so they can read better.

Differentiation: For **English language learners**, model and practice producing the sounds, exaggerating the shapes your mouth takes as it makes the sounds. For **above-level students**, select more complex patterns of the same sounds, such as *deal*, *peel*, and *these*.

✔ **Assessment Check:** Note which students can easily identify the chosen letter and sound combinations. They may need more challenging words, or they can hunt for more words in materials they can read that go along with those presented in the lesson. Keep track of students who need additional practice and guidance in learning to see and hear the combinations. Provide additional practice opportunities for them. Letter and sound correspondence knowledge is important for students to be able to independently decode.

Letters and Sounds of the Alphabet

Objective

Students will connect word study to reading by identifying words in their books with the letters of the alphabet and determining their sounds.

Preparation

1. Gather a set of alphabet letters (magnetic, plastic, or paper).

2. Lay the letters out in order on a table or the floor.

Procedure

1. Show students the letters and ask them to identify the ones they know by pointing to them and naming them.

2. Using the order on page 119, introduce each letter's name and have students suggest words that start with that letter.

3. After every five letters, have a "letter hunt" in the room. Tell students to look around the room and find each of the five letters you just discussed. They can look in books, on posters, on their name tags, or even on activity sheets they're completing. After they find the letters, they can come back to you and share what they found.

   Extend the mini-lesson into independent work by having students select one or more letters, label a page with the letter, and write words or draw pictures they know that begin with that letter.

4. On the next day, place one letter at a time on the table, using the recommended order from page 119. Ask students what sound each letter makes. Refer back to the activity from the previous day for words in the room that have the letter. Do the students hear the letter's sound in those words?

Differentiation: For **below-level students**, have a set of easy readers set aside in the classroom for them to use for their letter hunts. Have **above-level students** write silly alliterative sentences for the letters.

✔ **Assessment Check:** Keep track of students' participation. Some students may need additional experiences with knowing the letters and their sounds.

According to Piasta (2014), a specific order of learning letter names and their sounds exists and is recommended.

Recommended Order for Letter Names	Recommended Order for Letter Sounds
O	C-A
B	B
A	T-P-S
C	K-O-J-Z-F-D
X	M-V-E
P-S-H-E-T	G
W-M-R-K-D	L-H-N-R
F-L-Y-Z	Q
G-J-N-I-Q	I-W-X
U	U-Y
V	

K–2 Strategies

Reading

Punctuation

Objective

Students will identify punctuation marks and their purposes in reading.

Preparation

1. Select pages from a familiar text that have a variety of punctuation marks. Focus on one to four types of punctuation, depending on the level of text and students in the group.

2. Provide crayons to each student.

Procedure

1. Discuss how punctuation marks affect how you read texts. For example, a period means *stop*, a comma means *pause*, an exclamation point means *strong feelings*, and a question mark means *to ask*.

2. Tell students what punctuation marks you're focusing on for this mini-lesson. Have students find examples of these specific punctuation marks.

3. Read the sentences aloud and discuss the punctuation used.

> *Typical punctuation* learned in kindergarten through grade 2 (Fearn and Farnan 1998) includes periods (end of the sentence and abbreviations), question marks and exclamation points (end of the sentence), commas (in dates, a series, and addresses), apostrophes (in contractions and possessives), and quotes (in dialogue).

Extend the mini-lesson into independent work by having students use different color crayons to mark the punctuation marks on text, such as circling periods red and question marks purple.

Differentiation: Give **below-level students** small charts of the punctuation marks covered in the lesson for quick reference. For **above-level students**, create text without punctuation and have students add the punctuation marks.

✔ **Assessment Check:** Note which students quickly identify the requested punctuation marks. These students can be directed to their own writings to double-check for correct use of punctuation. Their independent work might involve circling punctuation marks in their journal or drafts to check for accuracy. Punctuation aids in comprehension, so helping students understand the purpose of each punctuation mark is useful for independent reading and writing.

Reading the News

Objective

Students will apply reading strategies learned in guided reading.

Preparation

1. Select a magazine, newspaper, or Internet text. Choose something related to content studies, such as a community story or an information article on a science topic. The text should include a number of words your students are not familiar with.

2. Enlarge the text and copy it for each student.

Procedure

1. Create a list of reading strategies students have learned, reviewing ways good readers solve word-reading problems, such as by sounding out, looking for word parts, and using the context.

2. Distribute copies of the text.

3. Tell students they are to read the text and as they do, circle any words they had to work to decode. If appropriate, have students label the strategy they used.

4. Discuss the strategies students used to read and understand some of the unfamiliar words they encountered.

Differentiation: For **below-level students**, read the text together aloud. Pause at words you want students to help you decode. At times, stop and verbalize the strategies you might use to decode the words. Making this process visible and explicit can assist these readers. For **above-level students**, have them color code the words they paused at by the strategy they used, such as circling words in red that were sounded out or in blue for words they took apart by base and affix.

✔ **Assessment Check:** Note the discussion of what strategies students use. See which students understand how to approach new words. For students who color-coded the words, note which strategies they use most often. You may want to see if they need an additional mini-lesson to learn other strategies. Applying knowledge of reading strategies in a variety of situations strengthens students' independent use of them.

K–2 Strategies

Reading

Tracing Character Development

Objective

Students will sequence events from a literature book.

Preparation

1. Have four to eight blank paper strips available.

2. Using a familiar literature text, make a list of story events. Use four to six events for kindergarten and six to eight events for grade 1 and grade 2.

3. Write the events in sentences, one per strip.

Procedure

1. Hold up each character card and have students describe the character's traits at the beginning of the story.

2. Discuss how events in the story changed the characters. Make notes on the board of ideas students add to this discussion.

3. Have students change the character drawings and/or add labels to reflect the character's end-of-story traits, such as brave, surrounded by friends, or obedient.

Differentiation: Have **English language learners** work in small groups together to determine how the characters changed and update the cards. Have **above-level students** find other stories where characters changed in similar ways.

✔ **Assessment Check:** Note who uses text evidence to describe the changes to the characters. These students are demonstrating more advanced reading strategies. Determine which students need more assistance in this area and provide direct instruction.

Sight Words

Objective

Students will practice identifying sight words.

Preparation

1. Select a familiar trade book that has many sight words in it. Choose some focus words from the *Top 100 High-Frequency Words* (page 266; hfwords.pdf).

2. Provide students with sheet protectors and erasable markers.

Procedure

1. Give each student a book, a sheet protector, and an erasable marker. Have students place the sheet protectors over pages in the books. If the books are small enough (and lay flat), the books can actually be slipped inside the sheet protectors. Otherwise, just make sure the plastic covers the pages of the books.

2. Explain that you will read aloud a sight word. Students are to find that word in their books and circle it on their sheet protectors. Do a quick check that everyone has correctly identified the word.

3. Have students wipe their sheet protectors before turning the page in their books to search for the next sight word you have selected.

   If time permits, ask students to use books they are independently reading to search for the same sight words. They can write lists of where these sight words show up in their books. This gives purposeful additional practice.

Differentiation: For **below-level students**, this lesson can be repeated with a different text and the same sight words. This will allow more time to ensure they are quickly identifying these key words. For **above-level students**, have them hunt for additional high-frequency words in this and other texts.

✔ **Assessment Check:** Keep track of students mastering these sight words and those who need additional practice and guidance with them. Provide additional words or additional practice, depending on the need. The goal is to quickly identify words, which assists in comprehension. The fewer times a reader must stop to analyze a word, the easier it is to remember what is read.

K–2 Strategies

Reading

Words with Common Features

Objective

Students will identify words with the suffixes –ed and –ing.

Preparation

1. Select four words with the suffixes –ed or –ing from a familiar text. Write these on note cards, one word per card.

2. Select two to four other words for students to compare that don't have suffixes but that end in –ing or –ed, such as *sing* which ends in –ing not acting as a suffix. Write these on note cards, as well.

Procedure

1. Show students two of the words that have the chosen suffixes.

2. Discuss the suffixes, what they mean, and how they change the word.

3. Show students other words, and discuss their meanings.

4. Show a word that has the letters but not the feature, such as the word *bed* which has –ed but has no suffix. Take suggestions of other words that have the same endings.

   Extend the mini-lesson into independent work by having students hunt for and create lists of words from their independent reading that fit the suffix patterns discussed.

Differentiation: Have **English language learners** identify the base words of the words you've written on the note cards. When discussing what the words mean, always refer back to the base words to make sure students have strong understandings of the parts of the words.

✔ **Assessment Check:** Note which students have trouble identifying the endings. Additional practice may be needed for those who are struggling. Knowing how to remove and add suffixes will help students as they approach new texts to read independently.

Reading

K–2 Strategies

Guided Reading in Grade 3 through Grade 5

Students in grade 3 through grade 5 are instructed in texts they can read that present some challenge but are not at their frustrational levels. Teachers should choose interesting texts that match students' instructional levels. As a reminder, word recognition according to Armbruster et al. (2001) and comprehension according to Betts (1946) are:

Independent Level: word recognition 95–100 percent; comprehension 90 percent

Instructional Level: word recognition 90–94 percent; comprehension at least 75 percent

Frustrational Level: word recognition below 90 percent; comprehension less than 50 percent

For students who might not yet be reading on grade level, be sure to select texts that are at both their instructional reading levels and their interest levels (Fresch and Harkins 2009). Picking easy books that are written for younger audiences can quickly create resistant students who do not want to read. Teachers have long been aware of the "fourth grade slump" (Chall 1983), the year when some students may still be transitioning from gaining decoding skills to using them. Students shift from learning *how* to read and write to *using* these skills to read and write. According to the National Assessment of Educational Progress (2015), one-third of fourth grade readers are below basic skills in reading. Unless addressed, these challenges are compounded by the time they reach fifth and sixth grade. So, being certain third, fourth, and fifth grade readers have full toolboxes to use when approaching *any* reading is crucial.

Assessing Readers

Teachers of grade 3 through grade 5 can use the QRI to assess students' word-attack and comprehension skills. As complex texts, new vocabulary, and critical reading become part of the demands at these grade levels, many students still struggle to decode. And teachers do, indeed, want to address any lingering decoding problems these students might have. The QRI allows teachers to watch students in action and can be used to record growth and development.

Planning Guided Reading Groups

Reading assessments provide assistance with analyzing student performance. Teachers may also use oral reading records to assist in examining students' word-attack skills. What cue(s) does the student seem to rely on, and which seem to be absent from his or her repertoire? You can use the

During observation time, notice the following:

- *Students who are still finger pointing as they read—Is the text too hard?*

- *Requests for help with unknown words—Are the unknown words or vocabulary too difficult?*

- *A student who is reading slower or faster than the majority of the group—Is it time to change groups for this student?*

- *Students who are studying the illustrations—Do they help them decode?*

- *Students who stop reading—Is the text at their frustrational level?*

Strategies Developed During Guided Reading

- *Predicting what will be learned, what will happen, and how thinking about prior knowledge will help.*
- *Making images in their heads helps them engage in reading.*
- *Self-monitoring and self-correction (fix-up strategies) helps with accurate reading.*
- *Selecting key ideas will help with comprehension.*
- *Drawing conclusions and/or inferences based on what they read.*
- *Using phonics knowledge to decode unknown words.*
- *Developing a summary of what they read.*

Class Oral Reading Record Form (page 311) to organize your guided reading groups by reading needs, as well as by level. Specific notes in each cell provide an easy way to see which students have common needs. Students needing more graphophonic knowledge can be grouped, but be certain they are reading texts that are appropriate for their reading levels. Pulling together students, regardless of reading levels, for the same mini-lesson can help you manage targeted instruction. For example, you may have students at various levels who ignore punctuation. A quick lesson on this will provide explicit instruction to all students needing to pay more attention to punctuation.

If your school uses an assessment to group students based on reading level, merge the information learned by completing oral reading records with the assessed reading levels of students.

Develop a list of skills and mini-lessons with which you want each group to work. Create a plan for which skills will be taught first, second, and so on. Having a plan of action for several weeks provides you with a clear overview of where your instruction is going to take students. Having this in mind allows you to take advantage of teachable moments. For example, if you know one of the strategies you want students to work on is breaking a word into prefix, base word, and suffix, and you are teaching a content lesson where the vocabulary would lend itself to the same instruction, use it! Remind students that they just did that sort of word work in their guided reading groups and how they can apply that knowledge to the content vocabulary word. The charts at the beginning of the Reading mini-lesson section (page 127), the correlation to the standards (standards.pdf), and the *Developmental Continuum Chart* (pages 337–339; continuum.pdf) provide guidance in selecting appropriate skills and mini-lessons. By creating an ordered list of strategies, you can plan across several days and weeks for each group.

Next, select a text for each group to read. Multiple copies are recommended so that each student can have a personal copy to allow for differences in reading pace. If that is not possible, then have student pairs share or have a large copy that several students can see. Alternately, project the text onto a screen. In this way, one copy is used, but students have a large version to share. The text should give opportunities for students to work on the skills they need to practice under your guidance. For students needing to work on context clues or graphophonic cues, be certain the text provides opportunities to address those skills. The text can be read in one sitting or have chapters that are read on a continual basis.

Lesson plans are essential to keep teachers on track with their plan of skills and strategies to be taught. As suggested in kindergarten through grade 2, you will want to organize each group's lesson plans in a three-ring binder. Make note of plans you want to repeat, students you might want to shift to a different group, or new texts you are thinking about introducing to the groups.

Reading

Suggested 3–5 Mini-Lessons

This section includes basic small-group strategy lessons for simple practice of the following skills for grade 3 through grade 5. Details regarding each strategy can be found on the subsequent pages. For additional lessons, download the Digital Resources. (See page 20 for the website address and access code.)

These guided reading mini-lessons are meant to expand students' experiences with texts. Teachers should have opportunities to explicitly teach skills and strategies to help students with the following skills:

- Make connections between prior knowledge and new texts they are reading.
- Pose questions of themselves (*How am I connected to this text?*), the text (*What structures help me understand the main idea?*), and the author (*Why did he write it* that *way?*).
- Draw inferences while they read and when they discuss the text after.
- Draw on key details to discover main ideas.
- Synthesize information across a number of texts.
- Realize they are not comprehending and use "fix-up" strategies (Harvey and Goudvis 2000).

You can easily connect any of the activities suggested for grade 3 through grade 5 in the Word Study section to specific words read during guided reading. Connect any of the writing approaches presented in the Writing section to reading. Also, look at the ideas presented in the kindergarten through grade 2 mini-lessons for students still working to develop particular reading skills.

Mini-Lessons

Lesson
Character Interviews (page 129)
Jump into the Book (page 130)
Key Ideas (page 131)
Point of View (page 132)
Text Set Creation (page 133)
Repeated Readings (page 134)
The Rhythm Walk (page 135)
Riddle Each Other (page 136)
Sentence Strip Sequencing (page 137)
Table of Contents, Index, and Glossary (page 138)
Text Features (page 139)
Vocabulary Boxes (page 140)

Digital Resources Lessons

Lesson
Book-Based Art (bookart.pdf)
Compare and Contrast (comparecontrast.pdf)
Fluency and Expression (fluencyexpress.pdf)
Summarizing (summarizing.pdf)
5 Ws & How Questions (whow.pdf)
Word Analysis (wordanalysis.pdf)

Some websites that serve to enhance instruction and provide additional opportunities for students to explore these various topics are:

- www.Internet4Classrooms.com
- www.smarttutor.com
- www.audacityteam.org/
- www.quia.com
- www.kids.niehs.nih.gov

Some apps that serve to enhance instruction and provide additional opportunities for students to explore these various topics are:

- Microsoft Photo Story 3.0 (Microsoft)
- K12 Timed Reading Practice Lite (K12 Inc.)
- Book Chat (Mobile Learning Services)
- Picturizr (ISBX)
- Reading Comprehension: Fable Edition (King's Apps)

Character Interviews

Objective

Students will deepen their comprehension by crafting questions.

Preparation

1. Select a familiar piece of literature.
2. Prepare a list of characters from the story.
3. Have chart paper and permanent markers.

Procedure

1. Review the main idea and key details from the text.

2. Create a list of the characters from the text on chart paper. Be sure to leave room next to each character's name to add questions.

3. Ask students how the characters interact or are connected in the story.

4. Ask students what questions they want to ask the characters. Begin a list of questions next to each character's name.

5. Have each student select one character and write additional questions to ask the character in an interview.

   Extend the mini-lesson into independent work by having students write a set of interview questions for another character.

> *If you want to show students how an interview might work, search the Internet for* Amazing Kids! Magazine.

Differentiation: Have **below-level students** use a voice application or software to help them transcribe their questions. Alternately, provide question starters. Have **above-level students** assume the characters' identities and answer the interview questions.

✔ **Assessment Check:** Note who can write good questions for characters. This mini-lesson helps demonstrate students' comprehension of the story. Collect students' questions to assess their appropriateness and connection to the story. As needed, provide additional opportunities to practice or teach a mini-lesson on the difference between sentence types (declarative, exclamatory, and interrogative).

3–5 Strategies

Reading

Jump into the Book

Objective

Students will develop their reading fluency.

Preparation

1. Select a familiar work of literature or informational text, such as a biography, where multiple copies are available. Be certain the book has several characters who use dialogue, so students can choose who they want to be.

Procedure

1. Distribute the text, and have students reread it.

2. Review the main idea and key details of the text, and have students name the characters.

3. Select one of the characters, and ask students to find where in the text that character speaks. Ask someone to read that part aloud.

4. Individually, have each student select another character and search the book for where that character speaks. Have students either directly read the speaking parts from the text (with you reading the other characters' parts if needed) or improvise what the characters might say.

5. Provide time for students to practice independently before reading their dialogue aloud to the group.

   Extend the mini-lesson into independent work by having students practice reading other parts for future performances. Students can collaborate to do the read-aloud parts.

Differentiation: For **below-level students**, have them circle the punctuation (commas, periods, questions marks, and exclamation points) and pay particular attention to these as they read. Then, have them read and reread the text over the course of several days to build their fluency. For **above-level students**, ask them to continue the dialogue between two characters after the story ends. What happens next? What do they say?

✔ **Assessment Check:** Note the fluency and expression used by students as they read. Additional opportunities will be necessary for students who read at a notably different rate from their conversational rate of speech.

Reading

3–5 Strategies

Key Ideas

Objective

Students will deepen their reading comprehension by asking and answering questions.

Preparation

1. Select a familiar text.

2. Inflate a beach ball.

3. Write the words *who*, *what*, *where*, *when*, *why*, and *how* around the ball's surface with permanent marker, one word per color or section.

Procedure

1. Show students the familiar text. Review the events or story line of the text.

2. Show students the ball.

3. Explain that you will toss the ball to a student. He or she must create a question about the text using the question word closest to either thumb. For example, if the thumb lands on "how," the student may ask, "How did Bob know the book was hidden in the old suitcase?" Other students will volunteer to answer the question.

4. The first student then tosses the ball to the student who correctly answers the question. Continue until all students have asked and answered questions correctly.

   Extend the mini-lesson into independent work by asking students to write their own questions using a different book.

Differentiation: Have **English language learners** create visuals to accompany each word, such as stick figures for *who* or a group of question marks for *why*. Have **above-level students** create written or visual summaries of the main idea of the text.

✔ **Assessment Check:** Evaluate students' participation. If a student does not volunteer an answer, you might say, "Jamal, you have not had a turn yet. What question would you ask about the text?" The questions posed by students are a good indicator of comprehension of key details.

Point of View

Objective

Students will deepen their comprehension of a text by discussing points of view.

Preparation

1. Select a familiar piece of literature where two or more characters play important roles in the story. Stories where characters have differing viewpoints are best. For example, you might choose a well-known fairy tale, such as *Three Billy Goats Gruff*. Choosing a read aloud you have presented works well, too.

2. Prepare a chart or board that has each character's name or picture and the words, "As I See It." Space these apart so students can add ideas to each.

Procedure

1. Review the story's plot and characters.

2. Tell students you want them to pretend they are different characters from the story.

3. Ask students how the characters acted or thought about something in the story. Why did they act that way? What was the character's specific point of view? For example, the troll did not want anyone walking on his bridge, so he tried to scare the goats away. He must have wanted peace and quiet!

4. Have students record their answers on the board. Continue until all the characters have been discussed.

Differentiation: For **English language learners** and **below-level students**, have them perform the story, assuming the identities of the different characters. Have **above-level students** engage in a debate about an event or issue in the story, assuming different characters' identities.

✔ **Assessment Check:** This strategy allows you to view a student's ability to connect with the characters in a story. Note who participates. If students struggle with this, additional discussions in small groups will help develop this skill.

Reading

3–5 Strategies

Text Set Creation

Objective

Students will deepen their understanding of a topic by creating text sets.

Preparation

1. Choose two familiar texts.

2. For one of the familiar texts, create a text set by finding other books that are connected to it. For example, if students read a story that takes place near an ocean, find poems and informational texts about the ocean, such as a biography about an oceanographer.

Procedure

1. Show students the familiar text and its text set.

2. Ask students to describe how the various texts are related.

3. Show students the other familiar text you selected, and ask if they know any related books that can be part of a text set for this text.

4. Have students look through your classroom library, their guided reading books, their basal readers and/or the Internet for possible text set pieces. If possible, give students time to visit the school library, having the librarian show them how to search for books.

5. Have students create lists or physically secure the other texts for their new text sets.

6. Share and discuss their findings. What genres did they find? What level of complexity does each set provide?

Differentiation: For **below-level students**, provide an array of possible texts for them to select from for their text sets. For **above-level students**, have them create text sets for diverse content-area topics.

✔ **Assessment Check:** Note the conversations about the possible text set books. Notice how closely students maintain the main topic of the familiar book as they search for a text set. Note the diversity of genres they are able to find. Additional guidance might be needed, and other opportunities to practice may be required for students to gain mastery.

> A **text set** is a group of related texts that expand the content and genre of a selected topic.

3–5 Strategies

Reading

Repeated Readings

Objective

Students will practice their reading fluency.

Preparation

1. Select a familiar text from a guided reading lesson.

2. Using PVC pipes, construct personal phones for each student in the group. Use two elbow pieces connected by a short, straight piece. Make these long enough to have the end of one elbow be at a student's ear and the other end by his or her mouth.

Procedure

1. Ask students to read the chosen text aloud using the phone. The phone amplifies the sound, so students end up speaking quietly and focusing on their own voices.

2. After practicing enough so that they think they sound fluent, have students record themselves in videos or podcasts. These can be posted online for family members or shared with other students.

Extend the mini-lesson into independent work by having students continue practicing their fluency with other books.

Differentiation: For **English language learners**, pre-teach unfamiliar vocabulary or letter/sound combinations by saying the words and having students repeat them. Where needed, briefly define the words as they pertain to the text. For **above-level students**, have them record whole books for younger students to listen to while reading.

✔ **Assessment Check:** Listen in as students read. Note their fluency as they read aloud. Hearing students read aloud provides information about how they are using the three cueing systems. For example, you may hear them sounding across a word or rereading a section to better understand a word. This may necessitate additional instruction or practice.

The Rhythm Walk

Objective

Students will practice their reading fluency.

Preparation

1. Select a variety of sentences from a familiar text.
2. Write or type/print the sentences onto tag board or other sturdy paper.
3. Cut the sentences into individual strips.
4. Place the strips spaced out, in order, on the floor so students can step over each sentence strip comfortably.

Procedure

1. Have students form a single file line in front of the first sentence strip.
2. The first student reads the first sentence out loud.
3. Have the first student step over the first sentence strip. The student then goes on to read the second strip, while the second student in line steps up to the first sentence.
4. Repeat until all students have reached the end of the sequence of sentences. (Adapted from Peebles 2007)

Differentiation: For **below-level students**, pre-read the sentences as a group. For **above-level students**, use dialogue, requiring students to express a range of emotions as they read each sentence.

✔ **Assessment Check:** Listen as students read each strip. Make note of any words they skip or take time to sound out, as this may indicate a need to further explore the vocabulary of the text. Listen for their fluency rates. Reading that is slow-paced may indicate that a text is too difficult.

3–5 Strategies

Reading

Riddle Each Other

Objective

Students will deepen their reading comprehension.

Preparation

1. Use a familiar text.

2. Select an event that happens in the story or a fact that is presented in the text, and create a riddle about it. For example, if the class read a book on oceans, a riddle such as *I am the ocean closest to California* is effective.

Procedure

1. Explain that students will write riddles about something from the text.

2. Read your model riddle, and have students answer it.

3. Have students discuss how riddles makes listeners think about what they read.

4. Write a new riddle together.

5. Then, ask students to create their own riddles to share with the group.

Differentiation: Above-level students can include multiple clues in their riddles, such as *I am the ocean closest to California, and I go all the way to Japan.*

✔ **Assessment Check:** Evaluate student-written riddles for clarity and connection to the text. A good riddle indicates that the student can think about the content in diverse ways. Students who struggle with this need practice inferring and using divergent thinking to answer questions.

Reading

3–5 Strategies

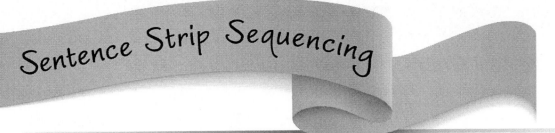

Sentence Strip Sequencing

Objective

Students will sequence text events.

Preparation

1. Select a variety of events from a familiar text.
2. Write the events on individual sentence strips.

Procedure

1. Lay the strips out in random order on a table or the floor.
2. Have students take turns reading the events to get familiar with them.
3. Ask students to work together to sequence the events. Or, provide multiple copies of the sentence strips and have students work individually.
4. Have students use the text as a reference to check for accuracy.

   Extend the mini-lesson into independent work by having students repeat the activity alone, gluing the finished order onto large paper so you can assess the results.

Differentiation: For **below-level students**, provide images as well as the written descriptions to help them sequence the text's events.

✔ **Assessment Check:** Listen to conversations as students work to order the strips. This is an ideal way to assess their logic and connection to meaningful content in a text. Use this information to guide new learning or reteaching opportunities.

3–5 Strategies

Reading

Objective

Students will identify the table of contents, glossary, and index in an informational text.

Preparation

1. Select a new informational text that students have not read. The text should have a table of contents, index, and glossary. Each student needs his or her own book or copy of the text.

2. Wrap each book in paper to hide the cover and title. Insert a bookmark or sticky note on the first page of the table of contents, the index, and the glossary. Consider using binder clips to clip the remaining pages together so that students cannot flip through the text.

Procedure

1. Distribute an unfamiliar book hiding the cover and title.

2. Have students use your bookmark to turn to the glossary and explore the words listed. Challenge student pairs to infer the topics that might be covered in the book based on the words listed in the glossary. Create a class list of topics.

3. Have students use your bookmark to turn to the index. Have students review the topics listed in the index. Cross off topics on the class list that are not similar to the actual topics in the index. Add important topics that were not listed.

4. Challenge student pairs to infer the chapter titles that might be included in the book based on the topics listed in the index. Create a class list of chapter titles.

5. Have students use your bookmark to turn to the table of contents. Have students review the chapter titles. Cross off titles on the class list that are not similar to the actual chapter titles. Add important titles that were not listed.

6. Reveal the book cover and title. Discuss the purposes and relationships between the table of contents, index, and glossary.

Differentiation: Have **below-level students** and **English language learners** create posters of the three text parts, explaining the purpose of each. Have **above-level students** create presentations to teach others about the function of each of these text components.

✔ **Assessment Check:** Note how well students utilize the table of contents to predict content. This strategy is important for students to prepare for when they are doing research, since a table of contents shows if the text will be relevant to a specific inquiry. Have students write the information when they do the same exercise independently so you can assess their competence and direct next learning steps.

Reading

3–5 Strategies

Text Features

Objective

Students will identify various text features.

Preparation

1. Select an informational text. The text should have headings, bolded vocabulary, captions for illustrations or photographs, and tables or other graphics.

2. Prepare a stack of note cards with a single text feature written on each card multiple times, such as *glossary* on four cards and *bolded vocabulary* on four cards.

Procedure

1. Shuffle the cards and place them facedown.

2. Flip the top card faceup.

3. Have students take turns drawing cards. They can choose either a face-up card or a face-down card. They must find examples in the text of the features written on the cards. Students keep the cards where they correctly identify the text features. If they do not correctly identify the features, they place the cards face up on the stack. The next student chooses either the face-up card or a face-down card.

4. Play continues until all cards are drawn. The student with the most cards wins.

Differentiation: Work with **English language learners** to add visual labels for each text feature to the cards. Have **above-level students** create multistep scavenger hunts for each feature.

✔ **Assessment Check:** Note who can find the features. Nonfiction text features are key to understanding content. Often, an author will put substantial information in a table or chart. We want to draw students' attention to these important text features. If students struggle, additional practice opportunities or guidance may be needed.

Vocabulary Boxes

Objective

Students will acquire and develop academic words.

Preparation

1. Select a new text.

2. Make a list of the words from the text that you would like to discuss with students, such as important content words.

3. Copy the *Vocabulary Boxes Chart* (page 313; vocabbox.pdf), one per student.

Procedure

1. Show students the text and *Vocabulary Boxes Charts*. Tell them you are looking for vocabulary words from the text that begin with each letter of the alphabet.

2. Suggest one word from your list and have students write it in the correct alphabet box, such as *oceanic* for *O*.

3. Ask students for a brief definition of the word to add to the *O* box. This will help them remember the words better. Continue with a couple more words in the same way.

4. Tell students that as they are reading the text and come across important words, they should write the words into the correct boxes along with their definitions. Their challenge is to find a strong word for each box.

Differentiation: When **English language learners** are working, use your prepared list to prompt them with word ideas they might be able to find.

✔ **Assessment Check:** Assess students as they define the words. If there are any words no student can define, you will want to help develop their knowledge about its meaning. It points to next learning steps in vocabulary instruction.

Reading

3–5 Strategies

Literature Circles in Grade 6 through Grade 8

In grade 6 through grade 8, students "are developing physically and emotionally, as well as cognitively" (Fresch and Harkins 2009, 12). Abstract thinking, concerns about the world around them, and diverse opinions drive their interests in reading materials. In a balanced literacy classroom, these grade levels are ideal for discussing and reading in literature circles, sometimes called book clubs. Groups set their own goals for reading, have specific roles to play in their groups, and meet about once a week with the teacher so skills can be assessed and considerations made about group assignments. The emphasis is on independent use of skills as readers to engage in reading, writing, discussion, and goal setting.

Best Practices in Literature Circles

Literature circles can be organized in two ways in grade 6 through grade 8. One way is to have students self-select groups based on interest in reading the same text. Reading ability is not the organizer; rather, groups are formed based on common interests. Teachers choose possible books and hold a book talk. The "book talk, a sort of movie trailer," grabs the interest of the listeners (Keane 2015, FAQ, para. 1). The teacher reads a particularly exciting part or poses questions that spark interest in the text. Only enough is told to entice a student to choose the book. The books are displayed for students to browse through after the initial book talk, and students rate the books in terms of their interest. Another approach to literature circles is to assess students and have those with similar reading levels work in the same groups. The groups have choices about the text they read from three or four books that are pre-selected by the teacher. The teacher offers a book talk about each book. The group members browse the books and rate them in order of interest for their group. Everyone must rank their choices and agree to read the same text. The ranking can also serve to inform a forward plan for the group in terms of what will be read first, second, and third.

Some classrooms, however, use both approaches. Homogeneous groups meet so the teacher can create appropriate mini-lessons to meet those particular students' needs. Then, heterogeneous groups form based on common interests of students. The organization that is best for a classroom depends on the time block for literature circles, the population of the class, the needs of students, and the purposes for reading. For example, a heterogeneous group may be formed to select a nonfiction book related to content studies.

Assessing Readers

In grade 6 through grade 8, students' reading accomplishments and needs have most likely been identified through school or district assessments. However, students can either improve or slip during the summer, so having a way to assess individuals can be a powerful tool for teachers. The QRI can provide needed information to address persistent issues in decoding, vocabulary, and comprehension. Using that information can help us plan needed mini-lessons with small groups of students. While these students may be reading different texts in different literature circles, pulling them together based on common need is the most efficient way to impact learning.

Planning Literature Circles

Students at this level are fairly independent in their reading abilities. During grade 6 through grade 8, teachers should organize the literature circles to give students more autonomy. Students should be reading books at the appropriate levels and lengths for extended reading and discussion. While teachers continue to guide the groups to provide explicit instruction as needed, students now have specific responsibilities to self-direct their reading.

Text choice is an important part of reading instruction. As noted previously, the circles are formed one of two ways: whole-class choices grouped by common interest in a book or several book choices presented to small groups of students with similar abilities. Book choice takes a bit of negotiation, but listen as students make arguments for or against particular books. This can give you some insights into the interest and leadership of the group members.

No matter which approach you choose, giving book talks not only provides previews of the texts for students but can also stimulate interest for even the most reluctant readers. Be certain you always pre-read any book you choose for literature groups. This allows you to add to group discussions, including posing critical-thinking questions, and it may help you devise integrated mini-lessons. For example, if a character in a story likes to write poetry, you can have a mini-lesson that requires writing a poem using words, ideas, and key details from the text. This also works as another comprehension check. If a character is caught up in a mystery, a mini-lesson on predicting ties in well.

Once groups are formed, several organizational patterns can be used. Students can read and then have specific meeting times to discuss the events. In this case, students agree on how far they will read by a certain date and then are individually responsible for meeting the deadline. A useful way to start students in their first experience with literature circles is to have them choose a specific role to carry out when reading. Have students volunteer for roles, randomly draw roles, or you can directly assign the roles. As they read, students make notes to bring to each group meeting. Students can have their assigned roles for one week and then switch, or you may want them to switch sooner. For smaller groups, you can choose between the roles you feel best suit your students. For larger groups, you can have two students do the same role. These roles can initially help organize the discussions within the groups, then slowly be eliminated as students understand their responsibilities in being prepared to discuss the books they read. As they read, students can complete the *Literature Circle Reading Log* (page 317) in preparation for the group discussion.

Students should meet weekly. Have spaces for students to meet, such as a group of desks or chairs. The space created by the chairs identifies the area as a group and allows you to move from group to group as needed to hold conferences and conduct mini-lessons. Using what they've included on the *Literature Circle Reading Log*, students discuss what they read since the last meeting. Each student should present what was required of his or her role for that day, if he or she has literature circle responsibilities. Have students spend about 15 minutes discussing what they've read. After the first meeting, students can plan how far they want to read for each week and when they will reasonably finish the entire book. This long-range planning helps with goal setting.

There are various roles to fill in a literature circle. Not every role needs to be filled every week. And, students can also create their own roles as they see needs for them. Some possible roles are as follows:

- **Discussion Director:** This person is the leader of the group for the week. What opening question or statement will start a discussion about what you read? What questions will you pose about what you read? How can you continue to encourage everyone in the class to participate? How will you bring the discussion to a close?

- **Passage Master:** The student is focused on the flow of the text. What passages will you read aloud because they were most powerful or interesting to you? What passages should you spotlight that are funny, puzzling, or important?

- **Wordsmith:** This is the vocabulary master. What important, new, or interesting vocabulary words should you remember? What are they, and what are their definitions?

- **Connector:** This person helps the rest of the group look for connections to themselves, other books, and the outside world. What else have you read or talked about that you are reminded of as you read this text?

- **Illustrator:** Students will love to fill this role. How can you draw or visually represent what you read? Be sure to include a description of what you drew.

- **Summarizer:** This role is a great starter for the discussion. What is the big idea of what you read for today?

- **Investigator:** The out-of-box thinkers will love this role. What other information should you look up now that you have read the text? What sort of inquiry project could you do?

- **Philosopher:** If there is a student who asks endless questions, this is the role for him or her. What does this text make you wonder about? What surprised you about what you read?

If possible, meet with each group during the 15-minute discussions. An easy way to manage checking in with students is to have groups have their weekly meetings on different days. Organize your records by having three-ring binders with each group's book title and a list of group members on the outside. In the notebook, keep lesson plan notes and individual records. The individual records can be transferred between notebooks when groups re-form with new texts.

When you meet with each group, do the following tasks:

- Listen to their conversations about the text. Ask about their interest in the text.

- Conduct a comprehension check about the material read thus far. Pose a few critical-thinking questions. These questions go beyond literal recall and ask students to connect what they read across several parts of a book or to connect something in the book to their lives.

- Be certain everyone has responsibilities, is following through on their roles, and is changing roles regularly.

- Ask a few students to read aloud from the chapter. This allows you to do a quick check of fluency and decoding strategies. Note any possible mini-lesson needs.

- Run through a mini-lesson as needed. Many suggestions are provided starting on page 145.

- Discuss future reading goals, make specific assignments based on the mini-lesson, and discuss an end-of-reading project for when the group finishes the text.

- Record observations about individual students. Notes can be transferred later to individual checklists. By keeping the lesson plans together in a three-ring binder, you can quickly review previous lessons and observe any continued issues or progress.

- See *Lesson Plan Template for Meeting with Literature Circles* (page 316) for a reproducible outline.

At the end of each week, review the notes from the meetings and decide when the next mini-lesson might be. What's next for this group of students? Are there just a few students in a group who need a focused mini-lesson? Might you combine students across groups for particular mini-lessons, regardless of the books they are reading? Subsequent book choices or groups may need reconsideration, depending on the skills and strategies of the members of each reading group. Also, be aware of students needing to move to a different group, either to provide more supportive reading or more challenging work.

Reading

Suggested Mini-Lessons

This section includes basic small-group strategy lessons for simple practice of the following skills for grade 6 through grade 8. Details regarding each strategy can be found on the subsequent pages. For additional lessons, download the Digital Resources. (See page 20 for the website address and access code.)

These guided reading mini-lessons are meant to solidify students' independence with the text. Teachers should have opportunities to explicitly teach skills and strategies to help students, yet they also need to allow students to self-select and self-direct as much as possible.

You can easily connect any of the activities suggested for grade 6 through grade 8 in the Word Study section to specific words read during guided reading. Connect any of the writing approaches presented in the Writing section. Also, look at the ideas presented in this section for grade 3 through grade 5 for students still working on reading skills.

Mini-Lessons

Lesson
Cause and Effect (page 146)
Character Trading Cards (page 147)
Compare and Contrast (page 148)
Critical Literacy Questions (page 149)
Figurative Language (page 150)
Inferences (page 151)
Justify Arguments! (page 152)
Self-Assessment (page 153)
So Many Choices! (page 154)
Time Line (page 155)
Web-Based Work (page 156)
Write a Review (page 157)

Digital Resources Lessons

Lesson
Anticipation Guide (anticipation.pdf)
Character Attributes (characattributes.pdf)
New Words (newwords.pdf)
Ordering Story Events (storyevents.pdf)
Personal Project (personalproject.pdf)
Posing Questions (posingquest.pdf)
Predicting What's Next (predicting.pdf)

Some websites that serve to enhance instruction and provide additional opportunities for students to explore these various topics are:

- www.prezi.com
- www.voki.com
- www.educreations.com
- www.goanimate.com
- www.evernote.com

Some apps that serve to enhance instruction and provide additional opportunities for students to explore these various topics are:

- Fotobabble (Fotobabble, Inc.)
- iMovie (Apple)

Cause and Effect

Objective

Students will deepen their reading comprehension by identifying cause-and-effect relationships in text.

Preparation

1. Make a list of cause-and-effect examples from a text students are reading.
2. Create a cause-and-effect chart, as below:

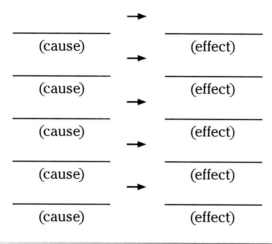

(cause)	→	(effect)
(cause)	→	(effect)
(cause)	→	(effect)
(cause)	→	(effect)
(cause)		(effect)

Procedure

1. Discuss and define the cause-and-effect relationship with students. Give some common examples, such as a thunderclap and their dog howling—the noise startled the dog (*cause*) and made him howl (*effect*).

2. Give a cause-and-effect example from the text.

3. Explain that understanding various text structures, such as cause and effect, enhances comprehension of the material.

4. Ask students for other cause-and-effect events from the text. List these on a poster so students can add additional events as they finish reading the text.

Differentiation: Have **below-level students** discuss the causes and effects in pairs before sharing with the group.

✔ **Assessment Check:** Note who contributes to the discussion. Those who do not may need additional guidance, practice, or instruction.

> *Cause and effect* is a text structure used in literature and informational texts. The relationship between one event and subsequent events demonstrates cause and effect.

Character Trading Cards

Objective
Students will engage in character analyses.

Preparation
1. Have enough large, blank note cards for each student.
2. Provide a variety of coloring supplies.
3. Have some sample sports trading cards (basketball, football, or baseball) available for demonstration purposes.

Procedure
1. Gather students together and discuss the format of sports trading cards.
2. Share the example cards, and ask students to note the information that is on the fronts and backs of the cards.
3. Make a list of this information for the students, asking them to decide which descriptors apply to characters in the books they are reading.
4. Have each student choose a character from literature and take notes about his or her key characteristics or facts about his or her life.
5. Provide time for students to create their character trading cards. Encourage them to add images of their characters.
6. Make multiple copies of the completed cards so students can "trade" them.

Extend the mini-lesson into independent work by having students work on the cards, information, and images after the format for making the cards is outlined in the mini-lesson.

Differentiation: Work with **below-level students** to locate the key characteristics or facts about their characters. Help them distinguish between the key facts and superfluous information. Have **above-level students** choose their own criteria and design their trading cards accordingly.

✔ **Assessment Check:** Assess students' abilities to determine key character features. This will determine whether guided practice or additional instruction is needed.

> *Character trading cards feature characters or real people to read about. The contents of the card can vary according to literature or informational text, but suggestions for the format are name, job or importance to the story, birth/death dates (if applicable), character traits, location (setting), and students' impression of the character.*

Compare and Contrast

Objective

Students will deepen their comprehension by comparing and contrasting two texts.

Preparation

1. Select two familiar texts about similar topics, such as animals cells and plant cells.

2. Make a list of how the two texts are similar and how they are different.

3. Copy the *Compare and Contrast Template* (page 312; comparetemp.pdf), one per student.

Procedure

1. Show students the two texts, and review the main points of each.

2. Discuss what it means to compare and contrast.

3. Have students list a few key similarities and differences between the two texts/topics.

4. Distribute copies of *Compare and Contrast Template* to students, and ask them to record their ideas of the two books on their own. Students should include at least five ideas in the outside circles and at least three ideas in the middle section.

Differentiation: Provide a written list of similarities and differences to **below-level students** as a reference to complete the template. Have **above-level students** add a third text to the comparison along with a third circle to their *Compare and Contrast Template*.

✔ **Assessment Check:** Note who can offer ideas about how the texts compare and contrast. Collect the templates to assess the independent work and determine who may need additional guidance, practice, or instruction.

Objective

Students will analyze a text.

Preparation

1. Review the text being read by a particular literature circle. Be sure the group has read enough of the book to meaningfully discuss the questions below.

2. Prepare answers for your questions so you can facilitate, but not direct, the discussion. Possible questions are:

   - *How does this text make you feel? Present evidence from the text to support your answer.*
   - *What question(s) would you like to ask the author? Cite the section of text that inspires your question.*
   - *Where did you imagine yourself as you read the text?*
   - *How did you visualize the events?*
   - *What does this text make you want to do in terms of writing or selecting other texts to read? Show where in the text you were encouraged to pursue this.*

Procedure

1. Gather the literature circle together.

2. Ask students the questions above, accepting oral answers. Encourage students to provide textual evidence about their thinking.

   Extend the mini-lesson into independent work by having students write answers to the questions discussed. They may write something different from what was discussed now that they have had time to consider and think about the questions.

Differentiation: Have **English language learners** use sentence stems or offer word banks to scaffold their responses. Have **above-level students** write analyses of the text, such as the effectiveness of the author communicating his or her point of view.

✔ **Assessment Check:** Note who can think about the questions and extend their comprehension by doing critical analyses of the readings. Assess the individual written responses to the questions to determine students' critical thinking about the book. Additional guidance may be needed for some students to gain a deeper understanding of the text.

6–8 Strategies

Reading

Figurative Language

Objective

Students will interpret the meaning and role figurative language plays in a text.

Preparation

1. On note cards, write six to nine figurative language examples from a text students are reading. Figurative language includes:

   - metaphors (comparison of two unrelated things, such as *His dad was the rock in their family.*)

   - similes (comparison of two unrelated things utilizing *like* or *as*, such as *hungry as a bear*)

   - idioms (figures of speech, such as *raining cats and dogs*)

   - hyperboles (exaggerated statements, such as *my bookbag weighs a ton*)

   - proverbs (simple sayings that express a truth based on experience, such as *Look before you leap.*)

   - personification (giving human qualities to animals or objects, such as *time flies*)

Procedure

1. Read one of the figurative language examples aloud. Have students define the type of figurative language the example illustrates.

2. Ask students to explain what the example means within the context of the book. For example, they can explain why the father of the story was the *rock*, or dependable person.

3. Distribute the other cards to pairs of students. Have them define the types of figurative language and discuss the examples. Students can switch cards and repeat the steps with other examples of figurative language

   Extend the mini-lesson by creating a figurative language bulletin board with headings for each type. Have students post examples from their independent reading.

Differentiation: Have **below-level students** examine predetermined pages to search for additional figurative language. **Above-level students can** locate sentences in their own books that do not contain figurative language. Have them rewrite those sections using figurative language.

✔ **Assessment Check:** Note who can define and discuss figurative language. These terms and examples are particularly difficult for English language learners, so additional work with these students will most likely be needed.

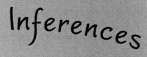
Inferences

Objective

Students will make inferences using textual evidence.

Preparation

1. Prepare a list of questions about possible inferences students can make from a familiar text, such as the following:

   - *What do we know about the character based on how he or she acts?*
   - *According to what you have read, what can you conclude about _____ ?*
   - *What generalizations can you make from the information you have?*
   - *What is the moral of the story?*
   - *What is the author's point of view?*

Procedure

1. Discuss and define the word *inference*.

2. Discuss how readers need to use textual evidence to support inferences. Ask students one of the questions from above. Encourage students to include text support for the inferences they give while answering the question.

3. Continue with each question. Discuss the questions as a group, or have students work in pairs.

4. Invite students to think of a question that requires inference they can ask other students.

   Extend the mini-lesson into independent work by having students write answers to those questions.

> *An inference is an informed guess based on the information provided.*

Differentiation: For **below-level students**, scaffold the activity by providing page numbers where textual evidence can be found to support their thinking for each question. For **above-level students**, have them locate additional pieces of evidence to support the questions.

✔ **Assessment Check:** Note who can contribute to the discussion. Inferencing is an important skill. It means students can use text evidence as well as background knowledge to support their thinking. Additional practice, scaffolding, or instruction may be needed.

6–8 Strategies

Reading

Justify Arguments!

Objective

Students will use text evidence to support their arguments.

Preparation

1. Gather lined paper, one sheet of paper per student.
2. Select a piece of text being read in a literature circle.
3. Make note of a few events or characters' actions to discuss. Consider using a controversial decision by a character or an event that surprised the reader.

Procedure

1. Distribute lined paper to students, and have them title it "In My Opinion."
2. Ask students to bring their current literature circle texts to meet together.
3. Discuss the meaning of the word *argument*.
4. Share the events or characters' actions you determined ahead of time, and ask students to form arguments about them.
5. Discuss why students feel the way they do. Ask them to find reasons, example, and evidence from the text to show how they made their decisions, and have them read the evidence from the text aloud.
6. Ask students to find other events or character decisions in the text that might make interesting discussion points.

   Extend the mini-lesson into independent work by having students write their arguments about particular events or characters.

Differentiation: Have **English language learners** discuss connections between these events or characters' actions to their own lives and experiences. Have **above-level students** write a letter to the author about their opinions on an event or character action of their choosing, including supporting text evidence.

✔ **Assessment Check:** When readers share an opinion, they loosely base their ideas on what they read, but they must think beyond the text. Assess the written arguments students create during independent work time. Determine who may need additional guidance in stating an arguments or providing text evidence. Additional instruction or practice may be required.

Self-Assessment

Objective
Students will self-reflect on their literature circle role.

Preparation

1. Copy and cut apart the *Literature Circle Self-Assessment Chart* (page 318; litself.pdf), one per student.

Procedure

1. Distribute the *Literature Circle Self-Assessment Chart* to each member of a literature circle.

2. Have students complete the self-assessment. Emphasize this is a self-assessment and will not be graded. Therefore, they need to consider each statement thoughtfully. They should take the time to comment on each statement.

3. Ask student pairs to briefly explain their answers to one another. For example, if they chose *no* or *sometimes*, ask students how they can improve. For any answer where they chose *yes*, ask students to explain how they were successful in completing those tasks.

   Extend the mini-lesson into independent work by having students revisit the self-assessment in two weeks and note any response changes and why they changed.

Differentiation: Have **English language learners** discuss their answers with you before meeting with their literature circles.

✔ **Assessment Check:** Assess how well each student is working in the group. Note if some of the groups need you to join them to help navigate their work as a literature circle. Note any students who might need individual assistance in contributing to the group.

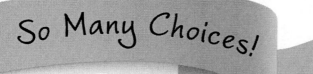
So Many Choices!

Objective

Students will practice analyzing character actions.

Preparation

1. Find a spot in a piece of literature being read as a class or in a literature circle group where a character must make a critical decision.

2. On poster paper or the board, create a three-column chart labeled *Choices*, *Pros*, and *Cons*. Have multiple markers available.

Procedure

1. Read the text up to the predetermined stopping point.

2. Have student pairs or groups brainstorm what options the character has regarding the critical decision he or she has to make.

3. Have students list the pros and cons of each decision in the three-column chart.

4. Discuss the decision as a group, and decide which choice the character should make.

5. Continue reading the text to see what the character decides to do or what other factors come into the decision-making process for the character.

Differentiation: For **English language learners**, relate the critical decision to decisions they might have to make in their own lives. This will help give the situation context for them. For **above-level students**, add a fourth column where students can list which other characters in the book will be most affected by the decision.

✔ **Assessment Check:** Note who contributes to the discussion. Those who do not may need additional prompting and guidance to make sure they are making decisions and supporting them with evidence from the text.

Time Line

Objective

Students will label events in a text with literary terms.

Preparation

1. Create an outline of major story events for a familiar text.

2. Gather enough note cards for the major story events you predetermined.

Procedure

1. Ask students to determine the major events in a story they are reading. Ask students to identify each major story event with the appropriate literary term such as *rising action*, *falling action*, *climax*, *problem*, or *solution*.

2. Have a student write each of these on a note card.

3. Shuffle the cards after students are done suggesting events and creating the cards.

4. Place them in a pile facedown on the table.

5. One at a time, have a student turn over a card, identify where the event happens in the story, and provide the corresponding literary term.

   Copy the major event cards, and extend the mini-lesson into independent work by having students order the events and write summaries of the stories.

Differentiation: For **below-level students**, provide the events and literary terms. Ask them to match and order them.

✔ **Assessment Check:** Note who contributes to the discussion. Assess the independent work for the correct order of events and follow up with students as needed.

6–8 Strategies

Reading

Objective

Students will increase their content knowledge.

Preparation

1. Locate appropriate websites students can use to look up setting maps of story locations, additional information related to informational texts, or research about new inquiries. For example, if a story takes place in Utah, link students to the Utah government website where they can read about the state.

2. Create a document with the URL addresses listed. Students can click on them to go directly to the sites.

3. Have chart paper available.

Procedure

1. Ask students what further information or additional perspective they might want to investigate connected to their current literature circle text.

2. On chart paper, make a list of suggestions.

3. Distribute the document of URLs you created to students.

4. Show students how to click on the URLs and/or safely search the Internet for further information.

5. Have students work together to find sites that connect to the text's content. Have them take note of interesting facts they learn. They should share this information in their next literature circle meeting to enhance the group's knowledge about the text.

   Extend the mini-lesson into independent work by having students finish the searching later in the day or at home.

Differentiation: Have **below-level students** use a predetermined list of topics to conduct their searches. Have **English language learners** search for corresponding videos of text-related topics.

✔ **Assessment Check:** Evaluate students' suggestions for text-related research topics. This is an indicator of both comprehension and critical thinking. Assess how well their thinking connects to the research. Provide additional practice opportunities or instructions as needed.

Reading

6–8 Strategies

Write a Review

Objective

Students will review books.

Preparation

1. Find a recent book review in a newspaper, magazine, or online. There are free online children's book review sites, such as *The Children's Book Review*, that include age-appropriate books with reviews.

Procedure

1. Meet with literature groups when they have finished their texts. Share the book review you located and discuss key characteristics of it. Explain that students are each to write a synopsis and review of the text their group is currently reading.

2. Discuss what should go in the synopsis, such as main characters, descriptions, plot or main idea, and key details.

3. Discuss adding personal ideas (or editorial comments), such as *It is spellbinding!* or *It has a surprise ending!* It is important to emphasize that the review should encourage others to read the book without giving away too much of the plot or ending.

   Extend the mini-lesson into independent work by having students write additional reviews. Have students read their reviews the next time groups meet. Groups can also create final reviews to post in the classroom.

Differentiation: For **below-level students**, provide an outline of key characteristics for them to follow as they write their reviews. Have **above-level students** with opposing reviews debate their opinions within their literature circles. Or, have students agree with or oppose published book reviews of the text.

✔ **Assessment Check:** Note who contributes to the discussion about the synopsis. This is a good indicator of overall comprehension. Read students' reviews and assess for connections to the book, crafting sentences, punctuation, and other written skills you might be currently teaching during Writer's Workshop. Follow up with additional instruction or provide other practice opportunities.

Modeled and Shared Read Alouds

Best Practices for Read Alouds

Read alouds are important at any age. The read aloud is a teacher's way of showing students the fun of reading as well as mentoring readers to help them develop independent comprehension strategies. While young readers need the modeling of how to read, "middle and high school students enjoy hearing read alouds, too. Yet we seldom think to include them in our instruction" (Richardson 2000, 3). In fact, "studies by education researchers, such as Stephen Krashen, Jim Trelease, and Janet Allen, have shown that reading to kids boosts their reading comprehension, increases their vocabularies, and helps them become better writers. In fact, students who are read to are more motivated to read themselves—increasing the likelihood that they will one day become independent, lifelong readers" (Blessing 2005, 44). Because the "work" for reading the text is done by the teacher during a read aloud, all students, regardless of reading ability, are drawn into understanding the text. While helping to develop listening skills, teachers are also developing students' ability to learn (Opitz and Zbaracki 2004). People can hear faster than they read, so read alouds level the playing field. As a result, below-level readers can participate in the same discussion, answer the same thought-provoking questions, and make the same predictions as their peers.

When the teacher reads aloud, the processes of reading and comprehending are modeled. The joy of reading can be conveyed through the teacher's approach. Smith (2006) reminds teachers that they must invite students to "join the club of readers" (113). Smith suggests the following advantages to students who are "club members":

- see what written language does in the world around them
- enter as neophytes with experts ready to coach them
- help all newcomers to the club, regardless of their own expertise
- participate in more and more activities in the club once they see how reading is "done" and they have experiences that help them
- identify themselves as a member of the group—they see themselves as readers (adapted from Smith 2006, 114–115)

Through modeling and an invitation to the "club," teachers allow students to see the possibilities and potential of being readers.

In younger grades, read alouds also include a shared responsibility for the reading. Students participate in a shared read aloud, and the teacher can coach students in "real time." Students are encouraged to predict, join in, and rehearse new strategies during this shared experience. Any number of strategies can be addressed under the mentoring of the teacher, and important skills are taught during this time. Knowledge of how print works has been shown to dramatically increase after shared read alouds (Piasta, Justice, McGinty, Kaderavek 2012), particularly for at-risk populations. Making the reading process explicit during the shared experiences encourages students to carry over important skills into independent reading time.

Modeled read alouds have a number of purposes across the curriculum. Besides the ability to model *how* one reads, teachers can engage students in deeper thinking about the text since the reading is being "shared." Oliveira found that first and second graders could transcend "passive reception of facts" (2015, 429) during science read alouds. Hurst and Griffity suggest that read alouds are not just for young students. The modeled read aloud "has positive implications for many middle school students by providing a helpful scaffold for lower ability readers with mature reasoning ability, allowing them to move their concentration from decoding words to the comprehension of new ideas found in texts. Teacher read alouds are a frequently overlooked but an appropriate and potentially valuable strategy for adolescent learners" (2015, 44).

There are several ways to use modeled read alouds:

1. **Share a book that is above the majority of the class's reading level.** While listening comprehension may enable them to learn from the book, some vocabulary may be new, preventing some students from independently approaching the book. This is particularly true of informational texts. Consequently, read alouds are particularly useful during content-area lessons. Below-level readers need to meet grade-level content standards but may not be ready to independently read texts at that level. With teacher scaffolding, students will be able to understand higher-level texts, thus encouraging student progress. In this way, the read aloud helps level the playing field.

2. **Share a book as an introduction to a theme or unit.** This common text allows students to have a shared learning experience. Students might then move into appropriate books for independent reading related to the same topic. Common experience builds prior knowledge and vocabulary to help them better understand their independent reading choices. The approach is also helpful for English language learners who may not have the same life experiences as other students.

3. **Share a book that stimulates an interesting discussion.** Formulating opinions based on information gained is an important skill for students to develop, regardless of their grade level. In modeled read alouds, teachers can explore forms of written text students may not normally choose, thus enabling them to decide if they want to try something similar for their independent reading.

4. **Share a book you personally enjoy.** Students love hearing teachers give voice and life to a book. During read alouds, teachers can model fluent reading, adding inflection and "voice" to the text.

During *shared read alouds*, teachers continue to model how to read but engage students in the process. Teachers want students to physically and verbally participate in the read aloud. A shared read aloud is best done with a large text that students can approach to point out particular elements as requested. In the early grades, big versions of books can be placed on easels where students gather around. If a big version of a particular book does not exist or teachers are working with older students, using technology to project the book onto a screen or whiteboard allows students to interact with the text.

Teachers can achieve a number of reading-related skills during shared read alouds:

1. **Teachers can explicitly demonstrate reading strategies.** Teachers can demonstrate mapping sounds with print or understanding complex ideas. Students can physically come to the board to point out the words, phrases, graphs, and charts.

2. **Teachers can stop, ask questions, and model what students should be doing independently.** They can see that they *are* readers. Students learn how to behave like readers, focusing on comprehension. Students who struggle with comprehension may be unaware of the way a good reader questions, predicts, and verifies content.

3. **Teachers can establish a community of helpers.** Knowing that others can support individual learning is important in developing confidence and skills.

4. **Teachers can show the enjoyment of reading.** Teachers build a sense of what success feels like and how all readers can have success.

5. **Teachers can refer back to the shared reading book.** Conversations about ideas and words will remain with students, and using the book in conjunction with their independent reading or content-area studies can provide support.

Selecting Books for Read Alouds

To select books for either type of read aloud, consider the emotional and social development of your students. Books need to captivate students, thus modeling how readers can learn while enjoying a good book. Also, consider the interest of students. Doing an interest inventory at the beginning of the year can help direct book choices.

Consider the length and complexity of the text. For example, should it be broken up over several days? What is the complexity of the story or facts presented? Will students understand well enough to later retell, recount, and discuss this text? Be certain students will be able to use their developing strategies to participate. If young students are not yet reading, be certain they can follow the story line to participate in discussions.

Use this time to introduce various genres. Literature choices should include narrative, realistic fiction, science fiction, historical fiction, poetry, fantasy, drama, and traditional stories. Informational text choices should include biographies, autobiographies, social studies/history, science, mathematics, the arts, and technical texts. You might also use sequential read alouds to examine the work of one author or illustrator. You might want to use picture books or other illustrated books to help add visual elements to the auditory experience. You can infuse multicultural books into your classroom during this time. The read aloud is a perfect time to choose books students may overlook on their own. Finally, consider if the reading is just for enjoyment or to extend the text into a curricular activity.

*An **interest inventory** can be taken orally (for young students) or in written form with questions, such as:*

- *What fun things did you do over the summer?*

- *What types of books do you like to read?*

- *What hobbies do you or your family have?*

- *Are there any authors you know and like?*

- *What are some topics you like learning about?*

Modeled Read-Aloud Lesson

Pre-read the read-aloud book. Opitz and Rasinski tell teachers not to skip this important step as "one intent of the read-aloud is for students to develop a sense of what fluent reading sounds like" (1998, 50). Opitz and Rasinski continue, stating "It is imperative that you read in a smooth and polished way—a presentation of the highest quality. Be sure to embed specific elements of expression into your presentation—increased and decreased volume, pitch of your voice, voice changes to signal different characters, change in speed at appropriate places—all for the purpose of showing students how the reader interprets the author's intended meaning" (1998, 50). While pre-reading, use sticky notes to mark some spots in the text where you want to model how to pause and ponder a question, make a prediction, or note an interesting event or fact. Stopping only a few times maintains the flow of the story. If you are reading a long book, start each day by asking students to recall the events or facts heard in previous chapters. This will refresh students' memories and update any students who were absent. Having students review what was read during the last session is also a good way to engage them and to do a quick comprehension check. If students have trouble providing some of the key details, use the post-reading time to compose a list that can be reviewed and shared during the next read aloud.

Remember to show how fluency, expression, and the use of punctuation help readers understand the tone and content of a text. There is much recent discussion on teaching "fluency." If you examine the origin of the term (Latin—*fluens* meaning "flowing"), it is clear to see the important links between fluency and comprehension (Pikulski and Chard 2005). The more fluently students read, the better their comprehension will be because effort will be concentrated on the meaning rather than the decoding. Model how reading should "sound" as you read a text aloud. Prosody, or the patterns of stress and intonation used in language, is an important part of fluency. Vary the volume (loud, soft, whisper), animation (voices, laugh, giggle, snore), and speed (fast, slow—consider the tempo of the text) in your voice to both entice listeners and show students the fun in reading.

You can also add "drama" to the reading beyond the tone of your voice. Darken the room for a mystery, wear something relevant to the main character (a hat, boots, or a vest), or bring an object related to the story (fishing pole or soccer ball). Bring students "in close"—that is, get them out of their desks and onto the floor near you. This assists in seeing illustrations and helps accentuate the "community" of learners. For young children, a tip for classroom management is to provide each student with a square of paper or inexpensive carpet square available at home improvement stores. Ask students to sit and stay on their squares.

Always follow read alouds with discussions connected to the text. Right after reading, simply invite students to react to the text. Then, you can use a few "in the book" or "in my head" questions. These can be brief, but reacting to the text, asking questions, and discussing the content all send the message that people read for enjoyment and to learn new things.

A read aloud can definitely include student participation as the readers. Suggest to students that they practice reading the book on their own first. This rehearsal alerts students to any words they may need assistance with before reading in front of the whole class. After read alouds, students may want to reread books you have shared. Modeled read alouds can be to whole classes, small groups, or as audio recordings to listen to at later dates. The approach gives credence to multiple readings of the same text, thus improving fluency and comprehension. Repeated reading improves prosody. Rasinski points out, "through repeated reading, readers become more adept and efficient at employing prosodic features into new passages not previously read" (2012, 519). Prosody helps develop automaticity or the quick and easy identification of words. The books can also be read to students in other classrooms, such as a younger grade, providing another reason for practicing fluent reading.

Shared Read-Aloud Lesson

Pre-read the shared read-aloud book. Make note where you want to pause to make a text-based prediction or ask students to participate in the reading. The following lesson plan gives general guidance, regardless of grade level.

Using the *Developmental Continuum Chart* (pages 337–339; continuum.pdf), select a strategy to focus on for a lesson. The choice of strategy can be guided by your assessment of the class or a small group and what you consider to be their needs. For example, first-grade students may be asked to read aloud a sentence they find that contains a particular sight word. (*Who sees a sentence with the word "about" in it?*) Fifth-grade students might be asked how context helps them understand a new vocabulary word. (*What in the sentence helps you to understand what* ecology *is?*) Seventh-grade students might be asked how a specific word helps to improve the overall mood of a scene. (*How does the word* erratic *help you to understand how the characters are feeling in the book and the overall mood in this passage?*)

Before reading, activate student background knowledge (for literature texts, about the author or what the title suggests; for informational texts, about the topic). Students can predict what the story will be about (literature) or what vocabulary and facts they might learn (informational). Additionally, if the book is informational, they can list what they already know about the topic along with some questions they hope will be answered in the text.

Strategies to Highlight

- *using context to figure out definitions*

- *using graphophonics to decode new words*

- *analyzing word parts (prefix, base, suffix, word family) to decode new words*

- *checking for understanding (Does what I read "make sense"?)*

During reading, invite students to participate. For example, first-grade students may be asked to read the first sentence on a page aloud. This can be read as a group or individually, which provides support for all readers. Group reading helps below-level students, and individual reading challenges above-level students. In older grades, students can be asked to read a paragraph or several sentences as the rest of the group listens. As with the read aloud, follow up with a discussion so that meaning takes center stage, showing how reading strategies help readers to understand texts. Alternate between you reading and asking students to read to keep the text moving along, maintain students' engagement, and allow flexibility in what students are asked to read. Just as in guided reading, the goal is to keep the reading purposeful and not just an exercise in reading words aloud.

After reading, circle back to the before reading discussion. Were student predictions accurate? Have a few "in the book" and "in my head" questions to pose. Ask students what questions they might pose for the group to answer. Older students can write these, then share them with the group. Some additional options are:

- **Ask students to summarize what was read.** Summarizing requires students to provide the main idea(s) with supporting details properly sequenced.

- **Discuss the text structures.** Was this text compare/contrast, problem/solution, or cause/effect? Can students recount the chronological sequence of events or facts?

- **Discuss text features.** In informational texts, these are headings, captions, charts, tables, and glossaries—anything that adds to understanding the text. In literature, point out how illustrations or the use of different type styles, such as italics or boldface, help readers to comprehend the author's meaning.

- **Discuss what students will do once they move back into independent work.** An extension to the book's content, illustrating something from what they read, working specifically with words from the text, and developing a reader's theater performance are beneficial after-reading tasks.

At some point in the lesson, take a few minutes to specifically analyze important words. What strategies were used while reading to decode words? What common features can you focus on to have students discuss and then go on a "scavenger hunt" in other texts to find similar features? Have students add to the word wall or keep personal lists of words that were particularly important from the shared read aloud that they might need in future reading and writing activities. See *Shared Reading Lesson Plan Template* (page 315) to customize your own shared reading lesson.

Independent Reading

Best Practices for Independent Reading

Every new skill that is learned, whether it is speaking a second language, playing a musical instrument, or reading a book, needs time for practice. People know that the more you practice something, the better you are at doing it. Gladwell (2008) provides compelling evidence of the power of practice. His study of successful people pointed to the difference practice made to moving someone from being a novice to an expert. Stanovich (1986) noted that students who do well practice more often, thus we see the "Matthew effect" (likened to the biblical saying that suggests the rich get richer and the poor get poorer). This "effect" notes that those who develop needed concepts practice them more often and become better at them. Students still struggling with skills often get more instruction in the skills and less practice in using them. And, of course, practice is more enjoyable when you have a say in how to spend your time. Sustained, independent reading allows students to immerse themselves in texts of their choice—where they can feel successful and maybe even stretch their new skills. It is also about reading for pure enjoyment. No book reports. No "looking up" vocabulary they are unsure about. No after-the-reading quiz. Just pure enjoyment (and practice, of course!). That's it.

Independent reading requires that students select their own texts to read—literature or informational texts—whatever will give them sustained time reading. Reviewing how to self-select books with students encourages them to pick appropriate books. As noted earlier, students have many reasons for picking a book. Use the *My Independent Reading Log* (page 314) as a way to keep track of students' choices, reasoning for the choices, and length of time spent with the books. This allows you to take a quick look at how the student is working in this self-directed reading.

As you check student reading logs, the following questions might be helpful:

- Is the student selecting appropriate books? An occasional "easy" book is okay, but you want students working in "just right" books.
- Is the student picking different types of books? You may learn a student's love of informational text by the choices he or she is making.
- Is the student focused on a topic?
- Is the student returning to a book for rereading? Sometimes students choose books they "know" they can read to build confidence.
- Is the student selecting books used during the class read aloud? Choosing a familiar book should build student confidence.
- Is the student reading each selection in a reasonable amount of time?

Organization

Providing a structure to the time students can read independently is important. Organizing how your students will read during this time will get everyone to the *work* of reading. "Research suggests that students spend a substantial amount of time transitioning between classroom activities, which may reduce time spent academically engaged" (Hine, Ardoin, and Foster 2015, 495). By managing the time to efficiently move students from one activity to the next, teachers can increase their students' independence and instructional time, while avoiding disruptions (Cameron, Connor, and Morrison 2005). Students know where they can read, what they can read, and how they should participate in independent reading. Whatever teachers can do to have students begin reading as soon as independent reading time begins, the more dedicated time students will have for the activity. There are many ways to designate independent reading in your classroom. Read aloud expert Jim Trelease (2013) provides some of the popular acronyms used to identify this specific reading time. The following are some examples:

- SSR = Sustained Silent Reading
- USSR = Universal Sustained Silent Reading
- DEAR = Drop Everything And Read
- DIRT = Daily Individual Reading Time
- SQUIRT = Sustained Quiet Uninterrupted Individual Reading Time

Typically, self-selected books are kept at school and not sent home, so students can be directed at any time to pull out their personal choices. Whatever you choose to name your independent reading time, be certain students know what this means. Students should understand the following:

- They are in charge of their own reading selections.
- They are to find spots to read and do so uninterrupted by other activities.
- They are to record their reading, choosing something new if they do not like their selection or they finish reading their choice.
- They have to give new choices "a fair shot." If during one or two sustained reading times they decide they do not like the book, they can make a new choice.
- They are reading for enjoyment and will not be tested or expected to perform an extension activity for the book, unless they voluntarily choose to do so.

Find a time in the day when students can read uninterrupted. This can be organized in a number of ways. You might ask students to use part of their independent work time for sustained reading, while you are meeting with other guided reading groups. Or, the entire class can take time in the day for independent reading. Some teachers like to do it immediately after lunch or recess. Some teachers like it while transitioning between different content areas, such as moving from guided reading to mathematics. When the entire class is reading, is also a good time for the teacher to read as well. Not only do you model reading for enjoyment, but you also show *how* sustained reading looks.

The amount of time for this sustained reading is dependent on the grade level. Much of this is subject to curricular requirements and how your school day is organized. The skills and stamina of your students are also important to consider. Students gain valuable practice in identifying vocabulary and using the three cueing systems. Students encounter many more words by reading silently in texts written at their independent levels. "The time allotted for SSR should begin small and gradually increase as the ability, attention, and motivation of students increase. For example, only five minutes of silent reading may be initially appropriate for a below-level reader. The time could then be increased by two minutes every three to four weeks until the student is reading independently for about 30 minutes" (Hairrell et al. 2010, 284).

How Independent Reading Informs Teaching

Not attaching assignments or assessments to reading does not mean teachers cannot learn about students' reading abilities. Independent reading can give information about book choices as discussed earlier. But, teachers can also use the power of observation to gain insights into students' literacy lives. Some key points to consider include the following:

- How engaged is the student during this time? Does the student stay on task?
- How often does a student change his or her mind about a book selection?
- What level of text difficulty does a student self-select?
- What reasons does a student note for book selection?
- If you observe a student during this reading time, do you notice finger pointing or lip movement?
- Does the student consult a resource, such as a dictionary, when reading?

Knowing the answers to these questions can be useful as you plan guided reading lessons. For example, you might want to tap into a student's favorite genre. This may provide an interesting change to the group reading and allow a student who excels in a particular genre to shine in his or her group. Or, you might review a lesson on using context to decode a new word if you see a student who seems to be making slow progress in his or her self-selected text.

Every few weeks, find time to hold a discussion with students. Have them open their reading logs to talk about their choices. Ask them to discuss how the reading is going, and what are the hardest and easiest parts of independent reading? Are there books they marked with four stars to recommend to other students? Are there books that several students read that they might do something special with, such as perform as reader's theater for the rest of the class? Are there books they want in the classroom library that are not currently available? Think back to the beginning of this section with Mr. Loomis getting "that" special book again for Isabella. Do students have any suggestions for improving or extending independent reading time? Class discussions such as these make it clear that your class is a community of literacy learners.

Conclusion

This section presented how to organize reading instruction in kindergarten through grade 8. Assessment drives reading instruction. Knowing what students *can* do as well as what they are still learning helps teachers know where to begin instruction. Students work in instructional texts to stretch their skills and "test the waters" of what they can do under teachers' watchful eyes. They also engage in independent reading to put their skills to use. Knowing which skills they can easily use and which need further work helps teachers decide on possible mini-lessons. In these lessons, teachers guide students to new learning and also take note of who still needs a nudge to gain mastery. Besides instruction in reading, teachers show students what it means to be *a reader.* The skills and strategies, along with the attitudes students develop under teacher guidance will last them a lifetime!

Reflection and Discussion Questions

1. Author Kate DiCamillo said, "Reading should not be presented to children as a chore or duty. It should be offered to them as a precious gift." How does your classroom offer reading as a gift?

2. After you have removed the child's name, share the oral reading record of a student you are concerned about with your colleagues. What do they think is the student's strength? What area needs more instruction?

3. Share ideas with post-book responses your students have done. Compile a list across the grade level of ideas to deepen student responses. What are your favorites?

4. How can you help someone who has students who are reluctant readers? Share stories about ways you entice readers to give a specific book a try or created a response after reading.

5. Consider creating a cross-classroom guided reading and/or literature circle with your above-level students. How can you provide students more autonomy of choice and responsibilities while still holding them accountable for grade-level standards?

6. How can you devise content-area literature circles? What units do you teach that would lead students to this? Can one teacher lead all students in reading informational texts and another lead literature? How can you switch this around during the day for students to get literacy and content instruction?

7. Share your most successful guided reading lessons. How did you help students improve specific skills?

8. Share your best management tricks with your colleagues. How do you keep all students engaged when you are working with a small group?

9. What are some graphic organizers you can share with your colleagues? Organize these by how they help focus students before, during, and after reading.

10. Discuss ways you focus on vocabulary building during guided reading or literature circles. Together, discuss ways to build academic vocabulary for your grade level using the books you use for instruction.

Introduction

"There is no greater gift a writing teacher can give than to help another person know he or she has a story to tell."
—Lucy Calkins

This section focuses on writing instruction. As with reading, writing has several plates to keep spinning to help students see the range of texts they can compose. While spinning the plates of writing instruction, teachers must have the word knowledge plates spinning in the background. How do you spell that word? How do you select just the right word to convey your meaning? Pointing out to students that what they learn in word study can help when writing enables them to cross their word knowledge over into real world applications. Teachers cannot assume students will see that the word study plates are spinning and are actively available for them to use when composing.

Modeled and shared writing provide support for students to develop skills in writing across the genres and across the curriculum. Understanding how and why they write begins with mentoring students in the writing process. Move students into independence during Writer's Workshop. Through conferencing and mini-lessons, you can assist students in their skills (Dorn and Soffos 2001). Finding ways to publish student work is often the motivator for reluctant writers. There are many easy, cost-effective ways to bring students' work to final, sharable versions that instill pride. Finally, consider the use of journals as another independent writing form. Journals can tap into content studies and writing. Your goal in writing instruction is to provide students with the breadth and depth of topics, genres, and skills needed to be comfortable with writing. Writing well is one skill that will serve them for a lifetime.

Writing

Meet Malik

Let's return to Mrs. Barton's classroom, where you listened in as Cameron read aloud from *Rosie's Walk* (Hutchins 1977). An agitated Malik jumps up from the library corner and stomps his way to where Mrs. Barton and Cameron are sitting. He hands her a book and proclaims, "I can't believe a guy got this published! All it says is 'I like, I like, I like!' That's not even a story!" He drops the book on the table, folds his arms, and stares at Mrs. Barton.

The book, *I Like* (Foresman 1971), is a supplemental reader from an old reading series the teacher found in the school's storage closet. These pre-primer books have limited vocabulary with highly supportive illustrations. This particular book has photographs grouped by theme, such as pets, fruits, vegetables, and toys. Under each page's photographs are the words "I like." Mrs. Barton stifles a chuckle. One month earlier, this was Malik's anchor book. (Remember Isabella's insistence about "her book" that Mr. Loomis returned to the library?) During independent reading time, Malik continually picked *I Like* from the library shelf. Deeply focused and pointing to the text, Malik read the book over and over—aloud at first and then eventually silently mouthing each word.

Malik's own "aha" moment connected his experiences in Writer's Workshop with reading.

> **Writer's Workshop** is one type of writing instruction in a balanced literacy classroom. Students apply what they have learned in modeled and shared writing to write independently. Writer's Workshop incorporates teacher coaching and conferencing, while students self-direct their learning. Writer's Workshop typically includes self-selected genres and topics, time to write and meet with peers, conferencing with the teacher, small group mini-lessons, and experiencing authentic opportunities to use and develop writing skills.

Mrs. Barton's writing instruction helped him define "story." Mrs. Barton asked Malik what she should do with the book. The power of these parallel literacy experiences was evident as Malik decided *I Like* did NOT belong on the library shelf. After all, he argued, it was not a story—it did not have a beginning, middle, and end. Most importantly, he stated, it had no "descriptive words to make the reader interested in the story." Mrs. Barton agreed, as did Cameron, who had been listening with great interest! Later in the day, during shared reading, Mrs. Barton asked Malik to explain his position on the book to the whole class. Again stating this was NOT a story, Malik asked that it be moved off the library shelf if everyone else agreed. Mrs. Barton used this teachable moment to discuss what defines "story." She tied in lessons about the writing the students were currently doing and asked if they agreed with Malik. By unanimous vote, *I Like* was "retired" to the storage closet.

Writing

Setting Up the Writing Classroom

Both Mrs. Barton and Mr. Loomis demonstrate how important reading and writing are in their classrooms. Both have library corners and reading zones for students to use for independent reading. Plenty of writing toools and author materials, including those suggested in the Word Study section, are readily available to students. Now, let's consider what materials specifically help students in kindergarten through grade 8 during the writing process.

Organization and Writing Tools

While this sounds fairly obvious, having materials ready reduces time students spend hunting for what they need. If various types of paper are accessible, you might intrigue a student to pick up a blank sheet and start writing. "Introduce lined paper only when a beginning writer has mastered the alphabet and forms letters that are the same size" (RIF, 1). Large spaced lined paper is particularly useful for students who are having difficulty with left to right and top to bottom concepts (Dierking and Jones 2003).

Creating a lined master and copying it on colored paper allows you to produce colorful options that entice students to write in different genres. Label the paper by color and genre, and place it in bins or box lids to organize the options. For example, pink paper for poetry, blue paper for narrative fiction, and yellow paper for informative/explanatory. For older students, more options can be made available, such as green paper for myths or fables, golden paper for realistic fiction, and gray paper for historical fiction. At a quick glance of a student's writing folder, you can see which genres he or she is selecting.

*Have a folder or notebook of interesting pictures you and your students have found to **inspire their writing** (intpics.pdf). Add a few questions to get students' thinking started.*

Students should have their own pencils or pens. Pencils allow for erasing, which some students prefer. Erasures signify that students are proofreading their own work, an important step in the writing process. When students use pens, encourage them to simply cross off what they want to change and write above it. This approach lets you see the word, spelling, or phrase first used by the student and then replaced. Having a jar of pencils and pens available can expedite work time. Find a pencil on the floor? Instead of hunting up the owner, just add it to the jar. If you think something different might inspire a reluctant writer, add crayons—especially good if a student has fine motor control issues—fine point markers, or colorful ink pens to the jar. Offer correction tape for editing.

Staplers, scissors, glue, a three-hole punch, student-appropriate magazines, and newspapers provide additional options for inspiring writing. Students can add new pages to their work, glue pictures to their writing, cut out letters and pictures from magazines to use, and so on. The more options you provide for creativity, the more inspired your students will be!

Some type of organizational system is key in implementing a successful writing program. Folders and three-ring binders are easy ways for students to quickly find their ongoing Writer's Workshop pieces or other assigned writing. You can also easily pull an individual folder or notebook to do an assessment of how a student is working.

Writing

The organization of current writing projects is helpful for "on the run" assessments. In many classrooms the organization includes a crate with hanging folders, where each folder is labeled with a student's name, or it might include a space on a shelf for the binders with students' names clearly written on the spines. Students can also place their folders or notebooks in one of four bins marked *Working on an New Idea*, *Ongoing Writing*, *Ready for a Conference*, and *Ready to Publish*. At the end of a day's Writer's Workshop, students can choose the status of their work. This organization is particularly helpful in middle school classrooms where more than one group of students may be in and out of the room. Students *ready for a conference* can be pulled together the next day to conference with you.

Conferencing allows teachers to look individually at student writing. A typical conference, depending on grade level, includes sitting beside the student so you can view the writing and letting the student speak first. You can prompt him or her by asking what the piece is about, where he or she is in the writing process, and if/how you can help. If the student needs help with revisions, talk about how they might change their writing or what they might change rather than telling them what to change. The more often you can turn the responsibility to the student, the sooner he or she will automatically consider this aspect of writing.

You can check in with students ready to start new writing projects to be sure they have strong ideas. If not, direct them to any of the idea generating locations in the classroom. Another way to keep easy track of where each student is in the writing process is with a daily status report. One visible way to create this is by using a pocket or wall chart. Going down the side of the chart, place labels in the left row: *Starting a New Project*, *Researching*, *Drafting/Writing*, *Revising*, *Needing a Conference*, and *Publishing*. Students have note cards with their names and simply place their cards in the proper rows. A quick glance lets you see where each student is in the writing process. For older students, use the *Status of the Class* form (page 320). Place this on a clipboard so students can easily mark where they are in the writing process. This allows both you and other students to see who is at the same place in the writing process, so students who want someone to peer review their work can find other students also ready to revise and edit.

Publishing Center

A place where students can polish a final piece of writing is often enough to inspire even the most reluctant writer. It may also be, according to Elbow (2002), one of the best ways to encourage students to revise and edit. "When we invite students to *make* something with writing instead of just asking them to write, they go about their work differently…[they] think of themselves as writers [and] achievement soars" (Ray 2004, 14). Stop at an appliance store for a large washer or oven-size box that can be decorated as The Publishing House for your younger students. Put a small table inside stocked with product supplies. For older students, a corner loaded with materials lets them choose how to finalize their writing, or team up with the art teacher for a book cover/illustration project. Whatever supplies you make available will help students remember that their writing has an audience. Indeed, "the basic concept of publication is that children learn to write for an audience" (Hughey and Slack 2001, 153). Card stock for covers, three-hole punchers with yarn to bind pages, and decorative materials such as markers, paints, crayons, glue, and tissue paper enable students to share their writing with others. Place the finished, decorated copies of student work in your school or classroom library. This proudly proclaims, "We are all authors!"

Resources

The Word Study section (pages 22–81) provides ideas for useful resources that cross from word study into writing. Older students can independently solve their own inquiries about words with an organized shelf of dictionaries and thesauri, while younger students need easy-to-access word walls. Students may want to keep individual lists of words they know they often struggle with but that they want to include in their writing, such as *friend*, *because*, and *there/their/they're*. These can be in their individual hanging folders or on a list compiled by the class and kept at the resource center.

*Check a local store that has **wallpaper books**. When new ones come in for display, the stores are often willing to donate the old sample books to teachers. The pages in these books make great covers because they are durable.*

Topic generation is often where students get stuck in the writing process. Create a place, such as a notebook or bulletin board, called *Bright Ideas* to offer topic suggestions. Any student can post intriguing questions, topic ideas, or share pictures that inspire writing. Add your own pages to keep the ideas fresh and provide new topics. These can connect to content studies or current events. Think of ways to pose questions that will intrigue students to do research before they write, such as the following:

- John Tyler was our 10th president, beginning in 1841. He has two grandchildren who are still alive today. How can that be? Research Tyler's life and tell us the story.

- When lava solidifies, it can form a light, porous rock called pumice. Pumice is a rock that can float. Can you explain the process? What can be made from pumice?

- Do you have a T-shirt with a picture of a favorite athlete, leader, or entertainer? Tell us something amazing that happened once when you wore that shirt.

- If unicorns existed and you owned one, what sort of pet would it be?

Remind students of the genre options they have for independent writing. Create a space on a wall, poster, bulletin board, or flip chart that defines the choices. The Common Core State Standards (NGA and CCSSO 2010) define four types of writing: opinion/argument, informative/explanatory, narrative nonfiction, and narrative fiction.

The purpose of *explanatory writing* is to teach, inform, reveal, or expand information about topics. Some common reasons to write explanatory include the following:

- analyze other pieces of writing
- give directions
- describe/explain the procedures for something
- give information about topics
- write reports on topics
- explain processes or opinions
- describe/explain how to do something
- provide detailed explanations

In explanatory writing, students should define or explain uncommon terms. They can't assume readers are experts. This writing must provide enough background information so that readers can understand the rest of the written piece. This is especially true in essays or research projects. If writing directions, writers should provide diagrams, pictures, maps, or charts, as needed.

The general characteristics of *narrative writing* include the following:

- plot structure
- conflict
- characterization
- setting
- theme
- point of view
- sequencing
- transitions
- tone

Plot structure includes:

- *introduction*
- *rising action*
- *climax*
- *falling action*
- *resolution*

In narrative writing, students should let characters talk. Dialogue makes the story active. A writer needs to remember to pick a point of view and let the reader see the story through a character's eyes.

Teachers can round out their students' experiences by adding poetry, since students are expected to read and respond to it. Poems share stories, ideas, feelings, or observations. There are many forms that rely, in differing ways, on the use of the sounds of words, rhythm, and rhyme.

- **Sounds of words** include similes (*silly as a goose*) and metaphors (*She is a walking encyclopedia.*), alliteration (*Betty Botter bought the butter.*), onomatopoeia (*whizz, snap, slurp*), and repetition.
- **Rhythm** includes syllable or word counts. For example, a Haiku is three unrhymed lines of five–seven–five syllables, a Cinquain is five unrhymed lines totaling 20 syllables, and a Diamante is seven unrhymed lines that create a diamond shape.
- **Rhyme** includes couplets, quatrains (*abab or abba pattern*), and limericks (five lines).

Free form poems do not adhere to rhythm or rhyme. However, some other poems do have specific rules when creating them. Acrostics use each letter of a word to begin the lines. And, concrete or shape poems are written to look like the topics that are written about, such as a poem about a flag written in the shape of a flag.

Since reading, writing, and speaking are "grounded in evidence from texts, both literary and informational" (NGA and CCSSO 2010, 1), having students create some of their own texts to meet the literature standards gives writing a double purpose and helps solidify understandings about genre.

Modeled and Shared Writing

Just as teachers need to instruct students in the skills of reading, they must also show students how and why people write. There are many forms of writing and many reasons to write. It is the teacher's responsibility to *teach* writing and not just *assign* it. Therefore, in a balanced literacy classroom, teachers utilize approaches to provide multiple, effective experiences in writing. There are two great ways to engage students in learning about writing through modeling and sharing the process.

When using *modeled writing*, teachers mentor novice writers in the process. "Students must attend to a model, code the information for retention, be capable of producing the demonstrated pattern, and be motivated to perform it. An important form of observational learning occurs through cognitive modeling, which incorporates modeled explanations and demonstrations with verbalizations of the model's thoughts and reasons for performing the actions" (Schunk 2003, 162). The teacher is the *active* writer, and students watch, listen, and learn through example. The teacher thinks out loud and lets students *see* and *hear* how writers approach tasks.

When using *shared writing*, students join in the process and help teachers craft the pieces. They share the decision making during all stages of the process. "The teacher typically records and scaffolds ideas while the children dictate" (Piazza 2003, 10). Shared writing "is suitable for learners of all ages, especially those who need to apprentice with an adult before writing on their own" (Piazza 2003, 11). These experiences then carry over into their independent writing that occurs all day long when teachers give decision-making responsibility to the students, such as during Writer's Workshop, journal writing, and content writing, both for note taking and research projects. With the skills developed in modeled and shared writing, students spread their wings of writing across the curriculum.

Introduction to Modeled Writing

Like the read-aloud, modeled writing allows teachers to provide real-time examples to students. Writing in front of your students demonstrates how to take an idea and put it into print. "Modeling accompanied by think-aloud helps [students] see that the teacher, too, struggles with word choice, syntax, and the like. The words don't just appear— shazam!—on the page. And rough drafts are rough!" (Read 2010, 51).

Explaining that writing allows people to keep memories, learn more about topics, have fun with story ideas, or express feelings are just some ways to show students the value of writing. This approach enables students to hear you think out loud about your writing— what is working, what needs to be revised, and how you want to find other words to express an idea. Students should know what a writer looks and sounds like after watching you write in front of them.

Best Practices in Kindergarten through Grade 2

During modeled writing lessons in kindergarten through grade 2, build your students' basic concepts about the writing process. This is best modeled on large paper with lines similar to what students use so they can easily see what they will do independently.

Graves (1983) reminds us to "make explicit what children ordinarily can't see: how words go down on paper" (45). Any large display of paper can be used so that students can follow as you write. Modeled lessons at this level should include how the writing process begins right through to creating finished products. You might spend several days modeling so students see how the process works. For example, you might address prewriting one day, drafting the next, revising and editing on a third day, and publishing on a fourth. Then, you can begin the process again, creating a different piece of writing. This continuous cycle of having students watch the writing process from drafting to publishing allows teachers to demonstrate a variety of genres.

Modeled writing lessons at this level cover the following skills:

Prewriting

- Get ideas or topics for writing. You might suggest something that happens over the weekend, your pet's antics, an upcoming school event, your interest in knitting, or a story about bees you want to recount. Show students how to keep a list of these ideas that refer to starting a new writing project.

- Make a list of words you want to use in the writing about the topic you choose.

Drafting

- Talk out loud about how you can start your writing. Specifically point out:
  - where you start writing
  - how you move from left to right and top to bottom
  - the importance of finger spaces between words
  - sounding out words before writing them
  - asking if a word you write "looks right"
  - using punctuation

- Reread your sentences aloud to check that the ideas are written correctly and you have all the words you need.

Revising

- Reread your entire story aloud.

- Comment where you think you need to change a sentence to tell more or have it make more sense. You might need to add something to help readers follow along better.
  - If it is a narrative, does it have a beginning, a middle, and an end?
  - If it is informational, does it begin with a main idea supported by details? Does it draw the information together at the end?

Editing

- Circle any words you need to check for spelling.
- Show students what resources can help, such as the word wall.
- Show how to cross off a word and correct the spelling.
- Double-check that all punctuation is correct.

Publishing

- Talk to students about how to rewrite or use a computer to create a final copy.
- Break up the story and leave space at the top of the page for an illustration, if appropriate.
- Talk about how the piece will be added to the classroom library as another text others can read during independent reading time.

What a Modeled Lesson Sounds Like

1. "Boys and girls, yesterday when I was going home from school, I noticed how the leaves on the trees are changing colors. They were really pretty. I know some people live in areas where there aren't a lot of trees that change color. I bet those prople would love to hear about what I saw. I need to begin a new writing project, so I think I'll write about the leaves. I want to remember all the colors I saw."

    Have a book or website about changing leaf color so you can reference before writing. For example, you might show *I Wonder Why Trees Have Leaves: and other questions about plants* (Charman 2003).

2. "What I need to do is start by brainstorming a list of some of the words I might use in the story, such as *yesterday*, *leaves*, *color*, *autumn*, *orange*, *yellow*, *red*, and *brown*." (Write the list on the board or somewhere students can see it.) "Now, I need to know a little bit about why leaves change colors, so I can add that to my story. Let me check a reference. At this website (or in this book), it says leaves are green because they have chlorophyll. In the fall, we have less daylight, the temperature is cooler, and the chlorophyll breaks down, so we see the other colors."

3. Add other words to the list, such as *colder*, *daylight*, and *chlorophyll*. "Let me take these words and organize them. That will help me as I write. Here is a concept map where I can put together some of my brainstormed words. I think I will organize them by three areas: appearance (how the tree looks), time and weather, and scientific information."

4. "Okay, I am ready to start drafting my story. *When I drove home, I saw tree of many colors. I saw red, yellow, and orange tree. They were very pretty.*" Write on large paper, a whiteboard, or other space that is large enough for students to easily follow along. Be sure to sound out the words, as you would want students to do. Refer to the list of words you made. Talk out loud about putting a period at the ends of sentences and capital letters for the first words.

5. "Let's see, what else should I write? I should probably tell my readers why the leaves change color. That would add detail and make it informative. *Leaves change colors because we have less daylight and colder temperatures. The leaves stop making chlorophyll are no longer green.* I would like to end this story in an interesting way. I was thinking about how much I like this time of year, so I'll write *I love this time of year, don't you.*"

Writing

6. "I like how that ends. It invites the reader into my story. Let's reread the whole piece to see if I need to change or fix anything. Boys and girls, I noticed I didn't tell the reader that it was yesterday that this happened, so I will add it to the first sentence *Yesterday, when I drove home.* Also, I see that I have the word *brown* on my list but did not use it. But I think I have told a lot about the colors already. I also notice that *The leaves stop making chlorophyll are no longer green* does not make sense. I need to add some words after *chlorophyll.* How about *making chlorophyll so they are no longer green*? Ok, now let's go back and be sure we have spelled everything correctly. Oh! I see I left the *s* off of trees. I'm going to add it. I also must check my punctuation. I think there should be a comma after *Yesterday,* and I asked a question in the last sentence, so there needs to be a question mark."

7. "I now want to make a final copy that I can share with others. I think I'll rewrite it, so it is three pages that I can illustrate. Page 1 will be, *Yesterday, when I drove home I saw trees of many colors. I saw read, yellow, and orange trees.* Page 2 will be, *Leaves change colors because we have less daylight and colder temperatures. The leaves stop making chlorophyll, so they are no longer green.* Page 3 will be, *They were very pretty to see. I love this time of year, don't you?* On page 1, I will draw me in my car driving by some trees. On page 2, I will draw a close-up of a leaf that is part green and part orange. On page 3, I will draw more trees, being sure to use all the colors I talked about in my writing. Maybe I will be standing by a pile of leaves, getting ready to jump into it to show another way I love leaves!"

Best Practices in Grade 3 through Grade 5

During modeled writing lessons in grade 3 through grade 5, teachers want to show the use of more complex grammar, descriptive words, more involved story lines, and content-related writing. Today's college and career readiness standards remind us that, "Each year in their writing, students should demonstrate increasing sophistication in all aspects of language use, from vocabulary and syntax to the development and organization of ideas, and they should address increasingly demanding content and sources" (NGA and CCSSO 2010, 1). Provide examples of your writing that are narrative, informational, and poetry. Students need to know what writers think about as they compose and revise their writing, so be sure to think out loud during the writing process to model how writers build on skills learned in previous years. You also want students to think more at this level about their audience. Twenty-first century standards suggest students, "adapt their communication in relation to audience, task, purpose, and discipline" (NGA and CCSSO 2010, 1), so demonstrating through modeled writing how writers approach these important aspects of writing is critical.

In modeled writing, you want students to understand that an idea can germinate from almost anywhere. You saw something interesting on television, you read a book that really interested you and want to write about that topic, or you sat outdoors under a tree and started thinking about nature. You can also talk about the use of "rehearsal" or talking with a peer about a story before beginning to write. Campbell and Hlusek's (2009) study found that storytelling and rehearsing a story before the writing process begins "enlivened the process of writing for a group of [fourth grade] students, most of whom were reluctant writers" (2). Finding ways to make students feel successful can engage otherwise resistant writers.

When writing, model aloud to remind students of the skills provided in kindergarten through grade 2 as appropriate. The stages of the writing process and what they entail are below:

Prewriting

- Get ideas or topics for writing. You might suggest something that happens over the weekend, animal antics, school events, hobbies, or funny stories you want to recount. Show students how to keep a list of these ideas that refer to starting a new writing project.
- Make a list of words to use for writing about the topic you select.

Drafting

- Write for a purpose.
- Use research notes to guide the development of writing.
- Write complete sentences.
- Use capital letters correctly.
- Use descriptive words and key details to elaborate ideas.
- Use more complex punctuation, such as commas in compound sentences and parentheses.
- Sequence ideas.
- Sound out more complex words by chunking syllables, affixes, and bases.

Revising

- Think about the audience. Who will read this? What is the purpose for writing?
- Revise for content.

Editing

- Use classroom resources to help make grammar, usage, and mechanics corrections.

Publishing

- Select a piece for a more formal finish, such as posting to a class site or typing and printing. Not all pieces need to be published in a formal way.

What a Modeled Lesson Sounds Like

1. "Boys and girls, I have my list of brainstormed ideas for possible writing projects. Today, I need to start a new piece of writing. I was going to use my list, but last night I heard a very funny noise coming from outside my front door. I thought oh, that is probably my cat, Milo, wanting in the house. I opened the door, and there was Milo by the front step making that funny noise. And guess what? A big red fox was standing right next to him! That made me think about writing what happened into a story, so I could tell my family who were all gone for the evening."

2. "By telling you about this, I have some idea of what I need to include in my story. Since this is going to be a narrative story, I need a beginning, a middle, and an end. To plan my story, I will jot down the events in the sequence they happened before I start drafting."

3. On chart paper, the whiteboard, or some other large viewing area, write:
   Watching *Wheel of Fortune*, lady won $5,000
   Noise at the front door
   Milo and the fox
   Yelled at Milo to get into the house!

4. "Okay, let's start the story, using my notes to help me. *Last night I was watching* Wheel of Fortune. *A woman won $5,000. Then, I heard a noise. I thought maybe milo, my cat, wanted inside. I opened the front door and there was Milo and a big red fox! The fox was licking its lips. I thought, 'Oh, oh, milo better get in the house!' So, I yelled, 'Milo!' and he ran write in the front door. I slamed the door, so the fox would not follow him."*

5. "Let's go back and reread the story to see if I included everything I wanted and what I might need to revise and edit." Read the story aloud.

6. "Now that I have read it, watching the game show and telling how much money the woman won is not really important to the story, so I'm going to cross off *I was watching* Wheel of Fortune. *A woman won $5,000.*"

7. "Now, the story starts, *Then, I heard a noise.* That doesn't make much sense. I need to tell the reader when it happened, so I'll cross off the word *Then* and make this new sentence: *Last night I heard a noise.*"

8. "I should tell what kind of noise I heard, so let's add a descriptive word. *Strange* is a good choice. I need to say where the noise was. Let's add *outside.* The sentence now reads *Last night I heard a strange noise outside.*"

9. "I also remember that the red fox was staring at Milo. That is how I knew my cat was in trouble. I think I will revise the sentence about the fox to read: *The fox was staring at Milo and licking his lips.*" Reread the whole story again.

10. "You know, I think it needs one more sentence to bring the story to an end. Let's see, I can say *I was scared* or *I'm glad Milo was safe.* I think I will add *I'm glad Milo was safe* to end the story. Now, let's go back and edit any errors I see. First, I see I did not capitalize Milo." Put three small horizontal lines under the lowercase *m* to denote it needs to be a capital *M*.

11. "I have a compound sentence here that is missing its comma. I will add it before *and.* (*I opened the front door, and there was Milo and a big red fox!*) I also notice I put *write.* While that sounds right, it is not the correct spelling of the meaning I used, so I need to fix that." Cross off *write*, and write *right* above it.

12. "I also see that *slammed* only has one *m*, so I need to insert another *m*. You know, I think the last sentence is an exciting end to the story and needs an exclamation mark."

13. "Finally, I do want to do something to finish this piece so others can read it. I think I will put a picture of a red fox and a picture of Milo at the top of a page. I will add the title *Milo and the Red Fox.* Hmmm, maybe I need something more exciting. How about *Milo's Escape from the Red Fox?* Then, I will type my story and paste it under the pictures and title."

Best Practices in Grade 6 through Grade 8

During modeled writing lessons in grade 6 through grade 8, teachers want to show the use of more complex grammar, descriptive words, complex story lines, content-area writing, and the use of various genres. "Beginning in grade 6, the literacy standards allow teachers of ELA, history/social studies, science, and technical subjects to use their content-area expertise to help students meet the particular challenges of reading, writing, speaking, listening, and language in their respective fields" (NGA and CCSSO 2010, 1). Connecting to content-area teachers for ideas of units of study can be meshed with the modeling you do. At this level, multiple page stories, outlines for the development of an expository piece, and more sophisticated vocabulary are expected.

Provide examples of your narrative and informational writing. Be sure to think aloud during the writing. Students need to know how writers think as they compose and revise their writing. Studying what authors do helps students develop awareness of their own writing strategies and provides a mentor approach to understanding genre, general composition, word choice, and more. "Having students recognize good writers' techniques positions them to infuse them into their own compositions" (Gallagher 2014, 29). Raising students' metacognitive awareness, or having them thinking about their thinking, helps them consciously monitor their ongoing writing. Teaching students how to think can positively transfer to their writing performance (Yu 2013). Therefore, explicitly modeling lessons helps students connect the author's craft to what they will do in their own writing. You want students to think about the audience of their completed writings. Particularly with older students, understanding "the concept of the unknown reader—the distant reader for whom the writer must hypothesize interest and knowledge" (Hughey and Slack 2001, 170) is an important aspect of their writing. When writing, model out loud to reinforce the same skills taught about the stages of the writing process (prewriting, drafting, revising, editing, and publishing) in earlier grades. Additionally, at this level students should do the following:

- Decide on a genre.
- Refer to research notes specific to content areas.
- Include appropriate vocabulary for the context.
- Think about tone and personal voice.
- Use proofreading skills.
- Analyze for organization and how the audience will perceive the writing.

What a Modeled Lesson Sounds Like

1. "The other day I was reading up on Australia when I learned you were studying different nations in social studies. I first thought about what big topics would be interesting to pick and I thought *Australia* is, indeed, a big topic. Then, I thought about *Australia*—what are some big topics I can research about that country?"

2. "I know land is an important topic, as well as animals. With two main topics, I started my research about the importance of two Australian topics."

Writing

3. "As I started to study Australia in the online encyclopedia and other articles I found some things that came up over and over in the areas of land and animals, so I started compiling a list."

4. Have this list of words projected so students can see them, such as on chart paper, a whiteboard, or on note cards posted on a board.

Continent, size of United States	*Kookaburra*
Kangaroos	*Snakes and spiders*
Koalas	*Crocodiles*
Sydney and the Blue Mountains	*Ocean and coral reefs*
Canberra	*Sharks*
Alice Springs and the desert	*Equator*
Boomerang	

5. "I see that I have lots of different ideas here. I can group some of these ideas into the bigger idea of land, so I'm going to circle all of those. My second category is animals. I'm going to draw a box around all of those words. I can have several different paragraphs where the grouped ideas can be put together. I have to decide which to write about first."

6. "Writing about the land first makes more sense as a writer and a reader." Use a computer on a screen or write on large chart paper so you can cut it apart to revise, edit, and move sentences easily. *Australia is both a country and a continent, equivalent in size to the United States of America. The Indian and Pacific Oceans surround it. It is known for its Great Barrier Reef. It has a large desert called the Outback. Australia also has some of the longest stretches of sand-covered coastline in the world.*

    Besides great land features, Australia is brimming with interesting animals. Kangaroos, crocodiles, kookaburras, koalas, sharks, snakes, spiders, and camels are among them.

7. "Okay, let's go back and read the entire text. What do I need to revise in the first paragraph? My information is general. I want to add more details. I also see that my sentences jump around, interrupting the flow of my ideas. I'll want to keep all of the sentences related to water and all of the sentences related to land together."

Add additional information and move sentences.

8. "My first paragraph now reads:

    Australia is both a country and a continent, equivalent in size to the United States of America. The Indian and Pacific Oceans surround it. It has some of the longest stretches of sand-covered coastline in the world. Australia is also known for the Great Barrier Reef—the largest living structure on the planet. Australia, however, is not all about coastal living. It has a large desert in its interior called the Outback where one finds the sculpted cliffs of Kings Canyon and ancient Aboriginal rock paintings at Kakadu National Park."

9. "Let's examine the second paragraph. It is short with two sentences. I will put land animals and ocean animals in separate sentences to make it easier to follow. My second paragraph now reads:

   Besides great land features, Australia is brimming with interesting animals. Kangaroos, kookaburras, koalas, and camels are among some of the land animals found in Australia. Sharks and crocodiles are some of its water animals."

10. "I think I should do some more research before finishing this. I can read about more animals, maybe even more about the land. Using only one book is a good start but should not be the only research I do. I think adding more will not only provide more facts, but also will make it more interesting to readers."

Introduction to Shared Writing

Shared writing is similar to modeled writing. The distinction is that in shared writing, students contribute to writing the text. Shared writing lessons can be introduced to students after modeled writing has provided experiences in observing writing expectations for their grade level. With younger students, do several modeled lessons, then try a shared writing experience with them. You want students to understand the process, so you can engage them in making decisions about content and mechanics. "Children become apprentice writers who work alongside an experienced writer—the teacher. The teacher and children share the authorship, and ownership, of co-constructed texts" (Mackenzie 2015, 36). As students develop more knowledge and independence in writing, shared writing is used alternately with modeled writing. Some days, if you are writing in a content area, you might have both types of writing. Consider what your students' literacy understandings are that will assist in the writing. As students develop more knowledge and skill at independent writing, they can assist more in shared writing. Use the *Developmental Continuum Chart* (continuum.pdf) to help you choose appropriate features of language and writing to use for these shared writing lessons.

For example, with kindergarten through grade 2, ask students join you where you are writing and write a letter, word, or punctuation mark. In doing so, you will learn about student understanding and mastery of letter sounds, spaces between words, and directionality. With older students, have them write more of the shared story, depending on their proficiencies. For example, if you are crafting a narrative and deciding what the character should say next, ask students in grade 3 through grade 5 to record the entire sentence on the chart or whiteboard. Students take turns doing the physical writing of what the group suggests. With students in grade 6 through grade 8, have them lead the entire process. Rather than the teacher guiding the students through every part of the writing, students can take turns leading the discussion for what's next and recording as they go. Across the grades, teachers initiate discussions about how to edit, what might be moved, revised, added, or changed. Discuss how readers will enjoy the story— thus showing how writers need to think about the audience. As students mature, their awareness expands outward to ever-expanding concentric circles of possible audiences (Fresch 2005).

Best Practices in Kindergarten through Grade 2

Engaging students in the process allows them to try on the author's "pen." Invite students to help you throughout the writing process. "The text is composed by the group, and the teacher guides the children as they write the text word-by-word on chart paper" (Tompkins 2008, 24). Use what you know about individual students to invite them into the process, so they can be successful. Even a student still learning the alphabet can put the capital letter at the beginning of a sentence or a period at the end.

What a Shared Writing Lesson Sounds Like

1. "Let's work together to write a story. Does anyone have any ideas for a story? What is something interesting that happened to you or something you heard or read about? Let's make a list of these topics on the board. Now, let's decide what story we want to write. (*Insert student name*), thanks for the idea of a story about picking apples. How should we start it?"

2. Begin to craft the story. While this is going to be based on what the students say, the following section gives you an idea of how it might sound.

3. "Great idea (*insert student name*)! (*Student name's*) family picked apples on Saturday. (*Insert student name*), why don't you write your name since it begins the sentence? Don't forget we need a capital letter, not only because it starts a sentence, but also because it is a name. (*Insert student name*), would you like to write the rest of the sentence? Who can help him/her spell *family*? Let's sound it out together. Oops, you have *e* at the end instead of *y*. Let's use this correction tape to fix that!"

4. Continue building the story, providing prompts as needed, such as what happened next? Should we think of something else to write about it? "Great idea (*insert student's name*) to put all of (*insert student's name*) family's names in the story. That will make it interesting and we can name our characters." As students work, be sure to sound out the words as you would want them to. Talk out loud about putting a period at the end of sentences and capital letters on the first word, and ask them to assist in putting in the punctuation. Talk about what you want readers to know.

5. "Let's find a way to bring this story to an end. Any suggestions? (*Insert student name*) suggested saying something about making applesauce. How should we write that? (*Insert student name*), do you want to write some of the sentence? Who can stand next to him and be his buddy to help as he writes?"

6. "Let's go back and reread the story aloud. Is there anything else we should add or anything we need to fix? Let's double-check our spelling and the punctuation." Have students participate in revising and editing.

7. "I will leave this story up for you to reread during independent reading time."

Best Practices in Grade 3 through Grade 5

Grade 3 through grade 5 students can collaborate to write a text together. If students have developed adequate keyboarding skills, they can take turns typing on a computer with a projected screen. This can be done in whole group or in small groups to allow the teacher to vary the amount of support needed to create the written piece. At this level, you want students to understand that you use writing to communicate for a variety of purposes. That is, one piece of writing may inform readers, so you need to be sure to include key details. Another piece of writing may be a narrative with the idea of entertaining your readers. You may write to persuade as well, so presenting a good argument is key. Teachers can scaffold the strategies students bring from the younger grades to develop their writing skills.

What a Shared Writing Lesson Sounds Like

1. "Boys and girls, get your writing idea lists. Who has an idea for a good piece that we can write together?"

2. Make a list on chart paper or a board for students to view.

3. "Let's brainstorm some other ideas. Where is a place you hope to visit one day? Who is your favorite person to spend time with? Why? Who made you laugh so hard it hurt? How did he or she do it? What topic fascinates you? Why? What other questions can we ask to get us started on a story?"

4. Add these ideas to the list. **Note:** For the purposes of this example, we will write about water on Mars.

5. "Thanks (*insert student name*). I did hear something on the news about finding water on Mars. But, who found it? Right, (*insert student name*), it was NASA scientists. Yes, that makes an interesting story if we think about going to Mars, (*insert student name*)! Let's start by reading about the discovery to give us more information and background for our story."

6. As you read the information aloud, charge students with taking notes and listing important words. Take suggestions for the opening sentence. Invite a student to come up and write that sentence. Continue working with students to suggest sentences, inviting them to write each sentence and reminding them to add punctuation. Tell them to refer to the notes, being sure to add more details about what you read. You may choose not to finish the story and, instead, have student pairs write an ending.

7. "Let's stop here where the rover is over the planet and spots the water. Let's go back and reread the story aloud. What might happen next?"

8. Take suggestions and either finish the story or have student pairs finish writing the story.

Writing

Best Practices in Grade 6 through Grade 8

In grade 6 through grade 8, students are honing their writing skills. College and career readiness standards point out that at this level, students must "gain adequate mastery of a range of skills and applications" and "should demonstrate increasing sophistication in all aspects of language use, from vocabulary and syntax to the development and organization of ideas, and they should address increasingly demanding content and sources" (NGA and CCSSO 2010, 1). Shared writing has been found to be successful beyond the primary grades to provide students "a chance to apply and experiment with new and more advanced writing concepts with the help and support of their peers (Wall 2008, 152). Mariage found this approach gave students "access and practice [to] the many writing skills and strategies that above-level writers routinely utilize" (2001, 184). Students who were still struggling with writing skills began to internalize many of the needed strategies because they were revisited so often during shared writing. Considering how lesson blocks in those grades are often arranged, shared writing at this level will be short lessons that emphasize particular aspects of writing teachers deem important for their particular groups of students. For example, if the teacher notices his or her sixth-grade students need work on using more relevant facts, details, and quotations to strengthen their argument writing pieces, then the shared writing will focus on that set of skills. "This will allow for the systematic instruction of writing development, organization, and style" (Fisher and Frey 2013, 98).

What a Shared Writing Lesson Sounds Like

1. "The other day I read the research reports you did in science. (*Insert science teacher's name*) and I were discussing how the reports compared and contrasted information but needed more details. I thought today we would compose a short written piece that compares and contrasts something in our lives so we can see what is important to include in order to help readers follow our thinking."

2. "Let's begin by brainstorming some ideas about something familiar we can compare and contrast. For example, what is your main source of music: the radio or your phone or tablet? Or maybe, what is your source of money: earning it or getting it from your parents? Or, how do you decide what to wear: based on trends or what you personally like? Any other ideas?"

3. Take ideas from students. **Note:** For the purposes of this example, we will compare and contrast music from a radio versus music downloaded to a personal device.

4. "Okay, we have a good topic to compare and contrast. Let's think about the differences and similarities between these two ways to listen to music. Let's think about the advantages and disadvantages of listening to a streaming radio station."

5. Project the list on a screen or write on large chart paper so students can see the list. "Okay, let's do the same with listening to songs that you have individually chosen and downloaded. What are the advantages? What are the disadvantages? Now, let's circle the items on the two lists that we want to compare as similar and box the items we want to contrast as different."

6. Once you are done, guide students to begin writing. "What should our opening sentence be? Remember, this is a big idea that will be followed by details."

7. Take ideas for the opener, having students write the sentence. Perhaps something such as, *Two ways to listen to music are through a streaming service and through individial downloads.*

8. Continue with the piece, asking for help in crafting the details from the list. Be sure to include the students in making decisions about sentence structure, word choice, and punctuation. The more involved you have students in the writing process, the more likely they are to carry these ideas over to their independent writing.

9. You might encourage students to do some research on the cost of downloading music versus streaming, or which services have contracts with the most artists.

10. "Now, let's go back and read the text aloud. How did we do with including details? Are there any sentences needing revision or additional information?" Depending on time, you can stop here and use the next day's lesson to edit.

Writer's Workshop

Writer's Workshop is an organized approach to independent writing. The environment supports and stimulates writing. Students self-select topics and genres for ongoing writing projects. Ideally, students write every day. Students know what is expected of them as they work independently. There is often a whole-group meeting before the workshop begins so that students can share where they are in their writing projects. The teacher identifies who needs a writing conference. The whole-group sharing is followed by a mini-lesson where the teacher explicitly explains aspects of the writing process students are still working to solidify.

The importance of a thoughtful writing program cannot be overstated. Instruction in writing is important, regardless of a student's grade level. Writer's Workshop specifically focuses on students using their developing skills for independent writing. We need students who are college and career ready, thus preparing them for a lifetime of writing (NGA and CCSSO 2010). "While the workshop is rooted in the *writing* process—prewriting, writing, revising, editing, and publishing—it includes much more. It sets the stage for writing as an ongoing *lifetime skill* with *multiple audiences and multiple purposes*" (Hughey and Slack 2001, 4). Students are never too young to begin thinking about how to express ideas on paper and never too old to hone their writing skills. At the same time, teachers want students to be excited about the writing process. One way to do that is to provide self-selection of topics. Self-selection adds joyfulness to the process, thus keeping students engaged in it. Writer's Workshop provides both structure (predictable work expectations) and freedom (through self-selection) for all students.

Introduction to Writer's Workshop

One important element of Writer's Workshop is the ability to meet the needs of individual students. Sturm (2012) found that the structure of Writer's Workshop was particularly useful for students with disabilities. The supportive atmosphere of seeing peers writing encouraged students who otherwise struggled to participate. Additionally, the Writer's Workshop structure helps English language learners develop proficiencies in writing (Kim 2015). Students should be explicitly taught workshop behaviors like self-selection of work and self-direction. Develop the rules for Writer's Workshop with students. Encouraging them to give their input empowers them as important decision makers and will help them remember the rules. Typical rules include the following: having a space on their paper where they can notify you of the need for a conference; using resources to solve their own problems, such as spelling while writing; and requesting peer assistance before looking for the teacher. Providing these guidelines about such procedures creates an efficient writing environment that maximizes time spent on writing.

Establishing these procedures at the beginning of the school year and then reviewing them regularly lets students understand the expectations for self-directed writing. The format for Writer's Workshop, depending on the age of the students, follows:

- Whole group mini-lesson (5–10 minutes of explicit instruction)
- Independent writing (15–30 minutes of self-directed writing)
- Conferencing (ongoing during independent writing)

- Small-group mini-lessons, as needed, during independent writing to address specific needs of small groups of students
- Whole-group sharing (5–10 minute status report of how writing is going or sharing of published pieces)

All stages of writing—prewriting, drafting, revising, editing, publishing, and sharing—are addressed in the suggested mini-lessons starting on page 193. A *Lesson Plan for Writer's Workshop Mini-Lesson* (page 336) is provided for support. Your lesson plans should reflect grade-level appropriate instruction in all stages of writing. The *Developmental Continuum Chart* (continuum.pdf) will help you select grade-appropriate instruction.

How to Organize for Writer's Workshop

Several decisions need to be made regarding Writer's Workshop in your classroom. While these decisions are rooted in the grade level you teach, generally all the following questions must be considered:

- **Where will students write?** You might choose to have students work at their own desks, computer stations, or at tables of their choosing. Laptops and tablets allow for flexible seating. Many teachers provide clipboards for students who are writing with pencil and paper, freeing them to choose where they would like to sit and write for the day. Remember, however, that you want to be able to easily move around for conferencing.

- **Where will students conference with you?** You may want to go to students based on a pocket chart status report—seeing which students are ready to conference. Or, you may reserve a table to sit at and ask students to come to you. You can use this space for any conversations, such as mini-lessons for students needing specific writing instruction.

- **Who will help the student with revisions?** Depending on the skill of the students, students can collaborate with each other to help in revisions. Students who have marked their pocket chart status or *Status of the Class* form (page 320) as *revising* can find each other. Students exchange written pieces. As they read, they can ask each other questions, note needed revisions, and check spelling and grammar. For older students, you may want to add a category on the status report pocket chart for *peer revision needed*.

- **How will you decide on which mini-lessons to teach?** Standards you must teach may direct your choice of mini-lessons. Of course, standards give the benchmark but not the instructional plan. So, you must consider the grade-level standard and a way to engage students in a short lesson to meet that standard. Keep in mind that students who are behind in writing skills may need additional mini-lessons to fill in learning gaps. The operative word here is *mini*. The lesson should be focused and brief. You can always pull together a small group of students needing further mini-lessons, either below or above standard, as you assess their writing. The grade-level discussions that follow provide additional guidance for these mini-lessons.

Writing

Best Practices in Kindergarten through Grade 2

This section includes basic Writer's Workshop strategy lessons for simpel practice of the following skills for kindergarten through grade 2. Details regarding each strategy can be found on the subsequent pages. For additional lessons, download the Digital Resources. (See page 20 for the website address and access code.)

At this level, encourage students to put ideas into print. Often students at this level draw first and then write as they experiment with creating print. As their skills progress, encourage students to lengthen their writing. Connect their attempts to the modeled and shared writing they have participated in under your mentorship, showing how to write in a variety of genres. Whole-group mini-lessons to support students' writing development should take about 5–10 minutes.

Mini-Lessons

Lesson
Add a Word (page 193)
A Personal Booklet (page 194)
Collect Ideas (page 195)
Concept of a Word (page 196)
Find It (page 197)
Grammar Basics (page 198)
How to Revise and Edit (page 199)
Matching Sound to Print (page 200)
Punctuation Matters (page 201)
Recalling Sight Words (page 202)
Sharing Ideas (page 203)
Use of Lines (page 204)

Digital Resources Lessons

Lesson
Considering Audience (considering.pdf)
Correct Formation of Letters (correctform.pdf)
Differences Between Genres (four-day lesson) (diffgenres.pdf)
Drawing versus Writing (drawwrite.pdf)
Helping a Buddy Edit (helpbuddy.pdf)
Publishing (publishing.pdf)

Some websites that serve to enhance instruction and provide additional opportunities for students to explore these various topics are:

- www.kidztype.com
- www.abcya.com
- www.storybird.com
- www.education.com

Some apps that serve to enhance instruction and provide additional opportunities for students to explore these various topics are:

- Toontastic (Launchpad Toys)
- Letter Cross Tracking (Visual Learning for Life)
- Bamboo Paper Notebook (Wacom)

Writing

Add a Word

Objective

Students will add details to writing.

Preparation

1. Create a short story to which students can add details. For example, *I have a dog. He sleeps in my room. I like my dog.*

2. Make a large enough copy of the story so that all students can see it.

Procedure

1. Show the story to students.

2. Read it aloud.

3. Ask students if there are words they can add to their stories to make them more descriptive.

4. As you reread the story, ask students to think of how to make the story more interesting. Take suggestions and add them to the story. For example, *I have a big, brown dog. He sleeps on a fuzzy rug in my room. I like my dog because he is playful.*

5. Have each student revisit one of his or her own pieces of writing to add details.

Differentiation: For **below-level students**, create a list of categorized adjectives together, such as color words, size words, and texture words. For **above-level students**, have them choose sentences from actual books and rewrite them to make them more interesting.

✔ **Assessment Check:** Note who can provide suggestions for the story. Those who do not participate may need prompting, guidance, or additional instruction.

K-2 Strategies

Writing

A Personal Booklet

Objective

Students will identify their own spelling needs.

Preparation

1. Create stapled booklets with at least 26 pages each front and back (7 pages folded in half).

Procedure

1. Ask students about the words they usually look up or need help spelling or distinguishing the meaning of, such as *said*, *because*, *your/you're*, and *there/their/they're*.

2. Explain that students will create personal word booklets to use whenever they are writing.

3. Distribute their booklets. Allow them time to create personalized covers. Then, ask students to label each page with a letter of the alphabet.

4. Have them add some words to the various pages of their booklets to get started, such as *was*, *grandma*, and *school*. They can walk around the room and use books, resources, or the word wall to find words to include in their booklets.

5. Discuss how and when students can add to their booklets. Suggest students use their ongoing writing, finished projects, and journals as sources for words. Encourage them to double-check every word before writing it in their booklets. They want to make sure every word is spelled right!

Differentiation: For **English language learners**, work with them to ensure their dictionary skills are strong. Or, give them access to dual-language dictionaries so they can look up words in their own languages and get them translated to record in their booklets.

✔ **Assessment Check:** Examine the words students put in their booklets. Note if there are common features that you can revisit in a mini-lesson, such as high-frequency words, contractions, or words with suffixes. Also, note if some of the words students record are below or above grade level expectations so you can provide further support or challenge to these students.

Writing

K–2 Strategies

Collect Ideas

Objective

Students will develop a list of writing topics.

Preparation

1. Place sheets of paper, one per student, on clipboards.

Procedure

1. Have students go outside with their clipboards and find comfortable spots to sit.

2. Ask students to listen carefully, paying close attention to what they hear.

3. Tell students to write down all the sounds they hear.

4. Then, gather together and share the sounds they heard.

5. Discuss the possible writing topics the sounds make them think of. Have students record these ideas on their papers. For example, birds chirping can result in an informational piece on a particular kind of bird, a siren can inspire a story about a brave firefighter, or a sanitation truck can turn into a mystery story about someone accidentally throwing away something important and how he or she has to work to get it back.

6. Have students place their lists in their writing folders for future writing periods.

Differentiation: Have **English language learners** color code their lists, such as green for will write about and yellow for might write about. Help **below-level students** create a comprehensive list by having them dictate part of their ideas.

✔ **Assessment Check:** Note how well students think of topics related to the sounds. Effective and efficient brainstorming takes practice, so think of other areas where you can take students to repeat this activity, such as the gym or lunchroom.

K-2 Strategies

Writing

Concept of Word

Objective

Students will develop concepts about word spacing.

Preparation

1. Select two anonymous writing samples. One should show correct spacing and one should not.

Procedure

1. Project the writing with correct spacing so students can see it.

2. Discuss how the spacing helps us tell one word from another when we read.

3. Show students the sample with incorrect spacing, and ask students where the spaces should go. Suggest to students that they put a finger on the paper at the end of each word to give enough space to begin writing the next word.

4. Have students assist you in creating a sentence about the importance of word spacing. Write the sentence on chart paper for younger students. Older students can write the sentence on paper themselves.

5. Have students count the number of words and the number of spaces in the sentence.

Differentiation: For **below-level students**, use their writing during an individual conference to show them one-on-one how to use a finger to help with spacing. For **above-level students**, ask them to look through their writing for any times they might have forgotten to apply correct spacing. Teach them the proper use of the proofreading symbol for add space (#). They can use this mark on their papers to edit their own work.

✔ **Assessment Check:** Make note of students who still need support with this important skill. Repeat the mini-lesson with those students.

Find It

Objective

Students will find classroom resources for writing.

Preparation

1. Look around your room at the placement of resources you want students to use, such as a word wall.

2. Create a list of questions regarding where you might find particular words or word features around your classroom, such as *Where can I find capital letters? Where can I find the word* saw? **Note:** You might need to provide a clue to the location, such as *Where can I find capital letters near the coat hooks?*

Procedure

1. Tell students they are going to be detectives. Explain that there are some places in the classroom that can help us when we are writing. We are going to find them.

2. Ask one of your questions. Continue to ask the questions and have students *hunt* through the room.

3. Have students work in small groups or pairs to create lists of the available classroom resources they can use while working in Writer's Workshop.

Differentiation: Above-level

students need less positional clues, such as *near the coat hook*. You might ask these students to find a resource they used that morning or when they were writing in their journals to give an indication of how they are using the classroom resources.

✔ Assessment Check: Note who

seems aware of the resources and who needs reminders. Additional guidance or instruction may be needed.

Grammar Basics

Objective

Students will sort and match nouns and verbs.

Preparation

1. Make note cards with the a mixture of nouns and verbs that can be joined together to make phrases. For example, *dog, dogs, cat, cats, he, we, girl, girls, bark, barks, meow, meows, jump, jumps, sing,* and *sings,* and then shuffle the cards.

2. On a space students can easily see, write *Noun—A Person, Place, or Thing* and *Verb—Action Word.*

Procedure

1. Gather students in front of the two parts-of-speech signs and read them.

2. Show students one word card at a time, and ask them if it is a noun or a verb. Reinforce the meanings of the words by providing definitions and/or example sentences. Continue with the remaining cards.

3. Ask students to look at the nouns and match them to correct verbs, such as *dog/barks*. Continue with all cards until all sets are made.

4. Have students look at how some nouns have verbs that end in *–s* and others do not. Ask them if they can explain why. Guide the discussion to reveal how singular nouns (*dog*) have verbs that end in *–s* (*barks*), while plural nouns (*girls*) have verbs that do not end in *–s* (*sing*).

5. Encourage students to look at their writing for any sentences with singular or plural nouns. Have them read these sentences aloud, checking for correct noun/verb agreement and making necessary corrections.

Differentiation: For **below-level students**, work with a small group to provide more support as they search their own writing for examples. For **above-level students**, have them work with irregular nouns, such as *mice nibble, mouse nibbles; children hop, child hops; foot kicks, feet kick.*

✔ **Assessment Check:** Note who can sort and match the nouns and verbs. Students who struggle may need additional support when editing their work to be sure nouns and verbs agree.

Writing

K–2 Strategies

How to Revise and Edit

Objective

Students will revise and edit pieces of writing.

Preparation

1. Create a simple story that has errors for students to revise and edit. For example, *Last week mi dad was a dog. It was yellow It had furry four leg. It was so big my dad saw afraid.*

2. Create a large version of the story, so students can see it in a whole-group setting.

3. Copy *Revision Marks Chart* (page 324; revision.pdf), one for each student.

Procedure

1. Show students the story. Tell students you want them to listen to it and see if you should revise any part of the story.

2. Read the story aloud.

3. Distribute the *Revision Marks Chart* and discuss the different editor's marks on the chart.

4. Ask students what is needed to improve the story. Ask them if you should change any of the content, such as where your dad saw the dog. Have individual students come up to the piece of writing an make any changes the group agrees to.

5. Then, have students to edit the story for grammar, usage, and mechanics. Guide each student in how to use the proper editing marks as they make the necessary changes.

6. Ask students to look back at pieces of their own writing to revise and edit. Encourage students to use the proper editing marks.

Differentiation: Have **above-level students** meet in small groups to extend the lesson. Ask them to read part of their writing aloud, and have the group decide what changes might be needed. Students should use the correct editing marks.

✔ **Assessment Check:** Note who assists in making the corrections. Students who are unable to participate may need more individualized support to revise their writing.

K–2 Strategies

Writing

Matching Sound to Print

Objective

Students will draw on phonemic awareness and spelling conventions as they write.

Preparation

1. Research and download images that begin or end with the same sound, depending on the skill level of your students. For example, kindergarten students might use *dog*, *doll*, *bat*, and *ball*. First-grade students might use *chicken*, *chain*, *church*, *shirt*, *shoe*, and *shower*. Second-grade students might use *fly*, *butterfly*, *monkey*, and *puppy*.

2. Print the images, one per page.

Procedure

1. Spread out the images and have students name them.

2. Take two images, and ask if the names of the images begin or end the same way. Say each name slowly, and encourage students to listen across the entire words.

3. Help students sort the words according to the same sounds in the same positions.

4. Show students how to write each word, listening across each sound as you write.

5. Have students think of additional words that begin or end like the ones sorted and add them to the list. Encourage students to listen across words as they write.

Differentiation: For **below-level students**, write the words as they identify the pictures. Point out the same letter(s) that makes the same sound(s). For **English language learners**, assess which sounds they are still working to hear and represent in print. Give additional experiences. For **above-level students**, use medial sounds.

✔ **Assessment Check:** Note who can assist in hearing the sounds and who cannot. Use this information to direct future mini-lessons to provide additional support for students still learning how to listen across the sounds of a word.

Punctuation Matters

Objective

Students will punctuate stories (. , ? !).

Preparation

1. Create a simple story with no punctuation, or reuse a modeled or shared writing piece by reprinting it without the punctuation. Make it large enough for all students to see when in a large group mini-lesson.

2. Have various colored markers available.

Procedure

1. Show students the story.

2. Read the story aloud in one continuous sentence. Say, "Oh, no! The punctuation bandit stole all the punctuation, and I need your help putting it back." Have students use the markers to add the missing punctuation. Use the same color marker for all the punctuation marks that are the same (one color for periods, another color for commas, another color for exclamation points, and another color for question marks).

3. Reread the story with the punctuation, pointing out how the meaning is affected by these marks.

4. Have students revisit pieces of their own writing and edit the punctuation as needed. Encourage them to use multiple colors also, so they can see which punctuation marks they most often miss.

Differentiation: For **English language learners**, overdramatize the effect of the unpunctuated story. Have them choral read it with you in this exaggerated way to internalize the important role punctuation performs in writing. For **above-level students**, have them work with a story that incorporates dialogue.

✔ **Assessment Check:** Note who added punctuation. For those who did not participate, further mini-lessons might be needed.

K–2 Strategies

Writing

Recalling Sight Words

Objective

Students will practice writing sight words.

Preparation

1. Copy *BINGO Board* (page 252; bingo.pdf), one per student.

2. Make a stack of note cards with nine sight words your students need practice with, such as *the, could, with, too, was,* and *bright.* Use a word twice if your students have limited experience with it. **Note:** You may want to have the *BINGO Boards* already filled in, just be sure each board has a different ordering of the words.

3. Provide colored pencils, at least one per student.

Procedure

1. Show students the sight word cards, one at a time. Have them randomly write the words in pencil on their boards, one word per square.

2. Shuffle the cards.

3. Have students play the first game with a light colored pencil, such as yellow or orange.

4. Select a card, show it, and call out the word. Have students trace over the word with their colored pencils.

5. Continue to call words until someone has five in a row (across, down, or diagonally) and calls, "*BINGO*" or "*Five in a row!*" Continue playing until other students also get five in a row.

   Extend the lesson by playing other rounds using slightly darker colored pencils, such as green.

Differentiation: For **above-level students**, do not show the card. Have them write the word from memory first, and then check it against your copy. For **below-level students**, choose six words and have them write each one four times on their boards. This gives additional practice with the words.

✔ **Assessment Check:** Assess who correctly marks their cards. Note which students need additional experience with some of the sight words.

Writing

K–2 Strategies

Sharing Ideas

Objective

Students will revise sentences to be more descriptive.

Preparation

1. On a space large enough for students to see, write simple sentences. For example, *He said hello to me.*

Procedure

1. Show students the sentences.

2. Explain that sometimes, when we write sentences, we write the first thing that comes to mind. But, when we reread the sentences, we see how to express our ideas in better ways.

3. Show the example sentence, *He said hello to me*, and ask students to imagine this interaction.

4. Ask students what they can do to make the sentence more expressive. Guide them to change and/or add a few words, such as *yelled* for *said*.

5. Ask students if they can add a word to tell *how* he yelled (*loudly*). Explain, or remind them that this descriptive word is called an *adverb*. It helps us better describe an action (verb). Continue with the rest of the sentences you have for students to review. Or have students revise the sentences in pairs and share what they create.

6. Ask students to look in their current writing folders or in their journals for sentences they can make more expressive and rewrite them.

Differentiation: For **below-level students**, create a word bank of descriptive and sensory words for them to use. For **English language learners**, provide cloze sentence frames to guide the placement of descriptive words.

✔ **Assessment Check:** Note how well students can add adjectives, adverbs, or more specific words. Additional small-group mini-lessons should be planned for students who need more experience with expressive language.

Writing

K–2 Strategies

Use of Lines

Objective

Students will observe and discuss writing on lined paper.

Preparation

1. Use two writing samples written on lined paper. One shows how writing is supposed to sit on the lines. The other shows some words sitting off the lines.

2. Make a large enough copy so that all students can see it.

Procedure

1. Show students the two writing samples.

2. Discuss the differences between the two. Point out how the sample with the letters written on the lines is easier to read.

3. Have students examine their own journals or writing pieces to see how well they use the lines. They should make corrections as needed.

Differentiation: Have **below-level students** practice by re-copying stories on lined paper, working to keep the words on the lines.

✔ **Assessment Check:** Assess who is working with lined paper and can consistently keep the words on the lines. Problems with this may indicate an eye-hand coordination issue that demands more attention and practice. Some students may need unlined paper for a while longer to develop this skill.

Best Practices in Grade 3 through Grade 5

This section includes basic Writer's Workshop strategy lessons for simple practice of the following skills for grade 3 through grade 5. Details regarding each strategy can be found on the subsequent pages. For additional lessons, download the Digital Resources. (See page 20 for the website address and access code.)

At this level, students are now able to write in a variety of genres. Awareness of audience encourages the writer to have different purposes for their writing. Honing skills in pre-planning, sentence writing, use of short paragraphs, and use of punctuation all develop for this level of writer. Connect their ongoing work to the modeled and shared writing they have participated in with your mentorship, showing how to write opinion, informative/explanatory, narrative nonfiction, and narrative fiction pieces. Whole-group Writer's Workshop mini-lessons to support students' writing development should take about 10–15 minutes.

Mini-Lessons

Lesson
Consider the Potential Audience (page 206)
Deciding on a Topic (page 207)
Expanding Sentences (page 208)
Finding the Apostrophe (page 209)
Helping a Friend Revise (page 210)
How to Transition Ideas (page 211)
Incorporating Technology in Composing (page 212)
Organizing Writing (page 213)
Punctuation Counts (page 214)
Self-Correcting Spelling (page 215)
Sight Words (page 216)
Using Classroom Resources (page 217)

Digital Resources Lessons

Lesson
Deciding on a Genre (five-day lesson) (decidegenre.pdf)
Developing and Using a Personal Word Bank (wordbank.pdf)
Grammar Fundamentals (grammarfund.pdf)
Publishing Final Copies (pubfinal.pdf)
Rereading Writing for Possible Revisions (rereading.pdf)
Revisions Make the Difference (revdifference.pdf)

Some websites that serve to enhance instruction and provide additional opportunities for students to explore these various topics are:

- www.kidblog.org
- reviewgamezone.com
- www.studygs.net
- www.learninggamesforkids.com
- www.eduplace.com

An app that serves to enhance instruction and provide additional opportunities for students to explore these various topics is Grammaropolis (Grammaropolis LLC).

Writing

Consider the Potential Audience

Objective

Students will identify the audience.

Preparation

1. Go to http://www.YouTube.com and search for *commercialsforKids*. Choose a video of interest to your students, making sure to show students who are about the same age as your students.

Procedure

1. Ask students to help you define *audience* and what it means to have one when writing.

2. Talk about how commercials are examples of opinion writing.

3. Tell students that as they watch and listen to the commercial they should think about the following questions:

   - *Who is the audience for this ad?*
   - *How does the ad draw in the viewer?*
   - *What does the ad use to persuade the viewer?*

4. Show the video and then return to the questions.

5. Discuss the use of emotion and/or facts to persuade.

6. Have students imagine that they are writing ads for their favorite foods.

7. Ask students what their favorite foods are, why someone should try it, who their audiences are, and what words will persuade their audiences.

8. Have students work in pairs to write their ads, keeping their audiences in mind.

   Extend the lesson, and have students create accompanying video ads.

Differentiation: Have **English language learners** create ads about topics with which they are very familiar, such as their cultures. Have **above-level students** add music to their videos for emotional effect.

✔ **Assessment Check:** Note who suggests the persuasive language and possible audience. At this level, students should be able to think beyond their immediate circle of audience (*self, family, and friends*). Additional modeling and guidance might be needed.

> ***Persuasive writing's*** *main goal is to persuade or convince readers that the point of view or course of action is valid. The writer must develop a limited topic that is well defined and debatable—or has more than one side. It is important that the author understand both sides of the position so that the strongest information is presented. Letters/ editorials, testimonials, and ads are common forms of persuasive writing. Researchers estimate that children view 40,000 TV ads each year (Committee on Communication 2006).*

Writing

3–5 Strategies

Deciding on a Topic

Objective

Students will select writing topics.

Preparation

1. Place sheets of paper on clipboards, one for each student.

2. Prepare a large sheet of chart paper, and have markers available.

Procedure

1. Give each student a clipboard.

2. Have students find comfortable spots to sit in the classroom.

3. Ask students to listen carefully, paying close attention to what they hear.

4. Tell students to write down all the sounds they hear.

5. Have students share their lists and compile a class list on chart paper.

6. Ask students to talk about what topics the sounds make them think of. For example, kids walking by the door can turn into a narrative about a school day or a car horn blowing might be an explanatory piece about sound.

7. Add potential topics next to each sound.

   Leave the list posted in the classroom to help students when they are in need of new writing topics.

Differentiation: Help **below-level students** prioritize their lists of topics based on their interests and knowledge. Have **above-level students** include genres, audiences, and output ideas next to each topic on their lists.

✔ **Assessment Check:** Note how well students think of topics related to the sounds. Brainstorming takes practice, so think of other areas you can take students to repeat this activity, such as the gym or the school's entrance.

Expanding Sentences

Objective

Students will write descriptive sentences.

Preparation

1. Prepare a list of simple sentences on chart paper or on a handout for each student. **Note:** You can also do both, so students have a copy to write on while viewing the whole-class chart. Simple sentences might include *I saw the dog. My team won the game. Mom made a cake.*

Procedure

1. Distribute the handout, or display the chart.

2. Ask a student to read the first sentence, *I saw the dog.*

3. Ask students how to change some words to more accurately express what happened. For example, *saw* can be changed to *spied* and words can be added to describe the dog, such as *furry, mean, ferocious, tiny, gray,* and *white.*

4. Continue with the other sentences, having students add additional words, such as adjectives and adverbs, to better express the ideas and help readers visualize the meaning.

Differentiation: For **below-level students** provide a suggested adjective and adverb word bank along with some guiding questions to ask themselves, such as *who, what, where, why,* and *how.*

✔ **Assessment Check:** Assess how well students add expressive language to the sentences. Compare this with what they do in their writing. Additional guidance or instruction may be needed.

Writing

3–5 Strategies

Finding the Apostrophe

Objective

Students will categorize words with apostrophes.

Preparation

1. Copy a newspaper article, one per student, or bring enough copies for each student to have an actual newspaper page. **Note:** Having students use content-related text aligns well with work in social studies and science.

2. Have two different color highlighters for each student.

Procedure

1. Ask students when an apostrophe is used. (*contractions* or *possessives*)

2. Discuss the difference. (*Contraction*: an apostrophe replaces a letter or letters, such as *don't*. *Possessives* show ownership, such as *Juana's house*.)

3. Distribute the article pages.

4. Ask students to circle all the words with apostrophes.

5. Have students use one color highlighter to mark all the contractions and another color to mark all the possessives.

6. Have students circle apostrophes in their own journal entries and writing pieces and highlight each according to its use, making any necessary corrections.

Differentiation: Provide a desktop chart for **English language learners** with examples of each apostrophe's use, including singular and plural possessives. Include example sentences and images for each. This will determine whether additional instructions or practice is needed.

✔ **Assessment Check:** Collect the handouts and see how well students were able to correctly categorize the words. This will determine whether additional instruction or practice is needed.

Helping a Friend Revise

Objective

Students will revise writing.

Preparation

1. Create a story needing revision, or have students use ongoing writing projects. If you are going to provide a story, make a copy for each student.

Procedure

1. Show students the story, or ask them to get their writing folders and choose stories to use.

2. Have student pairs of similar ability work together. Similar writing is easier to peer revise.

3. Tell the student pairs to read the stories or swap stories to read. Things to ask during their readings include:

   - Does it flow?
   - Does it need another sentence to make sense?
   - Does it need more descriptions?
   - Are all parts of the genre included?

4. Have students make lists of possible revisions.

   If using a single class story, then come together to share the suggestions. If using individual student stories, ask students to put their stories in their folders to use during Writer's Workshop.

Differentiation: Have **below-level students** use word processors. This can make the physical process of writing and revising more manageable. Guide **English language learners** by providing explicit goals for the revision, such as adding three adjectives, inserting one piece of dialogue, or changing one sentence in the introduction to a question.

✔ **Assessment Check:** Note who can assist in revisions. Note what suggestions they make, indicating an awareness of necessary revisions. Additional instruction and practice may be needed.

Writing

3–5 Strategies

How to Transition Ideas

Objective

Students will add transition words to stories.

Preparation

1. On a large sheet of paper, write a story needing transition words. For example, *Last night we baked a cake for my grandma's birthday. We broke eggs. We added milk. We put in some flour and chocolate. We put it in the oven to cook. It was delicious!*

2. On note cards, write the transition words *first*, *second*, *then*, *next*, and *finally*.

Procedure

1. Read the story aloud.

2. Discuss how the story will be more interesting and easier to follow if we add words to tell readers when things happened.

3. Read the words on the note cards. Spread them out and ask volunteers to choose ones they think helps the story. Guide them to add *First, we broke eggs. Second (or next), we added milk. Then (or next), we put in some flour and chocolate. Finally, we put it in the oven.* Use the caret mark to insert each word above the correct sentence.

4. Have students revisit their own work in their writing folders, using the caret mark to insert transition words as needed or circle the ones they previously used.

Differentiation: For **above-level students**, provide a list of additional transition words and phrases (*again*, *additionally*, *by the same token*, *in the same way*, *likewise*, *by and large*, and *all in all*) and have them revisit existing pieces of writing to revise accordingly.

✔ **Assessment Check:** Note who can assist in adding transitions to revise a story. Students not yet doing this may need more time practicing story composition to understand this concept.

Incorporating Technology in Composing

Objective

Students will practice keyboarding.

Preparation

1. Make plans to bring your students to a computer lab in your school. If this is not available, but you have a few computers in your room, create a schedule so all students can have turns practicing.

2. Have students use a word processing program, so they can type and print their work for you to assess.

3. Copy *Computer Composing* (page 321; compcomp.pdf). Print one teacher copy if conducted as a whole class, or one per student if completed independently. **Note:** You can audio record this and have students work at computer stations with headphones.

Procedure

1. Read the directions one step at a time if students are all at computers, or provide students with the *Computer Composing* direction sheet to self-direct this mini-lesson.

2. Tell students to place their hands so their index to pinkie fingers rest on the middle rows of alphabet keys (the home row). Tell them to rest their thumbs on the space bars.

3. Guide students in using the *Computer Composing* directions.

4. Have students print their work.

   Depending on the number of students, you can direct this while other students are in their independent work time in Writer's Workshop.

Differentiation: For **above-level students** already using keyboards, have them type one of their own Writer's Workshop stories on the computer for printing.

✔ **Assessment Check:** Assess how well students follow directions. Assess how comfortable students seem with the keyboards. You may want to provide extra experiences for those still learning to keyboard.

Writing

3–5 Strategies

Organizing Writing

Objective

Students will organize their ideas.

Preparation

1. Cut enough strips of paper so that each student has 10.
2. Cut 10 larger strips to use for students to see as a group.
3. Provide glue or tape for student use.

Procedure

1. Place the larger strips where students can see them.
2. Tell students you would like to write a story about something that just happened in your life, the school, or community.
3. Demonstrate how to write phrases or words about the topic on the strips.
4. Once the strips are done, show how you can move them around to organize your thinking before you begin writing. Ideas can be organized in many ways, such as big ideas to small ideas, chronological order, or opposing categories.
5. Ask students to do the same using their smaller strips of paper. Have them begin by thinking of something that happened recently, writing words and phrases on the strips of paper, and moving the strips of paper around in the order they want to use them in their writing.
6. Have students glue or tape their strips down in their writing folders to use for a future writing project.

Differentiation: Have **below-level students** create lists of writing topics. Pair students to brainstorm events to write on their strips of paper.

✔ **Assessment Check:** Assess how well students can turn events into lists of words and phrases. This is a good exercise in drafting and pre-planning their writing. Additional guidance or modeling may be needed.

3–5 Strategies

Writing

Punctuation Counts

Objective

Students will edit their written pieces for punctuation.

Preparation

1. Create signs with incorrect punctuation and word usage, such as *Private customer parking—all others will be toad*; *Kids partys*; *Your the best teacher ever*; *Employees, must wash hands, before returning, to work;* and *School Bored, Meeting Tonight.*

2. Post the signs around the room, on walls, doors, and windows.

3. Clip sheets of paper to clipboards, one per student.

Procedure

1. Distribute clipboards to the students.

2. Tell students there are signs posted around the room that need some punctuation and word usage corrections. **Note:** To increase the fun, tell students they are sign detectives and have to locate the errors.

3. Have students walk around to decide what needs fixing. They should write the correct language on the papers on their clipboards.

4. As a whole class, share the corrections. As you talk about each sign, use editing marks to make the corrections.

5. Have students look through their journals or writing folders to edit one of their own pieces.

Differentiation: For b**elow-level students**, provide a checklist to guide their edits. For **above-level students**, have them look online, in magazines, in school newsletters, or in newspapers for other errors they can correct.

✔ **Assessment Check:** Note who sees and makes corrections. This is an important time to work out usage errors, such as *to/too/two*, *their/they're/there*, and *your/you're*.

Writing

3–5 Strategies

Self-Correcting Spelling

Objective

Students will correct spelling errors.

Preparation

1. Create a piece of writing with spelling errors. You might target words that students often misspell.

2. Copy the story, one for each student.

3. Make a large copy (on chart paper or displayed via technology) that all students will be able to see.

Procedure

1. Show the story. Read the first sentence.

2. Ask students if they notice any spelling errors.

3. Ask them what previously taught spelling rules or available class resources could help them to correct the words without the help of a teacher. Think aloud as you use a student suggestion to help correct the spelling.

4. Have students continue reading on their own, crossing off words that are misspelled and writing the correct spellings above each one on their individual copies.

5. Gather students in front of the large copy when they are done correcting their individual copies. Work on each sentence, asking them for their corrections. If they missed a word, ask them to circle it on their individual copies.

Differentiation: Give **English language learners** a list of the specific words, phrases, or verb tenses that prove challenging to them. Have **above-level students** create individual lists of grammatical rules that are challenging to them.

✔ **Assessment Check:** Assess how well students proofread words that need to be corrected for spelling. Compare this to their own editing when working independently. Provide additional guidance and instruction as needed.

Sight Words

Objective
Students will practice writing sight words.

Preparation

1. Write sight words on the ends of craft sticks using permanent markers so every student can have two or three turns. This can be prepared as a whole-group mini-lesson or for a small, targeted group of students who need practice with these words. The words should be ones you want students to be able to quickly know when writing. **Note:** This mini-lesson can be used for both general sight words and content-specific words.

2. To record how students do during this mini-lesson, make a chart with students' names going down one side and the words across the top. (See below for an example.) This chart enables you to keep track of the words students know. For each incorrect word written, place an X next to the student's name and under the word read.

3. Provide individual whiteboards and markers, one per student.

Procedure

1. Have each student take a turn drawing a stick and reading the word on it aloud. If correct, he or she can keep the stick. If not, it goes back in the cup.

2. Continue play until all students have had two or three turns and all the sticks have been read.

3. Collect the sticks and distribute the individual whiteboards and markers.

4. Call out the sight words one at a time, having students write them. Spot check their work, and be sure to record on the chart whether they can spell each word correctly.

Differentiation: Help **below-level students** revisit their writing for misspelled sight words to add to their lists. Have **above-level students** add topic-specific vocabulary to their lists.

✔ **Assessment Check:** Use the chart to evaluate how students do. Some students may need additional exposure and practice with the words.

	together	often	different	friend	because	important
José	X			X		
Samuel		X				
Carl			X			
Maya					X	X

Writing

3–5 Strategies

Using Classroom Resources

Objective

Students will find classroom resources for writing.

Preparation

1. Look around your room at the placement of resources you want students to use, such as dictionaries, thesauri, rhyming dictionaries, and informational books with glossaries.

2. Create *what if* questions regarding where you might find particular resources, such as *What if I were writing a poem and trying to think of a rhyming word for* volcano? *Where would I look? What if I were writing a research report on snakes and needed to know how to spell* reticulated? *Where would I look? What if I were writing a story and wanted another word for* said? *Where would I find that?*

Procedure

1. Tell students they are going to play *What If?* Say, "There are some resources in the classroom that can help us when we write, so let's find them."

2. Ask one of your questions. Continue asking the questions and have students suggest the corresponding resources. Have a student go and pick up the resource to help others know exactly where to find it.

3. Have students write their own *what if* questions to share with the class.

Differentiation: For **below-level students**, write the questions on a handout and have them search the room and write their responses.

✔ **Assessment Check:** Note who seems aware of the resources and who might need reminders. This is a good time to assess who seems to self-direct his or her writing by knowing where classroom resources are. Additional guidance and support may be needed.

Best Practices in Grade 6 through Grade 8

This section includes basic Writer's Workshop strategy lessons for simple practice of the following skills for grade 6 through grade 8. Details regarding each strategy can be found on the subsequent pages. For additional lessons, download the Digital Resources. (See page 20 for the website address and access code.)

At this level, students are encouraged to become independent and proficient writers. Opportunities to write across the curriculum will encourage a wide selection of various genres, a broad use of more complex vocabulary, and deeper research skills. Connect students' ongoing work to the modeled and shared writing they have participated in under your mentorship, showing how to write argument, informative/explanatory, narrative nonfiction, and narrative fiction pieces. Whole-group Writer's Workshop mini-lessons to support students' writing development should take about 10–15 minutes.

Mini-Lessons

Lesson
Considering Purpose and Potential Audience (page 219)
Compound Sentences (page 220)
Genres, Genres, Genres (page 221)
Genre-Specific Writing (page 222)
Grammar Essentials (page 223)
Helping a Classmate Revise (page 224)
Organizing by Paragraphs (page 225)
Self-Correcting Spelling and Grammar (page 226)
Technology (page 227)
Using Editing Marks (page 228)
Vocabulary Choices (page 229)
Why Punctuate? (page 230)

Digital Resources Lessons

Lesson
Crafting Texts: Informational (craftinform.pdf)
Crafting Texts: Narrative (craftnarr.pdf)
Crafting Texts: Poetry (craftpoetry.pdf)
Cultivating a Personal Word Bank (cultivateword.pdf)
Determining a Topic (determine.pdf)
Homophones (homophones.pdf)
Putting it All Together (puttogether.pdf)
Recalling Familiar Words (familiarwords.pdf)
Transitions Make the Difference (transitionsdiff.pdf)
Using Correct Capitalization (correctcaps.pdf)
Utilizing Classroom Resources (classroomres.pdf)

Some websites that serve to enhance instruction and provide additional opportunities for students to explore these various topics are:

- www.ispot.tv
- www.discoveryeducation.com
- www.superteachertools.us
- www.studygs.net
- www.techlearning.com/

Some apps that serve to enhance instruction and provide additional opportunities for students to explore these various topics are:

- Pages (Apple)
- Educreations Interactive Whiteboard (Educreations, Inc.)
- Class Tools (Jeremy Cartee)

Considering Purpose and Potential Audience

Objective

Students will write persuasive slogans.

Preparation

1. Make a list of city and state slogans, such as Ohio's *So Much to Discover* and Chicago's *Second to None*. **Note:** An Internet search of each state's site will provide an interesting list. Choose your own state/city and several nearby. You can also do a screen shot of the site showing the slogan, and then project these for the students to see.

Procedure

1. Show students one slogan at a time.

2. Ask students what they think each slogan means.

3. Have students identify the intended audience.

4. Ask students what words were aimed at a particular audience.

5. Have students think about the authors' purposes in writing the slogans, such as to attract tourists. Continue through the list.

6. Ask students for ideas for a classroom slogan. Guide them with questions, such as, *Who would be the audience? What would be the purpose in writing a slogan about the classroom? What should be said to give the audience a good idea of what the classroom is like? What words might you use to describe our classroom in a slogan?*

7. Have students write their own slogans.

Differentiation: **Below-level students** can work in a small group under your direction to think about purpose and audience. Encourage **English language learners** to write a slogan that includes aspects of their cultural backgrounds.

✔ **Assessment Check:** Assess who is able to participate in the discussion. Who seems to understand the concept of *audience*? Additional support or guidance may be needed.

6–8 Strategies

Writing

Compound Sentences

Objective

Students will create compound sentences.

Preparation

1. Create a sign defining compound sentences, such as *Compound sentences are two sentences or independent clauses joined by a comma and conjunction (for, and, nor, but, or, yet, and so) or a semicolon.*

2. Copy onto cardstock and cut apart *Compound Sentences* (page 325; compsent.pdf).

Procedure

1. Review the definition of a compound sentence.

2. Distribute one card to each student.

3. Ask students to roam around the room and find a person with another sentence that can be joined to theirs with a comma and conjunction or a semicolon.

4. Once students pair up, have them record their new compound sentences. Then, have them continue around the room looking for other matches.

5. Share the sentences students created with the whole class.

6. Have students create their own compound sentence cards. They should write sentences on different cards and put them into a bag for drawing later in the day.

7. To continue this activity, have students repeat the exercise with sentences and clauses to create complex sentences.

Differentiation: Have **above-level students** create complex, compound sentences. These are sentences with at least two coordinate independent clauses and at least one dependent clause. Or, have students look through current reading materials to find these types of complex sentences.

✔ **Assessment Check:** Note how many students were able to accurately find partners to create compound sentences that made sense. Additional instruction or guidance may be needed.

Writing

6–8 Strategies

Genres, Genres, Genres

Objective

Students will categorize writing pieces according to genre.

Preparation

1. Select published writing that exemplifies each of the four writing genres—*argument, informative/explanatory, narrative nonfiction,* and *narrative fiction.* You can use newspapers, the Internet, or magazine articles from appropriate sources. Search for articles related to ongoing cross-curricular topics, if possible.

2. Print and copy these so students can read and respond to them.

Procedure

1. Distribute the articles.

2. Ask students to think about the four writing genres.

3. Explain that there is one article for each genre. Ask them to read and decide which article exemplifies each genre. Have them share their thinking with the whole group.

4. Create genre guidelines using the articles so students have an idea of how to proceed with their own writing in each of these genres. For example, argument pieces use supporting details. Informative/explanatory pieces give facts about topics. Narrative nonfiction pieces combine elements from informational and narrative fiction pieces, telling facts in a story-like manner. Narrative fiction pieces tell stories and have beginnings, middles, and ends.

5. Have students create lists of distinctive components for each genre. Extend the lesson by having students do Internet searches for additional examples of each genre.

Differentiation: Have **below-level students** or **English language learners** categorize their own finished writing pieces by genre. These pieces will have personal relevance to them and make this assignment meaningful.

✔ **Assessment Check:** Assess how well students classify the articles. If they are searching for more articles, how well do they match the genres and articles? Additional guidance and support may be needed.

6–8 Strategies

Writing

Genre-Specific Writing

Objective

Students will write genre-specific pieces.

Preparation

1. Make note cards that have topics (playing basketball, going into space, a magical pair of running shoes, or last night's dinner), one per student. You may choose to repeat topics.

2. Make another set of multiple note cards that provide genres, one per student. In addition to the four genres (*argument, informative/explanatory, narrative nonfiction,* and *narrative fiction*), you may include subgenres within each, such as historical fiction, science fiction, biography, poetry, and mystery.

Procedure

1. Choose a broad topic, such as basketball. Model using that topic to generate ideas for writing in different genres.

   - how basketball is safer to play than football (*argument*)
   - the origin of the game (*informative/explanatory*)
   - a day in the life of a professional basketball player (*narrative nonfiction*)
   - a basketball player who beats the odds even though he is very short (*narrative fiction*)

2. Distribute a topic card to each student.

3. Have students create short descriptions under each genre for what they might write using their topics.

4. Have students choose one of their ideas to use to create complete writing pieces during Writer's Workshop.

Differentiation: Have **below-level students** use graphic organizers to plan before writing their pieces, making sure all the genres' components are accounted for at the onset.

✔ **Assessment Check:** Assess how well students write on topics using specific genres. Did they use the features of that genre to write the story? Additional support may be needed.

Writing

6–8 Strategies

Grammar Essentials

Objective

Students will apply grammar rules in writing.

Preparation

1. Copy *Grammar List* (page 322; grammar.pdf), one per student.

Procedure

1. Pair students, distribute *Grammar List*, and explain that they are to write stories that include each of the listed grammar parts.

2. Direct students to type their stories using a computer. When they're finished, they should replace words that fit the grammar categories with blanks and the corresponding part of speech, such as

> *The* _____ *horse galloped*
> (adjective)
>
> _____ *over the* _____.
> (adverb)   (noun)

3. Tell students to print and exchange their stories with other student pairs.

4. Have the pairs fill in the correct types of words for the blanks.

5. Instruct the pairs that exchanged stories to discuss what they did to fill in the needed words.

6. Discuss how context helps writers. Ask students if there are words that fit but are not the exact words the authors wrote. Ask students to explain what that tells us.

Differentiation: Have **below-level students** complete this activity with existing pieces from their writing folders. Have **above-level students** write their pieces in a particular genre, such as informative/explanatory or narrative.

✔ **Assessment Check:** Assess how well students crafted stories needing the suggested grammar. How well did they fill in the words in the exchanged stories? Additional support or instruction may be needed. This lesson also gives insights into how students are using context clues when they read.

6–8 Strategies

Writing

Helping a Classmate Revise

Objective

Students will revise writing.

Preparation

1. Ask students to select one piece from their writing folders.

Procedure

1. Tell students they will have classmates listen to their pieces. They are to listen only to the narrative and not worry about spelling or other errors. As they listen, they should pay attention to the content of the piece.

   - *Does it make sense?*
   - *Does the writer tell all the necessary details?*
   - *What part of the piece works best?*
   - *What suggestions do I have for the author?*

2. Advise students to work on the writing and make changes based on peer suggestions.

3. Discuss how this is a strategy for having someone focus on the content and meaning of their story. This part of the writing shows their voice to readers, so the classmate revision process can be helpful.

Differentiation: Give **below-level students** directions or questions to guide their feedback. Have **above-level students** work together to create a list of writing techniques they want to hone in on in their feedback.

✔ **Assessment Check:** Note who is able to assist others during this revision discussion. Note who uses peer suggestions. Additional support and guidance may be needed.

Writing

6–8 Strategies

Organizing by Paragraphs

Objective

Students will organize their writing.

Preparation

1. Copy *Paragraph Outline* (page 323; paraout.pdf), one for each student. (**Note:** Students can use this outline for any topic. Consider having blank copies of this with your Writer's Workshop resources.)

Procedure

1. Have each student select a single sport to write about. It can be one they play, wish they played, or like to watch.

2. Explain that they will be writing informative/explanatory essays about their selected sports.

3. Distribute copies of *Paragraph Outline*.

4. Tell students that in each section they are to write phrases they can use in the final essays.

5. Provide time for students to work on their outlines.

6. Have student pairs talk about and share their outlines. Encourage them to add ideas after talking with their partners.

7. Discuss the format of the paragraphs, reminding them that transition words help the flow between paragraphs.

8. Have students add the outlines to their Writer's Workshop folders as ideas for future writing pieces, or have them finish the essays during class or as homework.

Differentiation: Provide **below-level students** with guidance for each paragraph. For example, paragraphs two through four ask for supporting details. Tell students to include sensory details focusing on the sights, sounds, and emotions associated with the sport. For **English language learners**, if sports are not relatable to students, guide them to select topics that are and draft their outlines accordingly.

✔ **Assessment Check:** Assess how well students adhere to the five-paragraph essay format by utilizing the outline. Additional guidance or instructions may be needed.

6–8 Strategies

Writing

Self-Correcting Spelling and Grammar

Objective

Students will edit writing pieces.

Preparation

1. Create a piece of writing with spelling and grammar errors.
2. Make copies of the written piece, one per student.

Procedure

1. Review a specific spelling or grammar rule you noticed the students are having trouble with.
1. Ask students to proofread the piece of writing independently, looking for and correcting spelling and grammatical errors.
2. Have students share what they find.

   This mini-lesson can also be done digitally by providing the piece in a word processing document and having students decide how to address the errors noted in green, red, or blue.

Differentiation: Have **above-level students** use pieces of writing from their journal entries or Writer's Workshop folders. Work in a small group with **below-level students** to proofread their pieces for errors.

✔ **Assessment Check:** Assess how well students proofread the piece. Note the types of errors that remain uncorrected. This may indicate the need for additional mini-lessons.

Writing

6–8 Strategies

Technology

Objective

Students will use technology to write.

Preparation

1. Plan time in the school's computer lab or set aside time during independent work time for students to use in-class computers.

2. See *Computer Composing* (page 321; compcomp.pdf) for explicit steps on how to help students learn keyboarding skills.

Procedure

1. Have students draft written pieces using a word processing program. Remind them that they are to use proper hand placement and not the hunt-and-peck system.

2. Ask them to note when the program alerts them of spelling or grammar errors. This will help them when they later return to the piece for revision and editing.

3. Display several published forms of writing (i.e., newspaper articles, magazine articles, blog posts, word clouds). Have students identify the differences in format such as font, text alignment, text colors, and columns. Discuss the impact of each.

4. Have students return to their saved writing and make formatting changes so their final published pieces have the desired impacts.

Differentiation: For **below-level students**, have them use pieces they have already written by hand and transfer them to the computer, keeping font, text alignment, text colors, and columns in mind. For **above-level students**, have them pare their pieces down to a Twitter-friendly 144 characters, using multiple text features.

✔ **Assessment Check:** Assess how well students are able to use the keyboard while typing their stories. Are they using proper hand placement? They may need additional practice, particularly if they do not have access to computers at home.

6–8 Strategies

Writing

Using Editing Marks

Objective

Students will edit their writing.

Preparation

1. Create a humorous writing piece that needs revision, or use a book students enjoy, such as *Schooled* (Korman 2007). If you opt for the book, take a passage from it and retype it with errors your students commonly make, such as grammar, text sequence, or lackluster descriptions. Remember to cite the book at the bottom so students understand the importance of giving credit to published work.

2. Make copies of your own piece or the book's original passage and the one with errors, one per student.

3. Make copies of *Revision Marks Chart* (page 324; revision.pdf), one per student.

Procedure

1. Distribute copies of the humorous story with errors.

2. Have students read it.

3. Distribute copies of *Revision Marks Chart*, and have them reread the story, looking for errors to be corrected.

4. Ask them to use the editing marks to make their corrections. When they are done, provide students with the correct version to compare.

5. Discuss the changes students made and the ones they overlooked.

6. Discuss the role the editing marks play when they revise and/or edit.

7. Have students edit one of their own pieces, using *Revision Marks Chart*.

Differentiation: For **below-level students**, provide a checklist of specific errors to look out for and correct.

✔ **Assessment Check:** Note who makes corrections. Students who are unable to participate may need more individualized support to revise their writing.

> Teach students now that borrowing the work of others without giving them recognition is not appropriate. A good way for them to remember is to share the origin of the word, **plagiarism**. It is Latin—*plagiarius, meaning kidnapper.* This creates a memorable way to share that using someone else's words is kidnapping if they don't properly cite them.

Writing

6–8 Strategies

Vocabulary Choices

Objective

Students will use outstanding vocabulary.

Which Word Is Best?	
Average	**Outstanding!**
ask	interrogate
rise	ascend
sweat	perspire
smell	odor
buy	purchase
answer	response

Preparation

1. Copy *Which Word Is Best?* (page 326; whichword.pdf), one per student.

Procedure

1. Distribute *Which Word Is Best?*. Ask students to create sentences using words from the *Average* column, such as, *I want to* buy *paper for school.*

2. Ask a student to say the same sentence with an *Outstanding!* word in place of the *Average* word, such as, *I want to* purchase *paper for school.*

3. Discuss how the word choice changes the sentence. Explain that the *Average* column words are Anglo-Saxon (Old English) in origin, and the words in the *Outstanding!* column are Old French or Latin in origin. Typically, simpler words are Anglo-Saxon.

4. Assign pairs of words to students. Have them decide which word in each pair is Anglo-Saxon and which is Old French or Latin. You'll need to mix the order of the pairs. You can alternatively provide other word pairs, such as *follow/ensue, chicken/ poultry, cow/beef, pig/pork, fall/autumn, wisdom/prudence, forgive/pardon, folk/ people, wish/desire, span/distance, tumble/somersault,* and *freedom/ liberty.* The first word in each pair is Anglo-Saxon, and the second word Old French or Latin.

5. Have students revisit their own writing to replace some of their *Average* words with *Outstanding!* words.

Differentiation: Have **English language learners** color code the words. For example, the *Average* words can be circled in red, while the *Outstanding!* words can be circled in green. Have **above-level students** research and find more pairs of Anglo-Saxon and French or Latin words to add to the list. Post them in the classroom for reference when students are writing.

✔ **Assessment Check:** Listen as students discuss the words. What do they base their decisions on for sorting the words? Their answers may indicate that additional support or instruction is needed.

> ***Fun fact!*** *We have words that are "on the hoof" (cow, chicken, pig, deer) and ones that are "on the plate" (beef, poultry, pork, venison). At one time, these words related to the social class one belonged to. For example, if you were poor, you probably raised the animals ("on the hoof"), whereas if you were rich, you probably ate them ("on the plate").*

6–8 Strategies

Writing

Why Punctuate?

Objective

Students will punctuate their writing for meaning.

Preparation

1. Gather copies of *Eats, Shoots and Leaves: Why, Commas Really Do Make a Difference* (Truss 2006), *The Girl's Like Spaghetti: Why, You Can't Manage Without Apostrophes!* (Truss 2007) and *Twenty-odd Ducks: Why, Every Punctuation Mark Counts!* (Truss 2008). If you cannot access the books, Amazon lets you "look inside" some of their products, so you can project pages and complete this mini-lesson.

Procedure

1. Have students (in small groups or pairs) read through the books.

2. Ask students to discuss the differences that punctuation makes.

3. Have students craft their own pairs of sentences where the punctuation shifts, therefore changing the meaning. Remind them that simple changes like apostrophes (*brothers'*, *brother's*) are an easy place to start in crafting their sentence pairs.

4. Share the sentences, either as a class or in small groups.

Differentiation: For **below-level students**, provide them with some newspaper headlines and ask them to change the punctuation, such as *The boy's in trouble* versus *The boys in trouble*. For **above-level students**, have them move commas around. For example, "Let's eat, David" and "Let's eat David." In one, we eat with David, and in the other we actually eat David!

✔ **Assessment Check:** Note who can assist in writing the sentence pairs. Assess how well the move in punctuation changes the meaning of the sentences. Provide further guidance or instruction.

Writing

6–8 Strategies

Assessment in Writer's Workshop

Assessment at the kindergarten through grade 2 level should include checklists and simple rubrics. Checklists allow you to keep track of a student's progress as well as the status of the class on particular mini-lessons needed. Use the *Mini-Lessons Class Checklist (K–2)* (page 333) to keep track of the mini-lessons. Pull together small groups based on the formative assessments you completed during or after each mini-lesson. Through observation of students' participation and their ongoing writing, you can choose the order of mini-lessons as well as the need to repeat the topics. Use the *Individual Record Sheet for Writing* (page 328) to keep track of when the student appears to regularly apply the concepts taught in the mini-lesson in their independent writing. As needed, follow up with individuals or small groups. Using the class checklist, you can easily see who to pull together for a small group lesson. You might mark a student as *A* (accomplished), *T* (trying), *N* (not yet) or some other coding that lets you easily see who you can group for additional mini-lessons. Another form of assessment is rubrics. Students can be guided by and assessed with rubrics as appropriate. Rubrics should reflect the goals and standards set by your school, district, and/or state. For example, kindergarten through grade 2 students might have a 3-point scale for some aspect of the writing, such as concept of word or matching sound to text. The scale might be 1 = does not attempt; 2 = attempts, shows some understanding; and 3 = attempts, nearly or completely mastered. Sit with your student, showing him or her how the work was scored and why. This can often be the very way to help students improve their work.

Grade 3 through grade 5 students can be assessed using checklists and rubrics. Use the *Mini-Lessons Class Checklist (3–5)* (page 334) to keep track of when and what mini-lessons are taught. Small groups can be created for any of the mini-lessons that might need to be repeated. Through observation of students' participation in the lesson, along with ongoing independent writing, you can choose the order as well as the need to repeat topics. Use the *Individual Record Sheet for Writing* (page 330) to keep track of when a student appears to regularly be able to apply the concepts taught during mini-lesson instruction. The formative assessments suggested in the mini-lessons serve as quick indicators of mastery levels. As needed, follow up with individuals or small groups with additional instruction in the mini-lesson topics. Using the class checklist, you can easily see who to pull together for a small group lesson. At this level, students can also be responsible for self-evaluations. Have them keep a *My Writing Record Sheet (3–5)* (page 329) with their writing folders. You can have them use this as an ongoing record, or use it once a quarter and give them time to reflect on how they are doing. They will also benefit from comparing a previously filled-in record sheet to a new one. This enables them to chart growth in their own work over time.

Rubrics should reflect your district, school, or state standards. When creating a rubric, consider the criteria. Categories of how you will assess students should be shared ahead of time. This is the road map for their work. If you want them to write narratives and create categories, such as *beginning, middle (climax), end (resolution), setting*, and *character (protagonist, antagonist)*, give the range of how these will be graded. (*1 = does not show understanding of establishing setting, 2 = attempts to establish setting, but needs further development, 3 = establishes setting*). Also, the possible scores for each writing aspect should be accompanied by specific descriptors. This way both students and the

Writing

teacher understand what the score really means. For example, a rubric might offer three scores for the level of detail in a paragraph—3 = one or two broad ideas with at least two descriptive details including a mix of adjectives, sensory details, similes, metaphors, or hyperbole; 2 = one or two broad ideas with at least two descriptive details using simple adjectives; and 1 = one or two broad ideas. A student who receives a score on this rubric knows what he or she did well and knows what he or she can add to the next writing piece to improve.

Letting students know the level of quality you will accept is important, thereby making the rubric instructional (Andrade 2000). Sharing how a student was scored afterwards develops metacognition (Skillings and Ferrell 2000). When students learn to talk about and reflect on their writing, the goal is to have them apply new concepts during their independent writing.

Grade 6 through grade 8 students can be assessed using checklists, self-evaluation checklists, and rubrics. Use the *Mini-Lessons Class Checklist (6–8)* (page 335) to keep track of when you provide mini-lessons. Small groups can be created for any of the mini-lessons. Through observation of students' participation in the lesson along with ongoing independent writing, you can choose the order as well as the need to repeat particular topics. Use the *Individual Record Sheet for Writing* (page 331) to keep track of when the student appears to regularly be able to apply the concepts taught during the mini-lesson. The formative assessments suggested in the mini-lessons can be a quick indicator of who is mastering or still needs to master particular skills. As needed, follow up with individuals or small groups with additional instruction. Using the class checklist, you can easily see who to pull together for a small-group lesson. Students should also be responsible to self-evaluate at this level. Have them keep *My Writing Record Sheet* (page 332) to self-evaluate. You can have them use this as an ongoing record, or use it once a quarter and give students time to reflect on how they are doing. They will benefit from comparing a previously filled-in record to a new one to evaluate growth in their own work.

Rubrics should reflect your state, district, or school standards. When creating a rubric, consider the criteria you consider important. Categories of how you will assess students should be shared ahead of time. This is the road map for their work. If you want them to write informative/explanatory pieces, create categories, such as *main idea (focus)*, *organization (structure)*, and *evidence*, and the language that gives the range of how these will be graded. Rubrics can have three to six levels with descriptors of quality (Tompkins 2002). Letting students know the level of quality you will accept is important, making the rubric both instructional and for assessment (Andrade 2000). Students can also self-assess and meet with you later to compare how you scored the rubric (Tompkins 2013). When students talk about and reflect on their writing, their development of metacognition assists them in applying new concepts during independent writing.

Journals

Introduction to Journal Writing

Journals are the perfect writing place for students to play with ideas, form, and words, as well as pose questions about the world around them. "Journal writing engages students' thinking through different cognitive processes such as prediction, brainstorming, reflection, and questioning. It encourages students to express their interests, thinking and curiosity about the world around them, and discover new ideas" (Al-Rawahi and Al-Balushi 2015, 368). It should be a safe place to express ideas, not worry about trying the spelling of an unknown word, and provide the place to think "out loud" on paper. Journals are an excellent opportunity for expressive writing. "Children's journal writing is often spontaneous and loosely organized, and it contains more mechanical errors than other types of writing because children are focusing on thinking, not on spelling and other mechanical considerations" (Tompkins 2008, 102). An important management issue of using journals in your classroom is to decide what the purpose is of this type of writing.

1. Do you want students to have a place for writing with less structure that does not need revision and editing?

   - *Kindergarten through grade 2* students can draw first, and then write. Ten minutes can be set aside in the literacy block to allow everyone, including you, to focus on their journal writing. Model for students how you get started, thinking about something in your life, something you read that reminded you of something else. In this format, any topic is appropriate.

   - *Grade 3 through grade 5* students can write about topics of personal concern and interest. These can be connected to their lives or something occurring at school. Sometimes, this is where we get a hint about bullying or a stressful home situation.

   - *Grade 6 through grade 8* students can use it as a diary. Have students write entries about what is going on in their lives, or as a place to ponder, question, and think about the world around them.

2. Do you want students to write about topics of choice, or do you want to offer some topics that can be chosen if they are stuck for an idea?

   - *Kindergarten through grade 2* students can suggest topics that relate to students' lives, such as the school play or an upcoming holiday.

   - *Grade 3 through grade 5* students can pose questions that connect to their lives and the world around them, such as wonder questions (*I wonder what Mars is like?*), rhetorical questions (*Do I really want to own a dog?*), and *what if* questions (*What if I woke up and was invisible to my family?*).

   - *Grade 6 through grade 8* students can pose questions that challenge them to think, such as critical questions about values and norms (*Should all students be tested? What do I feel would be the perfect day?*), and problem-solving questions (*What would make college accessible to more students?*).

3. Do you want a journal where you can dialogue with students or they can dialogue with a friend?

- *Kindergarten through grade 2* students can flag any pages they want you to read and respond to.

- *Grade 3 through grade 5* students can flag pages they want you or another student to respond to. Use different color sticky notes to signal who the reader should be. Ask students to pick one entry each week for you or a friend to read.

- In *grade 6 through grade 8* students can flag a page for a peer to read and write a response to. Plan a short time each week or every other week for this journal exchange.

4. Do you want students to use their journal to reflect and respond to specific topics, such as a book (read aloud or independent) or a field experience?

- *Kindergarten through grade 2* students can draw or write, as appropriate, their favorite part of the story or field experience.

- *Grade 3 through grade 5* students can write about a topic or book you want them to respond to.

- *Grade 6 through grade 8* students can make suggestions of topics they want to write about, such as 100 Things I Like. You can add your own, including a shared read aloud, and offer a menu of options for students to select from for their entries.

5. Do you want them to use the journal as a learning log for a class project?

- *Kindergarten through grade 2* students can draw or write, as appropriate, something new they learned.

- *Grade 3 through grade 5* students can write a summary of what they learned each day, using the new vocabulary they are learning.

- *Grade 6 through grade 8* students can to reflect on something learned in another class. What still puzzles them? What surprised them? Encourage them to use the new vocabulary they are learning.

Best Practices for Journal Writing

There are various ways to organize journals in your classroom, and it depends a great deal on the type or types of journals you have students write, as well as how they can best be accessed and used by students. Any of the following might be perfect for your classroom:

Students keep a bound journal. Here they enter ideas they are thinking about, which can later be used as inspiration for assigned writing. Students can write about problems they are wrestling with and activities in their lives they want to talk about.

Students keep an organized three-ring notebook. Pages can be added and sections can be divided with tabs labeling the entrie. Example sections should be *Writing Ideas, Inspirational Pictures, Cool Words I Heard Today, My Word Bank, Things I Wonder About, Book Responses,* and *My Life.* Pages can also easily be taken out of the notebook and handed in if they are asking you to respond or you are checking their entry if you assigned a topic. This approach is easier to manage for you as well—no avalanche of notebooks!

Students can dialogue with you and/or other students. This is easily accomplished when the student paper clips a page he or she wants you to read and respond to. You can write back or use time during a writing conference to dialogue about the entry.

Students can respond to independent reading books. Ask them to write about the ending, the characters, or about what surprised them, puzzled them, or confirmed what they guessed might happen.

Students can use their journal to keep a record of books read independently. *My Independent Reading Log* (page 314) can be kept in a three-ring binder journal.

Students can keep a record of writing topics of pieces they have already written. You can encourage them to consult their journals not only for inspiration but also for a check on the topics already used.

Get the Year Started with Journals

1. Say, "Students, today we are going to start our journals. This journal will be a place where we can think and write. I'm going to write down three things that happened in my life." Write several events, such as attending your sister's soccer game, riding the bus into the city, or eating lunch with a new teacher.

2. Say, "Next, let's take this list and turn each of the events into a beginning sentence about what happened. For example, *Yesterday I went to my sister's soccer game.* Okay, now I need to decide which one I am going to write about and list the sequence of events connected to it. What happened first? Then what? My ideas are: *drove to the field, stood on the sidelines, started to rain, mud!* Now, let's turn those into sentences. I have to add some transitions and more details to make a complete entry. I think I'll write, *Yesterday I went to my sister's soccer game. We had to drive across town at rush hour. We were nervous that we wouldn't make it on time, but we did! We stood on the sidelines and cheered and cheered for the team. But, soon it began to rain. We ran to the car to get umbrellas. The field got very muddy. My sister slid in to make a goal and got very muddy! But they won the game!*"

3. Say, "Okay, everyone, let's have you try to write a journal entry of your own. Begin by listing at least three events from your own life." Circulate to assist students as needed.

Many **children's books** can be used during mini-lessons as models of journal writing, such as the following:

- *The Diary of a Worm* by Doreen Cronin (2003)

- *Diary of a Wimpy Kid* series by Jeff Kinney (2007)

- *Amelia's Notebook* by Marissa Moss (2006)

- *The Journal of Douglas Allen Deeds: The Donner Party Expedition* by Rodman Philbrick (2002)

Writing

4. Say, "Now, I would like you to pair up and share. Read your list of events to each other, and help each other pick one to write about." Circulate as student pairs talk, assisting as needed.

5. Exclaim, "Great! Everyone has picked one event to write about. Now, I want you to list the sequence of events connected to that one. What happened first? Then what? Write down your ideas." Circulate as the classmates talk to assist students.

6. Say, "Good, now let's share this new list with our friend. Does he or she think I have enough details to write about? Make suggestions or ask questions of each other." Circulate as students talk and assist as needed.

7. Say, "Now that we have reviewed that list, I would like you to take your sequence of events and turn them into sentences. You might need to add transitions (*next*, *and then*, and *finally*) or more details to complete the entry. When you are done, share with your partner."

Journal Use Ideas

- Have students use their journal entries for story ideas. An entry about a soccer game, for example, can become a narrative about a family, an explanatory piece of the sport, or a poem about a game.

- Give students 5–10 small (1" × 2") pieces of card stock. Ask them to comb through their entries to find interesting words. Ask them to write those on the cards. You can thumbtack them to a bulletin board or use spray adhesive and add them to magnets. Put them all together and let students move them around to make poetry. Have some blank cards so they can add other words.

- Ask students to bring in a family photo and staple it to a journal page. How does that inspire an entry?

- Ask students to take an entry and make a comic strip of the events they wrote about.

Conclusion

This section addressed how to organize writing instruction in kindergarten through grade 8. By having a multifaceted approach to teaching writing, teachers give students many opportunities to learn skills and expand their expertise. As they watch modeled writing lessons, they help them consider how to write under various circumstances. In shared writing, they ask students to step up and take part under tutelage. Success abounds in shared writing because you can choose who assists where and how much they participate, and you can craft a lesson that teaches and engages students. During Writer's Workshop, students spread their wings and independently write. Applying what they learned in modeled and shared writing, students can assume responsibility for their writing. Journals provide a place for thoughtful, free flowing writing or guided responses. Without a doubt, learning to write well is a skill that will serve students throughout their lives.

Reflection and Discussion Questions

1. Discuss Anaïs Nin's (1976, 13) quote, "We write to taste life twice, in the moment and in retrospect." How can you apply this idea to what you do with your students when discussing their writing?

2. Share writing prompts you have used that were particularly successful. Why do you think students responded so well?

3. How can you help someone who has reluctant writers in his or her classroom? Share stories about the ways you inspire students to write.

4. Share books that you read to the class that prompted writing from your students. What about the book appealed to them?

5. How can you develop grade-level rubrics to evaluate student writing? How will they differ according to genre?

6. Gather writing samples. Share your evaluation of how students are meeting grade-level-standards. What more can you do to improve some particular skill in writing? Use Appendix C in the Common Core State Standards (http://www.corestandards.org/assets/Appendix_C.pdf) to compare your students' work with those presented to critique skills.

7. What are some graphic organizers you use to help your students during the prewriting phase? How did the students like using them? Are there some you would recommend?

8. Share some students' published pieces. Do you see this part of the Writer's Workshop as important for your students? How often do they publish?

9. Discuss the use of mentor texts. How can we inspire students with such texts, without limiting their creativity?

10. Share personal writing, such as a story, poem, or journal entry, and respond to each other's writing. Start a dialogue journal between your grade-level teachers.

Writing

References Cited

Ada, Alma Flor. 2004. *With Love, Little Red Hen.* New York, NY: Antheneum Books for Young Readers.

Adams, Marilyn J. 1990. *Beginning to Read: Thinking and Learning About Print.* Cambridge, MA: Massachusetts Institute of Technology Press.

Adams, Marilyn J. 1998. "The Three-Cueing System." *Literacy For All Issues In Teaching and Learning,* 73–99. New York, NY: Guilford Press.

Adler, Bill. 2002. *Kids' Letters to Harry Potter From Around the World.* Philadelphia, PA: Running Press.

Al-Rawahi, Nawar M., and Sulaiman M. Al-Balushi. 2015. "The Effect Of Reflective Science Journal Writing On Students' Self-Regulated Learning Strategies." *International Journal Of Environmental and Science Education* 10(3): 367–379.

Allred, Ruel A. 1977. *Spelling, the Application of Research Findings.* Washington D.C.: National Education Association.

Allington, Richard L, and Anne McGill-Franzen. 2003. "The Impact of Summer Reading Setback on the Reading Achievement Gap." *Phi Delta Kappan.* 85 (1): 68–75.

Andrade, Heidi Goodrich. 2000. "Using Rubrics to Promote Thinking and Learning." *Educational Leadership,* 57.(5): 13–18.

Armbruster, Bonnie B., Fran Lehr, and Jean Osborn. 2001. *Put Reading First: The Research Building Blocks for Teaching Children to Read Kindergarten through Grade 3.* Washington, D.C.: National Institute for Literacy, National Institute of Child Health and Human Development, US Department of Education.

Baumann, James F. and Edward J. Kame'enui. 1991. "Research on Vocabulary Instruction: Ode To Voltaire." In *Handbook of Research on Teaching the English Language Arts,* edited by James Flood, Diane Lapp, Julie J. Jensen, and James R. Squire. 1:604–632. New York, NY: MacMillan.

Baumann, James, George Font, Cathleen A. Tereshinski, Edward J. Kame'enui, and Stephen Olejnik. 2002. "Teaching Morphemic and Contextual Analysis to Fifth-Grade Students." *Reading Research Quarterly* 37 (2): 150–176.

Bear, Donald E. and Shane Templeton. 1998. "Explorations in Developmental Spelling: Foundations for Learning and Teaching Phonics, Spelling, and Vocabulary." *The Reading Teacher* 52 (3): 222–242.

Beck, Isabel and Margaret McKeown. 1991. "Conditions of Vocabulary Acquisition." *Handbook of Reading Research (Vol. 2),* edited by Rebecca Barr, Michael L. Kamil, Peter Mosenthal. and P.David Pearson. New York, NY: Longman.

Beck, Isabel, Margaret McKeown, and Richard Omanson. 1991. "The Effects and Uses of Diverse Vocabulary Instructional Techniques." *The Nature of Vocabulary Acquisition,* edited by Margaret G. McKeown and Mary E. Curtis. Hoboken, NJ: Taylor and Francis.

Beck, Isabel L., Margaret G. McKeown, and Linda Kucan. 2013. *Bringing Words to Life: Robust Vocabulary Instruction.* New York, NY: Guilfor.

Appendix A

Betts, Emmett A. 1946. *Foundations of Reading Instruction, with Emphasis on Differentiated Guidance.* New York, NY: American Book.

Biemiller, Andrew. 2010. "Size and Sequence in Vocabulary Development: Implications for Choosing Words for Primary Grade Vocabulary Instruction." *Teaching and Learning Vocabulary: Bringing Research to Practice*, edited by Elfrieda H. Hiebert. Mahwah, N.J.: L. Erlbaum Associates.

Blessing, Candy. 2005. "Reading to Kids Who Are Old Enough to Shave." *School Library Journal* 51 (4): 44–45.

Borden, Louise. 2004. *Sea Clocks: The Story of Longitude.* New York, NY: Margaret K. McElderry Publishing.

Bruner, Jerome. 1986. *Actual Minds, Possible Worlds.* Cambridge, Mass.: Harvard University Press.

Calkins, Lucy. 1985. *The Art of Teaching Writing.* Portsmouth, NH: Heinemann.

Cameron, Claire E., Carol McDonald Connor, and Frederick J. Morrison. 2005. "The Effects of Variation in Teacher Organization on Classroom Functioning." *Journal of School Psychology* 43(1): 61-85.

Camp, Deanne. 2000. "It Takes Two: Teaching with Twin Texts of Fact and Fiction." *The Reading Teacher* 53 (3): 400–408.

Campbell, Terry A., and Michelle Hlusek. 2009. "Storytelling and Story Writing." *What Works? Research into Practice.* Ontario, Canada: Ontario Ministry of Education.

Chall, Jeanne S. 1967. *Learning to Read: The Great Debate; an Inquiry into the Science, Art, and Ideology of Old and New Methods of Teaching Children to Read, 1910-1965.* New York: McGraw-Hill.

Chall, Jeanne S. 1983. *Stages of Reading Development.* Fort Worth, TX: Harcourt Brace.

Chall, Jeanne S., and Vicki A. Jacobs. 1990. *The Reading Crisis: Why Poor Children Fall Behind.* Cambridge, Mass.: Harvard University Press.

The Charles A. Dana Center at the University of Texas at Austin and Agile Mind, Inc. 2015. "Culture of Learning." *Learning and the Adolescent Mind.* Accessed September 22, 2015 http://learningandtheadolescentmind.org/ideas_community.html.

Charman, Andrew. 2003. *I Wonder Why Trees Have Leaves: And Other Questions About Plants.* New York, NY: Kingfisher.

Chomsky, Noam, and Morris Halle. 1968. *The Sound Pattern of English.* New York, NY: Harper and Row.

Clay, Marie. 2006. *An Observation Survey of Early Literacy Achievement.* Portsmouth, NH: Heinemann.

Committee on Communications. 2006. "Children, Adolescents, and Advertisting. *Pediatrics,* 118(6): 2563–2569.

Coxhead, Averil. 2000. "A New Academic Word List." *TESOL Quarterly* 34(2) 213-238.

Coyne, Michael, Deborah Simmons, Edward Kame'enui, & Michael Stoolmiller. 2004. "Teaching Vocabulary During Shared Storybook Readings: An Examination of Differential Effects." *Exceptionality* 12 (3): 145–162.

Cronin, Doreen. 2000. *Click, Clack, Moo Cows That Type.* New York, NY: Little Simon and Schuster.

Cronin, Doreen. 2003. *Diary of a Worm.* New York, NY: HarperCollins.

Crystal, David. 2011. "From Riddle to Twittersphere: David Crystal Tells the Story of English in 100 Words." *The Telegraph.* Telegraph Media Group.

Cunningham, James, W., Stephanie A. Spadorcia, Karen A. Erickson, David A. Koppenhaver, Janet M. Sturm, and David E Yoder. 2005. "Investigating the Instructional Supportiveness of Leveled Texts." *Reading Research Quarterly* 40(4): 410-427.

Cunningham, Patricia M., Dorothy P. Hall, and Margaret Defee. 1998. "Nonability-Grouped, Multilevel Instruction: Eight Years Later." *Reading Teacher* 51 (8): 652–664.

Cunningham, Patricia M., and Richard L. Allington. 1999. *Classrooms That Work: They Can All Read and Write.* 2nd ed. New York, NY: Longman.

DiCamillo, Kate. 2000. *Because of Winn-Dixie.* New York: Candlewick Press.

DiCamillo, Kate. 2003. *The Tale of Despereaux.* New York: Candlewick Press.

DiCamillo, Kate. 2001. *The Tiger Rising.* New York: Candlewick Press.

Dierking, Connie Campbell, and Sherra Ann Jones. 2003. *Growing up Writing: Mini-lessons for Emergent and Beginning Writers.* Gainesville, FL: Maupin House.

Dolch, Edward William. 1936. "A Basic Sight Vocabulary." *The Elementary School Journal* (36): 456–460.

Dorn, Linda J., and Carla Soffos. 2001. *Scaffolding Young Writers: A Writers' Workshop Approach.* Portland, ME: Stenhouse.

Duke, Nell. 2000. "3.6 Minutes Per Day: The Scarcity of Informational Texts in First Grade." *Reading Research Quarterly* 35 (2): 202–224.

Dymock, Susan, and Tom Nicholson. 2010. "High 5! Strategies To Enhance Comprehension Of Expository Text." *The Reading Teacher* 64 (3): 166–178.

Dzaldov, Brenda Stein, and Shelley Peterson. 2005. "Book Leveling and Readers." *The Reading Teacher* 59 (3): 222–229.

Edwards, A.W. F. 2004. *Cogwheels of the Mind: The Story of Venn Diagrams.* Baltimore, MD: John Hopkins University Press.

Ehri, Linnea C. 1991. "Development of the Ability to Read Words." *Handbook of Reading Research.* edited by Rebecca Barr, Michael L. Kamil, Peter Mosenthal. and P.David Pearson. New York, NY: Longman.

Ehri, Linnea C. 2005. "Learning to Read Words: Theory, Findings, and Issues." *Scientific Studies of Reading* 9(2): 167-188.

Ehri, Linnea C. 2004. "Teaching Phonemic Awareness and Phonics: An Explanation of the National Reading Panel Meta-analysis." *The Voice of Evidence in Reading Research,* edited by Peggy McCardle and Vinita Chhabra. Baltimore, MD: Paul H. Brookes.

Ehri, Linnea C., and Theresa Roberts. 2006. "The Roots of Learning to Read and Write: Acquisition of Letters and Phonemic Awareness." In *Handbook of Early Literacy Research, Vol. 2*, edited by David K. Dickinson and Susan B. Neuman. 113–131.

Ehri, Linnea C., Simone Nunes, Dale Willows, Barbara Valeska Schuster, Zohreh Yaghoub-Zadeh, and Timothy Shanahan. 2001. "Phonemic Awareness Instruction Helps Children Learn To Read: Evidence From The National Reading Panel's Meta-Analysis." *Reading Research Quarterly* 36(3): 250-287.

Elbow, Peter. 2002. "Writing to Publish is for Every Student." In *Publishing With Students: A Comprehensive Guide*, edited by Chris Weber. Portsmouth, NH: Heinemann.

Eldredge, J. Lloyd. 2004. *Phonics for Teachers: Self-Instruction, Methods, and Activities, 2nd edition.* Upper Saddle River, NJ: Pearson.

Encyclopedia of Children's Health. "Auditory Discrimination Test." Accessed December 22, 2015 http://www.healthofchildren.com/A/Auditory-Discrimination-Test.html.

Fearn, Leif and Nancy Farnan. 1998. *Writing Effectively: Helping Children Master the Conventions of Writing.* Boston, MA: Allyn and Bacon.

Fisher, Douglas. "Close Reading and the CCSS, Part 1." *Common Core State Standards Toolbox.* McGraw Hill. Accessed on September 13, 2015. http://www.mhecommoncoretoolbox.com/close-reading-and-the-ccss-part-1.html.

Fisher, Douglas and Nancy Frey. 2013. "A Range of Writing Across the Content Areas." *The Reading Teacher*, 67(2): 96–101.

Flesch, Rudolph. 1955. *Why Johnny Can't Read and What You Can Do About It.* New York: Harper & Row.

Ford, Michael P., and Michael F. Opitz. 2008. "Guided Reading: Then and Now." *An Essential History of Current Reading Practices.* Edited by Mary Jo Fresch. Newark, NJ: International Reading Association, 66-81.

Foresman, Scott. 1971. *I Like.* Glenville, IL: Scott Foresman.

Fountas, Irene C., and Gay Su Pinnell. 1996. *Guided Reading: Good First Teaching for All Children.* Portsmouth, NH: Heinemann.

Fresch, Mary Jo. 2014. *Engaging Minds in English Language Arts Classrooms: The Surprising Power of Joy.* Alexandria, VA: ASCD.

Fresch, Mary Jo. 2003. "A National Survey of Spelling Instruction: Investigating Teachers' Beliefs and Practice." *J. of Literacy Res. Journal of Literacy Research HJLR* (1): 819–48.

Fresch, Mary Jo. 2005. "Observing the Self-Selection of an Emerging Literacy Learner." *Reading and Writing Quarterly,* 21(2): 135–149.

Fresch, Mary Jo. 1995. "Self-Selection of Early Literacy Learners." *Reading Teacher.* 49 (3): 220–227.

Fresch, Mary Jo. 2007. "Teachers' Concerns About Spelling Instruction: A National Survey." *Reading Psychology* (1): 301–30.

Fresch, Mary Jo, and Aileen Wheaton. 2002. *Teaching and Assessing Spelling: A Practical Approach that Strikes the Balance Between Whole-group and Individualized Instruction.* New York, NY: Scholastic.

Fresch, Mary Jo, and David L. Harrison. 2013. *Learning Through Poetry: Consonants.* Huntington Beach, CA: Shell Education.

Fresch, Mary Jo, and Peggy Harkins. 2014. "Picture Books Across the Curriculum: Meeting the Challenges of Intermediate Grade Learners." *The Dragon Lode* 33 (1): 46–62.

Fresch, Mary Jo, and Peggy Harkins. 2009. *The Power of Picture Books: Using Content Area Literature in Middle School.* Urbana, IL: National Council of Teachers of English.

Frey, Nancy. 2010. *The Effective Teacher's Guide: 50 Ways to Engage Students and Promote Interactive Learning.* New York, NY: Guildford Press.

Fry, Edward. 2002. "Readability Versus Leveling." *The Reading Teacher* 56.3: 286-291.

Gallagher, Kelly. 2014. "Making The Most Of Mentor Texts." *Educational Leadership,* 71(7): 28–33.

Gladwell, Malcolm. 2008. *Outliers: The Story of Success.* New York, NY: Little, Brown and Co.

Goodman, Kenneth S., and Yetta M. Goodman. 1979. "Learning to Read Is Natural." *Theory and Practice of Early Reading*, Vol. 1. Hillsdale, NJ: Erlbaum.

Graves, Donald H. 1983. *Writing: Teachers and Children at Work.* Portsmouth, NH: Heinemann.

Graves, Michael. 2000. "A Vocabulary Program to Complement and Bolster a Middle-Grade Comprehension Program." *Reading for Meaning: Fostering Comprehension is the Middle Grades*, edited by Barbara M. Taylor, Michael Graves, and Paulus Willem van den Broek. New York, NY: Teachers College.

Graves, Michael F. 2006. *The Vocabulary Book: Learning & Instruction.* New York, NY: Teacher's College.

Gray, William S. 1919. "Principles of Method in Teaching Reading, As Derived from Scientific Investigation." In *The Eighteenth Yearbook of the National Society for the Study of Education, Part II: Fourth Report of the Committee on Economy of Time in Education*, edited by Guy Montrose Whipple. Bloomington, IL: Public School Publishing.

Gray, William S., and May Hill Arbuthnot. 1946. *Fun with Dick and Jane.* Chicago: Scott, Foresman and Company.

Gunning, Thomas G. 2013. *Creating Literacy Instruction for All Students. 9th Edition.* Boston: Pearson.

Hairrell, Angela, Meaghan Edmonds, Sharon Vaughn, and Deborah Simmons. 2010. "Independent Silent Reading for Struggling Readers: Pitfalls and Potential." In *Revisiting Silent Reading: New Directions for Teachers and Researchers*, edited by Elfrieda H. Hiebert and D. Ray Reutzel. 275–289.

Harris, Theodore L., and Richard E. Hodges, editors. 1995. *The Literacy Dictionary: The Vocabulary of Reading and Writing.* Newark, DE: International Reading Association.

Harrison, David L. 2003. *Oceans: The Vast, Mysterious Deep.* Honesdale, PA: Boyds Mills Press.

Hart, Betty, and Todd R. Risley. 1995. *Meaningful Differences in the Everyday Experience of Young American Children*. Baltimore, MD: P.H. Brookes.

Harvey, Stephanie and Anne Goudvis. 2000. *Strategies that Work: Teaching Comprehension to Enhance Understanding*. Portland, ME: Stenhouse.

Henderson, Edmund H. 1992. *Development of Orthographic Knowledge and the Foundation of Literacy: A Memorial Festschrift for Edmund H. Henderson*, edited by Shane Templeton and Donald Bear. Hillsdale, NJ: L. Erlbaum Associates.

Henderson, Edmund H. 1981. *Learning to Read and Spell: The Child's Knowledge of Words*. DeKalb, IL: Northern Illinois UP.

Hine, Jeffrey F., Scott P. Ardoin, and Tori E. Foster. 2015. "Decreasing Transition Times in Elementary School Classrooms: Using Computer-Assisted Instruction to Automate Intervention Components." *Journal of Applied Behavior Analysis* 48(3): 495–510.

Hodges, Richard E. 1977. "In Adam's Fall: A Brief History of Spelling Instruction in the United States." In *Reading & Writing Instruction in the United States: Historical Trends*, edited by H. Alan Robinson. Newark, NJ: International Reading Association.

Hoffman, Mary. 1991. *Amazing Grace*. New York, NY: Reading Rainbow Books.

Horn, Ernest. 1926. *A Basic Writing Vocabulary, 10,000 Words Most Commonly Used in Writing*. Iowa City, IA: University of Iowa College of Education.

Hughey, Jane B. and Charlotte Slack. 2001. *Teaching Children to Write: Theory into Practice*. Upper Saddle River. NJ: Prentice-Hall.

Hugo, Victor. 2009. *Les Miserables*. Translated by Julie Rose. New York, NY: Random House.

Hurst, Sylvia and Priscilla Griffity. 2015. "Examining the Effects of Teacher Read-Aloud on Adolescent Attitudes and Learning." *Middle Grades Research Journal* 10 (1): 31–47.

Hutchins, Pat. 1977. *Rosie's Walk*. New York: Scholastic.

Keane, Nancy. 2015. "Book Talks—Quick and Simple." Accessed September 18, 2015. http://nancykeane.com/booktalks/faq.htm.

Kim, Soo Hyon. 2015. "Preparing English Learners for Effective Peer Review in the Writer's Workshop." *The Reading Teacher*, 68(8): 599–603.

Kinney, Jeff. 2007. *Diary of a Wimpy Kid*. New York, NY: Amulet.

Korman, Gordon. 2007. *Schooled*. New York, NY: Hyperion.

Mackenzie, Noella M. 2015. "Interactive Writing: A Powerful Teaching Strategy." *Practical Literacy: The Early and Primary Years*, 20(3): 36–38.

Mariage, TV. 2001. "Features Of An Interactive Writing Discourse: Conversational Involvement, Conventional Knowledge, And Internalization In 'Morning Message.' *Journal Of Learning Disabilities* 34(2): 172–196.

Math Is Fun. 2015. "Cube Net (with tabs) Template." Accessed April 20, 2015. http://www.mathsisfun.com/geometry/cube-model.html.

McKeown, Regina G, and James L. Gentilucci. 2007. "Think Aloud Strategy: Metacognitive Development and Monitoring Comprehension in the Middle School Second-Language Setting." *Journal of Adolescent and Adult Literacy* 51 (2): 136–147.

McLaughlin, Maureen and Glenn L. DeVoogd. 2004. *Critical Literacy: Enhancing Students' Comprehension of Text*. New York, NY: Scholastic.

Miller, Beth M. 2007. *The Learning Season: The Untapped Power of Summer to Advance Student Achievement*. Accessed December 7, 2015. http://dmlcentral.net/wp-content/uploads/files/Learning_Season_ES.pdf.

Morrisette, Sharon. 2012. *Toads and Tessellations*. Watertown, MA: Charlesbridge.

Moss, Marissa. 2006. *Amelia's Notebook*. New York, NY: Simon and Schuster.

Nagy, William, and Anderson, Richard. 1984. "How Many Words are There in Printed School English?" *Reading Research Quarterly*. (19): 304–330.

National Governors Association Center for Best Practices (NGA), Council of Chief State School Officers (CCSSO). 2010. *Common Core State English Language Arts Standards*. Washington D.C.: National Governors Association Center for Best Practices, Council of Chief State School Officers.

National Institute of Child Health and Human Development. 2000. *Report Of The National Reading Panel: Teaching Children to Read: An Evidence-Based Assessment of the Scientific Research Literature on Reading and Its Implications for Reading Instruction*. Washington, DC: U.S. Government Printing Office.

National Reading Panel, National Institute of Child Health, and Human Development. 2000. *Report of the National Reading Panel: Teaching Children to Read: An Evidence-Based Assessment of the Scientific Research Literature on Reading and Its Implications for Reading Instruction: Reports of the Subgroups*. National Institute of Child Health and Human Development, National Institutes of Health.

Nin, Anaïs. 1976. *In Favor of the Sensitive Man and Other Essays*. San Diego: Harcourt Brace.

Oliveira, Alandeom W. 2015. "Reading Engagement in Science: Elementary Student Read-Aloud Experiences." *International Journal of Environmental and Science Education* 10 (3): 429–451.

Opitz, Michael F., and James Erekson. 2015. *Understanding, Assessing, and Teaching Reading: A Diagnostic Approach*. Boston, MA: Pearson.

Opitz, Michael F., and Matthew D. Zbaracki. 2004. *Listen Hear! 25 Effective Listening Comprehension Strategies*. Portsmouth, NH: Heinemann.

Opitz, Michael F. and Timothy V. Rasinski. 1998. *Good-bye Round Robin: 25 Effective Oral Reading Strategies*. Portsmouth, NH: Heinemann.

Orloff, Karen Kaufman. 2004. *I Wanna Iguana*. New York, NY: G. P. Putnam.

Ortiz, Rosario, Adelina Estévez, Mercedes Muñetón, and Carolina Domínguez. 2014. "Visual and Auditory Perception in Preschool Children at Risk for Dyslexia." *Research in Developmental Disabilities* 35(11) 2673–2680.

Peebles, Jodi L. 2007. "Incorporating Movement with Fluency Instruction: A Motivation for Struggling Readers." *The Reading Teacher* 60(6): 578–581.

Philbrick, Rodman. 2002. *The Journal of Douglas Allen Deeds: The Donner Party Expedition*. New York, NY: Scholastic.

Piasta, Shayne B. 2014. "Moving to Assessment-Guided Differentiated Instruction to Support Young Children's Alphabet Knowledge." *The Reading Teacher* 68 (3): 202–211.

Piasta, Shayne B., Laura M. Justice, Anita S. McGinty, and Joan N. Kaderavek. 2012. "Increasing Young Children's Contact With Print During Shared Reading: Longitudinal Effects of Literacy Achievement." *Child Development* 83 (3): 810–820.

Piazza, Carolyn L. 2003. *Journeys: The Teaching of Writing in Elementary Classrooms*. Upper Saddle River, NJ: Pearson.

Pikulski, John J. and David J. Chard. 2005. "Fluency: Bridge Between Decoding and Reading Comprehension." *The Reading Teacher* 58 (6): 510–519.

Pinnell, Gay Su, and Andrea McCarrier. 1994. "Interactive Writing: A Transition Tool for Assisting Children in Learning to Read and Write." In *Getting Reading Right from the Start: Effective Early Literacy Interventions*, edited by Elfrieda H. Hiebert and Barbara M. Taylor 1:149–170. Needham, MA: Allyn and Bacon.

Raphael, Taffy E., and Kathryn H. Au. 2005. "QAR: Enhancing Comprehension and Test Taking Across Grades and Content Areas." The Reading Teacher 59(3) 206-221.

Rasinski, Timothy V. 2012. "Why Reading Fluency Should be Hot!" *The Reading Teacher* 65 (8): 516–522.

Rasinski, Timothy, Nancy Pedak, Rick Newton, and Evangeline Newton. 2008. *Greek and Latin Roots: Keys to Building Vocabulary*. Huntington Beach, CA: Shell Education.

Ray, Katie Wood. 2004. "When Kids Make Books." *Educational Leadership*, 62(2):14–18.

Read, Charles. 1971. "Pre-School Children's Knowledge of English Phonology." *Harvard Educational Review* (1): 1–34.

Read, Sylvia. 2010. "A Model For Scaffolding Writing Instruction: IMSCI." *The Reading Teacher,* 64(1): 47–52.

Reading is Fundamental. 2015. *Encouraging Young Writers*. Accessed 23 September 2015 http://www.rif.org/us/literacy-resources/articles/encouraging-young-writers.htm.

Rice, Joseph. 1897. "The Utility of the Spelling Grind." *The Forum.* (23): 409–419.

Richardson, Judy S. 2000. *Read it Aloud Using Literature in the Secondary Content Classroom*. Newark, DE: International Reading Association.

Rog, Lori Jamison, and Wilfred Burton. 2002. "Matching Texts and Readers: Leveling Early Reading Materials for Assessment and Instruction." *The Reading Teacher* 55 (4): 348–356.

Rosenstock, Barb. 2014. *The Streak: How Joe DiMaggio Became America's Hero*. Honesdale, PA: Calkins Creek.

Rowling, J.K. 1998. *Harry Potter and the Sorcerer's Stone*. New York, NY: Scholastic.

Ruddell, Robert B. 2009. *How to Teach Reading to Elementary and Middle School Students: Practical Ideas from Highly Effective Teachers*. Boston, MA: Pearson.

Schunk, Dale H. 2003. "Self-Efficacy for Reading and Writing: Influence of Modeling, Goal Setting, and Self-Evaluation." *Reading and Writing Quarterly*, 19(2): 159–172.

Skillings, Mary Jo and Robbin Ferrell. 2000. "Student-generated Rubrics: Bringing Students Into the Assessment Process." *The Reading Teacher*, 53(6): 452–455.

Smith, Frank. 2006. *Reading without Nonsense*. 4th ed. New York: Teachers College Press.

Smith, J. Lea and J. Daniel Herring. 1996. "Literature Alive: Connecting to Story Through the Arts." *Reading Horizons* 37 (2): 102–115.

Snow, Catherine E. 2002. *Reading for Understanding Toward an RandD Program in Reading Comprehension*. Santa Monica, CA: Rand.

Standiford, Natalie. 1989. *The Bravest Dog Ever: The True Story of Balto*. New York, NY: Random House.

Stanovich, Keith E. 1986. "Matthew Effects in Reading: Some Consequences of Individual Difference in the Acquisition of Literacy. *Reading Research Quarterly* 21(1): 360–407.

Stanovich, Keith E. 1993. "Romance and Reality." The Reading Teacher 47(4): 280-291.

Sturm, Janet M. 2012. "An Enriches Writers' Workshop for Beginning Writers in Developmental Disabilities." *Topics in Language Disorders*, 32(4): 335–360.

Swanborn, Machteld S.L., and Kees De Glopper. 1999. "Incidental Word Learning While Reading: A Meta-Analysis." *Review of Educational Research* (1): 261–85.

Taylor, Barbara M., P. David Pearson, Debra S. Peterson, and Michael C. Rodriguez. 2003. "Reading Growth In High-Poverty Classrooms: The Influence Of Teacher Practices That Encourage Cognitive Engagement In Literacy Learning." *Elementary School Journal* 104 (1): 3–28.

Taylor, Wilson L. 1953. "Cloze procedure: A New Tool for Measuring Readability." *Journalism Quarterly* 30: 415–433.

Tomlinson, Carol Ann. 2014. "The Bridge Between Today's Lesson and Tomorrow's." *Educational Leadership* 71 (6): 10–15.

Tomlinson, Carol Ann. 2014. *The Differentiated Classroom: Responding to the Needs of All Learners*. 2nd ed. Alexandria, VA: ASCD.

Tomlinson, Carol Ann, and Jay McTighe. 2006. *Integrating Differentiated Instruction & Understanding by Design Connecting Content and Kids*. Alexandria, VA: Association for Supervision and Curriculum Development.

Tompkins, Gail E. 2013. *Language Arts: Patterns of Practice*. 8th edition. Boston, MA: Pearson.

Tompkins, Gail E. 2008. *Teaching Writing: Balancing Process and Product*. Upper Saddle River, NJ: Pearson.

Tompkins, Gail E. 2002. *Literacy in the 21st Century*. Upper Saddle River, NJ: Prentice Hall.

Trelease, Jim. 2013. *The Read-Aloud Handbook, 7th edition*. New York: Penguin.

Truch, Stephen. 1994. "Stimulating Basic Reading Processes Using Auditory Discrimination in Depth." *Annals of Dyslexia* 44(1): 60-80.

Truss, Lynne. 2006. *Eats, Shoots and Leaves: Why, Commas Really Do Make a Difference*. New York, NY: G.P. Putnan's Sons Books for Young Readers.

Truss, Lynn. 2007. *The Girl's Like Spaghetti: Why, You Can't Manage Without Apostrophes!* New York, NY: G.P. Putnan's Sons Books for Young Readers.

Truss, Lynn. 2008. *Twenty-odd Ducks: Why, Every Punctuation Mark Counts!* New York, NY: G.P. Putnan's Sons Books for Young Readers.

United States National Commission on Excellence in Education. 1983. A Nation At Risk: The Imperative for Educational Reform: A Report to the Nation and the Secretary of Education. Washington, D.C.: The Commission.

University of North Carolina at Chapel Hill Writing Center. 2012. *Transitions.* Accessed December 11 2015 https://writingcenter.unc.edu/files/2012/09/Transitions-The-Writing-Center.pdf.

VanTassel-Baska, Joyce, and Tamra Stambaugh. 2005. "Challenges and Possibilities For Serving Gifted Learners In The Regular Classroom." *Theory Into Practice* 44 (3): 211–217.

Venezky, Richard L. 1970. *The Structure of English Orthography.* New York, NY: The Guilford Press.

Vygotsky, Lev. 1978. *Mind in Society: The Development of Higher Psychological Processes.* Cambridge, MA: Harvard University Press.

Wall, Heather. 2008. "Interactive Writing Beyond The Primary Grades." *The Reading Teacher* 62(2): 149–152.

White, E.B. 1952. *Charlotte's Web.* New York, NY: Harper and Brothers.

White, Thomas G., Joanne Sowell, and Alice Yanagihara. 1999. "Teaching Elementary Students to Use Word-Part Clues." *The Reading Teacher* 42 (4): 302–308.

Wiliam, Dylan, and Marnie Thompson. 2007. "Integrating Assessment with Instruction: What Will It Take to Make It Work?" In *The Future of Assessment: Shaping Teaching and Learning,* edited by Carol Anne Dwyer. 1:53–82. Mahwah, NJ: Erlbaum.

Willingham, Daniel T. 2008/2009. "What Will Improve a Student's Memory?" *American Educator* 32 (4) 17-25, 44.

Wylie, Richard E., and Donald D. Durrell. 1970. "Teaching vowels through phonograms." *Elementary School Journal* 47, 787-791.

Yousafzai, Malala. 2013. "Malala Yousafzai's speech at the Youth Takeover of the United Nations." Accessed December 23, 2015. https://secure.aworldatschool.org/page/content/the-text-of-malala-yousafzais-speech-at-the-unit`ed-nations/.

Yu, Eunjyu. 2013. "Empowering At-Risk Students as Autonomous Learners: Toward a Metacognitive Approach." *Research and Teaching in Developmental Education* 30(1) 35–45.

Appendix A

Additional Resources

Websites

ABCYA: Educational Games for Kids
http://www.abcya.com

Apple's GarageBand
http://www.apple.com/mac/garageband/

Audacity
http://www.audacityteam.org/

ClassZone
http://www.classzone.com

Digital Graphic Organizer
http://www.edhelper.com/teachers/graphic_organizers.htm

Discovery Education
http://www.discoveryeducation.com

Education.com
http://www.education.com

Education Place
http://www.eduplace.com

EduCreations
http://www.educreations.com

Evernote
http://www.evernote.com

Flashcard Stash
http://www.flashcardstash.com

Fun English Games
http://www.funenglishgames.com

GoAnimate
http://www.goanimate.com

Internet4Classrooms
http://www.Internet4Classrooms.com

iSpottv
http://www.ispot.tv

Just Books Read Aloud
http://www.justbooksreadaloud.com/

Kidblog
http://www. kidblog.org

KidzType
http://www.kidztype.com

Kubbu
http://www.kubbu.com

Learning Games for Kids
http://www.learninggamesforkids.com

Lit2Go
http://etc.usf.edu/lit2go/readability/flesch_kincaid_grade_level/

Many Things
http://www.manythings.org/cts/

National Institute of Environmental Health Sciences: Kid Pages
http://www.kids.niehs.nih.gov

Online Etymology Dictionary
http://www.etymonline.com

PBS Kids Between the Lions
http://www.pbskids.org/lions

Prezi
http://www.prezi.com

PrimaryGames
http://www.primarygames.com

Quia
http://www.quia.com

Quizlet
http://www.quizlet.com

Reading is Fundamental
http://www.rif.org

Review Game Zone
http://www.reviewgamezone.com

Sadlier Connect
http://www.sadlierconnect.com

Smart Tutor
http://www.smarttutor.com

Starfall
http://www.starfall.com

Sight Words
http://www.sightwords.com

StoryBird
http://www.storybird.com

Storyline Online
http://www.storylineonline.net/

Storynory
http://www.storynory.com/

Study Guides and Strategies
http://www.studygs.net

Study Ladder
http://www.studyladder.com

Super Teacher Tools
http://www.superteachertools.us

Tech & Learning
http://www.techlearning.com/

Vocabulary.Co.Il
http://www.vocabulary.co.il

VocabularySpellingCity
http://www.spellingcity.com

Voki
http://www.voki.com

Web English Teacher
http://www.webenglishteacher.com

WISC-Online
http://www.wisc-online.com

Word Sift 2
http://www.wordsift.com

Worlde
http://www.wordle.net

Apps

Abby Phonics
(Arch Square)

Bamboo Paper—Notebook
(Wacom)

Book Chat
(Mobile Learning Services)

Class Tools
(Jeremy Cartee)

Educreations Interactive Whiteboard
(Educreations, Inc.)

Fotobabble
(Fotobabble, Inc)

Grammaropolis
(Grammaropolis, LLC)

Homophones Free—English Language Arts Grammar App
(Abitalk Incorporated)

iMovie
(Apple)

K12 Timed Reading Practice Lite
(K12 Inc.)

Letter Cross Tracking
(Visual Learning for Life)

Long Vowel Word Study
(Thomas Wilson)

MeeGenius Children's Books
(Houghton Mifflin Harcourt)

Microsoft Photo Story 3.0
(Microsoft)

Middle School Vocabulary Prep
(Peekaboo Studios LLC)

My Spelling Test
(Mathan Education)

Pages
(Apple)

Pango FREE
(Studio Pango)

Picturizr
(ISBX)

Reading Comprehension: Fable Edition
(King's Apps)

Sight Words: Kids Learn
(Teacher Created Materials)

Sight Words List—Learn to Read Flash Cards & Games
(Innovative Mobile Apps)

SparkleFish
(Whoseagoodboy Partners)

Spelling City
(Spelling City)

Spelling Magic 3
(Preschool University)

Toontastic
(Launchpad Toys)

WordTree 3D Free
(Apple Learning)

File Folder Pocket Instructions

1. Lay the folder on the table with the fold toward you.

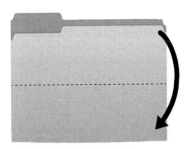

2. Fold down the top edge of one side of the file, until it meets the base.

3. Crease.

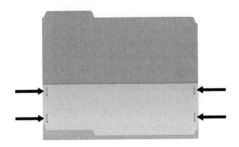

4. Staple at the open sides.

5. This creates a pocket.

BINGO Board

	Free Space	

Appendix C

Blends and Digraphs

Blends

BL	blend	blood	blue	blush
BR	brick	brook	brush	brown
CL	clam	clock	climb	clown
CR	cry	cross	creek	crown
DR	drip	draw	drive	drove
FL	floor	flute	flap	flour
FR	free	from	friend	front
GL	glad	glass	glide	glow
GR	grass	green	grey	great
PL	plain	place	play	plain
PR	prize	pretty	price	proof
SC	scoot	scarf	scatter	score
SK	skip	sky	skid	skirt
SL	slap	slow	slab	sleek
SM	small	smile	smart	smug
SN	snake	snap	snow	snore
SP	spot	spy	spend	spill
SPL	splash	split	splatter	splint
SPR	spray	spread	sprain	spree
ST	star	still	stack	stamp
SW	swan	swap	sweet	sweat
TR	trap	tray	trash	true
TW	twig	tweet	twenty	twice

Digraphs

CH	chill	chick	charm	cheese	bunch	each	bench	much
SH	sheep	show	shout	shadow	bush	crash	dish	wash
PH	phone	phrase	phonics	graph	elephant	gopher	alphabet	trophy
TH	that	this	these	thing	with	both	fourth	teeth
WH	what	when	while	whisper	wheel	whale	nowhere	whiskers

Basketball Hoops

Basketballs

Who Belongs Together?

Who Belongs Together? Answer Key

baby	ball	boy
bat	bag	pig
bus	pizza	pan
pot	puzzle	pen

Appendix C

Hop to It! Note Cards

at	bit	can	cap
cub	cut	dim	fin
fir	hat	hid	hop
hug	kit	mad	mat
pet	pin	rid	rip
rob	rod	sit	stag
tap	tub	us	wag

The Magic of E

e	e	e	e	e	e
e	e	e	e	e	e
e	e	e	e	e	e
e	e	e	e	e	e
e	e	e	e	e	e
e	e	e	e	e	e

Presto Wands

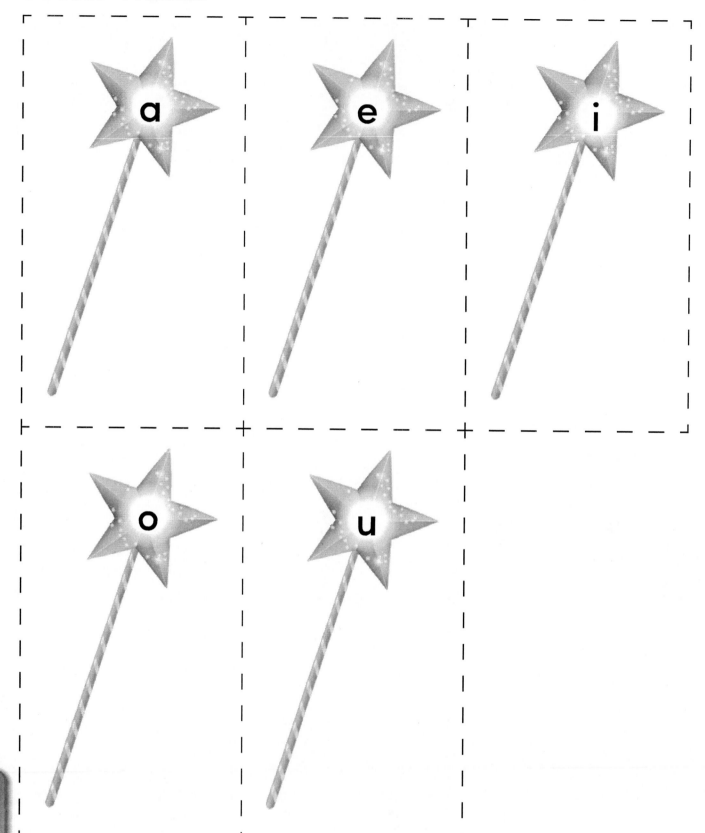

Appendix C

Build a Word Sample List

look	*ing*	help	*ing*
look	*ed*	help	*ed*
mix	*es*	duck	*s*
wish	*es*	kick	*s*

Appendix C

Mix and Match Compound Pairs

Appendix C

Mix and Match Compound Pairs (cont.)

Mix and Match Vocabulary

bird	house	wrist	watch
sail	boat	back	pack
rain	coat	pan	cake
dog	house	foot	ball

Appendix C

Compound Pairs

birdhouse

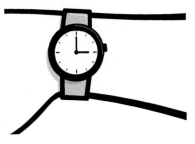

wristwatch

sailboat

backpack

raincoat

pancake

doghouse

football

Appendix C

Top 100 High-Frequency Words

the	is	a	to	go
in	of	you	that	it
he	was	for	on	are
made	her	his	they	I
and	be	this	have	from
at	or	one	had	work
by	but	what	all	were
we	when	your	can	said
there	use	an	each	which
she	how	their	if	not
will	up	other	about	do
many	then	these	so	out
some	with	would	like	water
him	into	time	look	them
two	more	day	over	see
number	no	way	could	people
my	call	has	been	make
than	who	first	sit	now
find	long	down	did	write
get	come	as	many	part

Vowel House Template

Roof   A

Roof   E

Roof   I

Roof   O

Roof   U

Wall   A

Wall   E

Wall   I

Wall   O

Wall   U

Roof Wild Card

Wall Wild Card

Vowel Alternations List

admire	admiration	angel	angelic
deal	dealt	metal	metallic
compose	composition	agile	agility
mean	meant	reduce	reduction
volcano	volcanic	nation	national
aristocrat	aristocracy	athlete	athletic
reveal	revelation	invite	invitation
geometry	geometric	confide	confidence
creep	crept	compete	competition
clean	cleanse	aspire	aspiration
serene	serenity	realize	realization
oppose	opposition	divide	division

Circus Rings

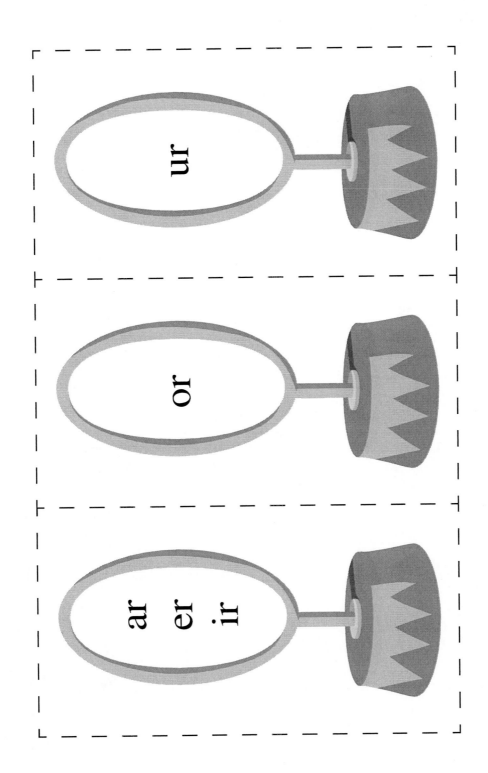

Circus Animals

Appendix C

Circus Performers

Circus Words

ar	er	ir	or	ur
are	her	bird	for	fur
arm	ever	fir	or	hurt
bar	enter	first	born	sure
cart	herd	girl	corn	burn
bark	fern	firm	fork	purr
hard	perk	stir	fort	turn
harm	over	sir	horse	surf
jar	never	shirt	more	purple

Quiet Letters Cards

abst__n	b__con	conc__t	copyr__t
__lment	bl__cher	conc__ve	enl__ten
acqu__nt	cr__mery	dec__t	sl__t
expl__n	dis__se	perc__ve	l__tning
m__ntenance	fr__k	rec__ver	fr__tful
pr__se	rev__l	s__zure	twil__t
p__nstaking	decr__se	sl__gh	outr__t
str__ght	__vesdrop	b__ge	del__tful

Quiet Letters Cards (cont.)

appr__ch	bell__	barbec__
c__stal	minn__	discontin__
c__x	overgr__n	iss__
r__ch	overthr__	purs__
thr__t	st__away	resid__
l__ves	tomorr__	reven__
b__stful	will__	subd__
stagec__ch	marshmall__	val__

Appendix C

Football Jersey

Football Field

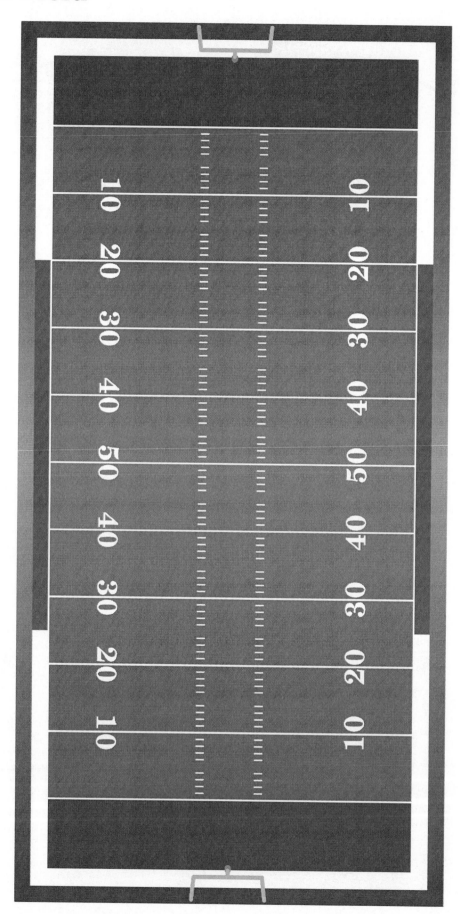

Automobiles

Awesome Automobile Words

au	aw	ou
author	paw	bought
haul	fawn	sought
cause	claw	brought
August	thaw	ought
autumn	yawn	fought
fault	withdraw	thought
taught	jigsaw	cough
saucer	spawn	trough

Double Consonant Cards

flipping	slammed	plodded	permitted	zipping
dragging	wrapping	winner	babysitter	drummer

Meatballs Template

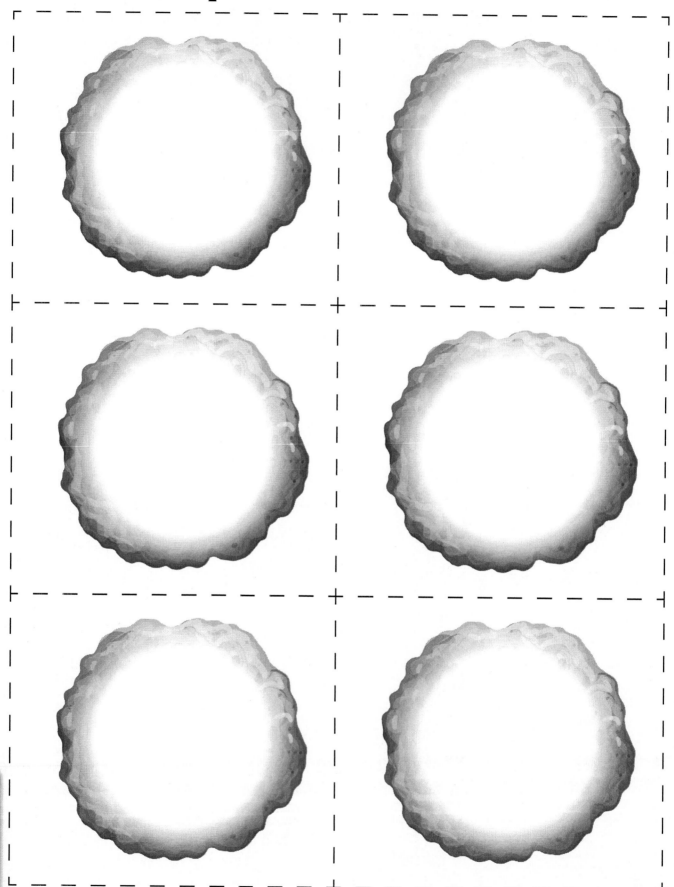

Appendix C

VCV and VCCV Word Suggestions

Example VCV Word

super

VCV Words for Sorting

tiger, zebra, vapor, minus, human, cubic, bacon, secret, spoken, major, minor, climate, motive, meter, crater

Example VCCV Word

supper

VCCV Words for Sorting

kitten, cotton, fossil, muffin, tennis, happen, funny, blizzard, blossom, common, message, mammal, dipper

Doubled or Dropped Word List

hopping	hoping
staring	starring
sloping	slopping
gaping	gapping
caning	canning
robing	robbing
pinning	pining
taping	tapping
waging	wagging
baring	barring
riding	ridding
moping	mopping

Arrow Template

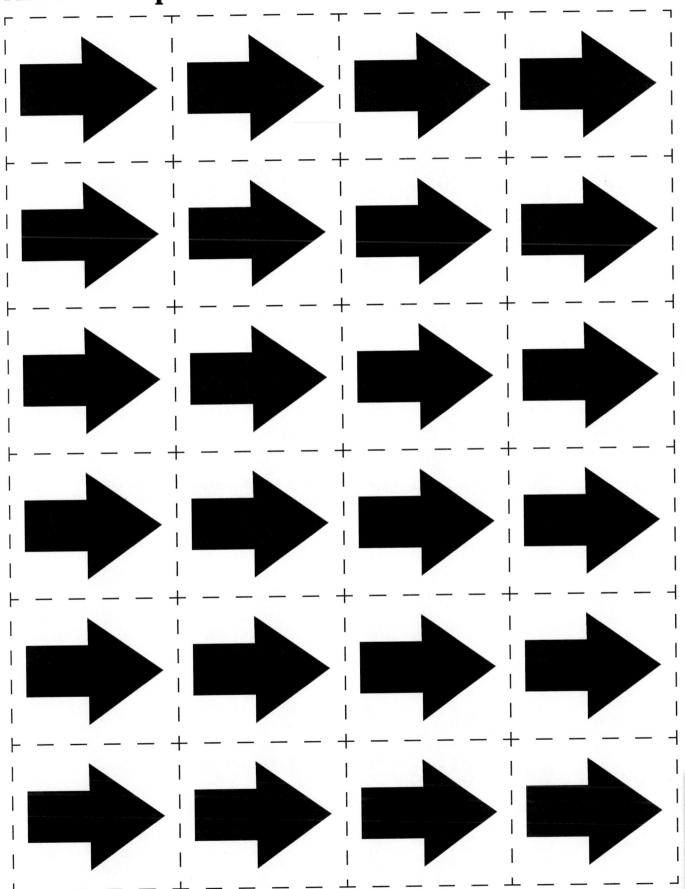

Ant Template

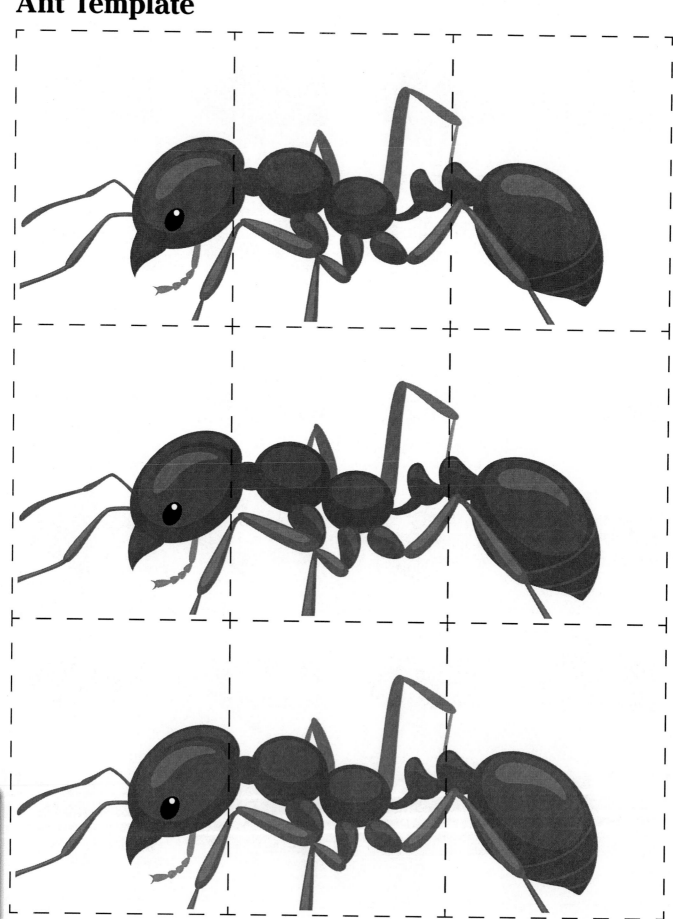

Appendix C

Pancake Compounds

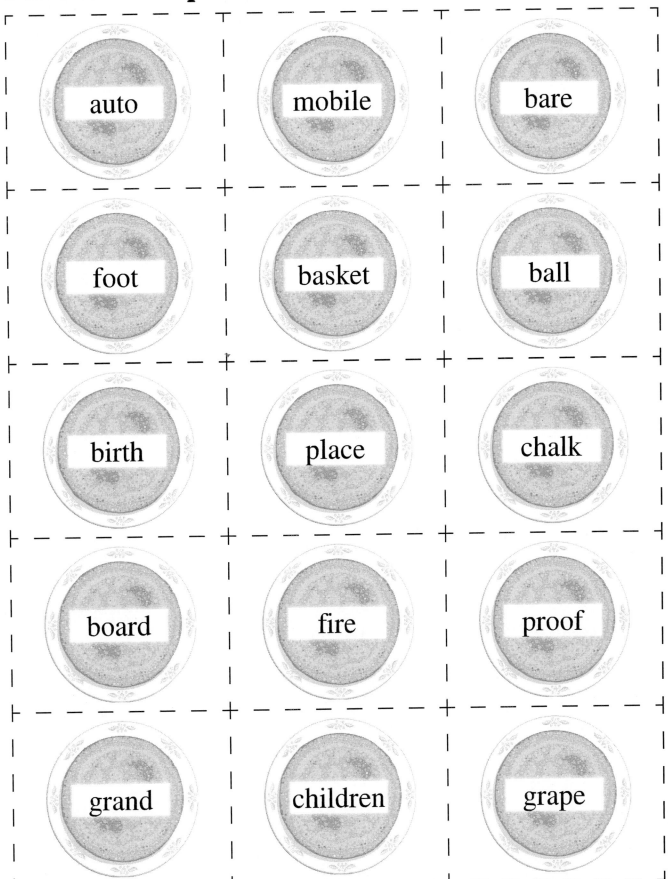

auto	mobile	bare
foot	basket	ball
birth	place	chalk
board	fire	proof
grand	children	grape

Pancake Compounds (cont.)

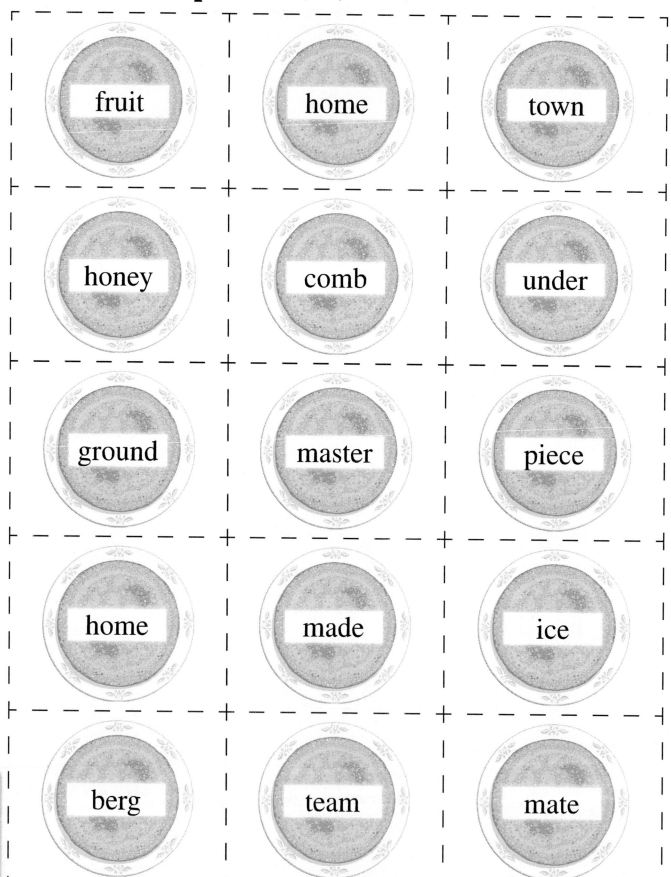

fruit

home

town

honey

comb

under

ground

master

piece

home

made

ice

berg

team

mate

Appendix C

Comparatives and Superlatives List

Word	Comparative	Superlative
tall	taller	tallest
short	shorter	shortest
old	older	oldest
close	closer	closest
far	farther	farthest
funny	funnier	funniest
long	longer	longest
clean	cleaner	cleanest

Pear Template

Word Pairs

Homophones	Antonyms	Synonyms
words that sound alike but have different spellings and meanings	*words with opposite meanings*	*words with similar meanings*
tale/tail	big/small	cold/icy
plane/plain	noisy/quiet	large/big
wring/ring	calm/excited	said/replied
hour/our	lost/found	happy/glad
their/there	add/subtract	small/tiny
write/right	above/below	afraid/scared
rode/road	hot/cold	house/home
sail/sale	clean/dirty	neat/tidy
toe/tow	east/west	center/middle
beat/beet	start/end	rock/stone
cent/sent	awake/asleep	rest/relax
threw/through	open/close	carpet/rug
wait/weight	day/night	sad/unhappy
fur/fir		under/below
dough/doe		ill/sick
past/passed		
pole/poll		
heal/heel		
sun/son		

Top Hat Template

Appendix C

Hit or Miss Chart

	1	2	3	4	5	6
D						
C						
B						
A						

Vocabulary Word Template

Vocabulary Word	Definition

Vocabulary Word	Definition

Appendix C

Make-a-Word Cards

in	cred	ion	ation	stand
ing	pro	lax	in	con
ceed	ion	ation	ject	ing
trans	port	struct	re	under
ible				

Word Cards

-tion Endings

direct	examine	reduce	react	educate
consider	integrate	adopt	promote	communicate
suggest	vacate	reject	act	relate
moderate	complete	protect	populate	

-sion Endings

discuss	impress	televise	confess	invade
intrude	collide	compress	conclude	diffuse
elude	comprehend	explode	possess	admit
commit	transmit	succeed	concede	proceed

Explanation Signs

–tion

- most common
- all are nouns (from a verb)
- Drop *–e*, if at end of word, and add *–tion*.
- If ends in *–t*, add *–ion*.

–sion

- If ends in *–d*, *–de*, or *–se*, drop those endings and add *–sion*.
- If ends in *–ss*, add *–ion*.
- If ends in *–mit*, drop *t* add *–ssion*.
- If ends in *–cedel* or *–ceed*, add *–ssion*.

Bases and Affixes

vert	con	ible	intro
re	ical	di	

sign	al	ature	de
ify	ate		

duct	in	aque	con
de	ab		

man	ual	acle	age
euver	ly		

cycle	bi	tri	re
uni	motor		

Greek and Latin Bases

Base	Definition
acro	height
polis	city
phobia	fear
bat	to walk
nym	name
vis	to see
re	again
in	not
ible	can; able to
super	over
or	one who

Word	Definition
acropolis	a citadel that is on high ground
acrophobia	fear of heights
acrobat	someone who entertains by performing dangerous acts (walking on high apparatus)
acronym	a name derived from the first (or high) letters of words, such as NASA—National Aeronautics Space Administration
revise	to see again
invisible	not able to be seen
supervisor	one who oversees

Word Hunt Cards

We're going on a word hunt for a synonym for _____.

I found _____. We're going on a word hunt for a synonym for _____.

I found _____. We're going on a word hunt for a synonym for _____.

I found _____. We're going on a word hunt for a synonym for _____.

I found _____. We're going on a word hunt for a synonym for _____.

I found _____. The hunt is over!

Appendix C

Word Hunt Cards (cont.)

We're going on a word hunt for an antonym for

_____.

I found _____.
We're going on a word hunt for an antonym for

_____.

I found _____.
We're going on a word hunt for an antonym for

_____.

I found _____.
We're going on a word hunt for an antonym for

_____.

I found _____.
We're going on a word hunt for an antonym for

_____.

I found _____.
The hunt is over!

Synonyms and Antonyms

Synonym Suggestions

empty—vacant	respect—honor
job—occupation	value—worth
rush—hurry	eat—consume
guess—estimate	thought—idea
final—last	problem—nuisance

Antonym Suggestions

sharp—blunt	shrink—swell
quarrel—agree	question—answer
difficult—simple	innocent—guilty
attack—defend	success—failure
unique—common	liquid—solid

Appendix C

Base Template

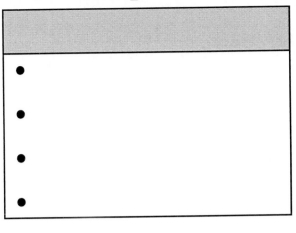

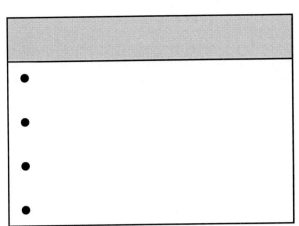

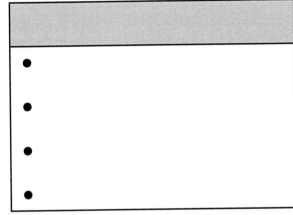

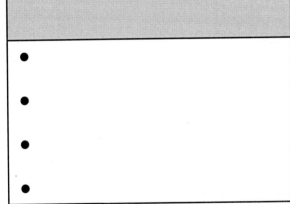

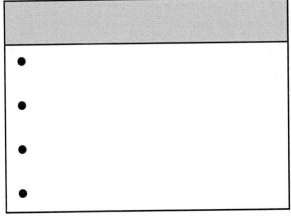

Base Examples

vis/vid (to see)
- video
- visual
- visible
- visor

scop (a watcher or viewer)
- telescope
- microscope
- stethoscope
- horoscope

sign (to mark)
- signature
- design
- signal
- significant

ped (foot)
- pedal
- pedestrian
- pedestal
- pedigree

aster (star)
- asterisk
- asteroid
- astronaut
- disaster

scrib/scrip (to write)
- describe
- inscribe
- scribble
- postscript

man (hand)
- manual
- manipulate
- mange
- maneuver

voc (call)
- vocal
- advocate
- vocabulary
- vocation

Base Examples (cont.)

rupt (to break)

- erupt
- rupture
- interrupt
- bankrupt

spir (to breathe)

- inspire
- expire
- respiration
- conspire

volve (turn)

- volume
- evolve
- revolve
- evolution

cap (head)

- captain
- capitol
- capitalize
- decapitate

tang/tact (to touch)

- tangible
- tangent
- contact
- tactile

Appendix C

Bookmark Template

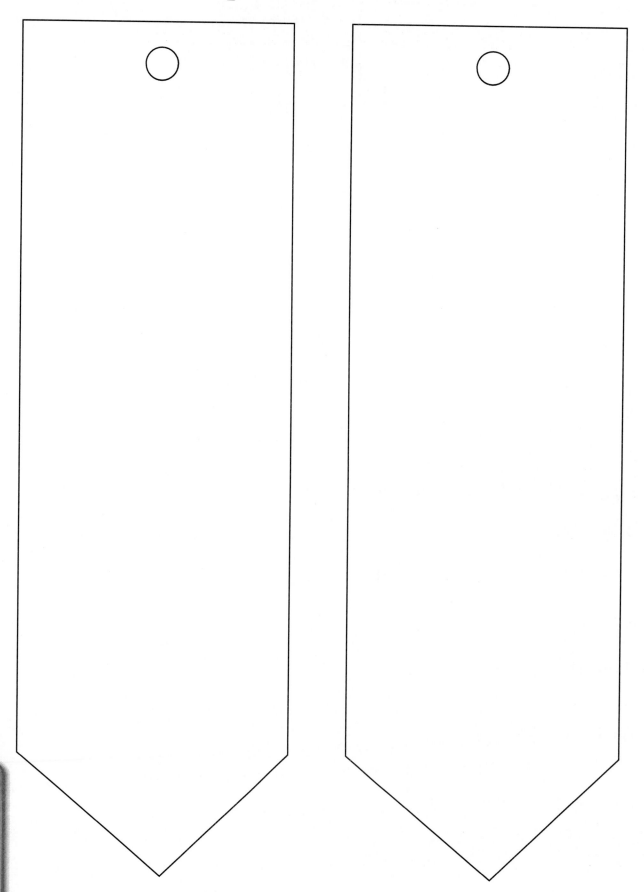

The Five-Finger Rule

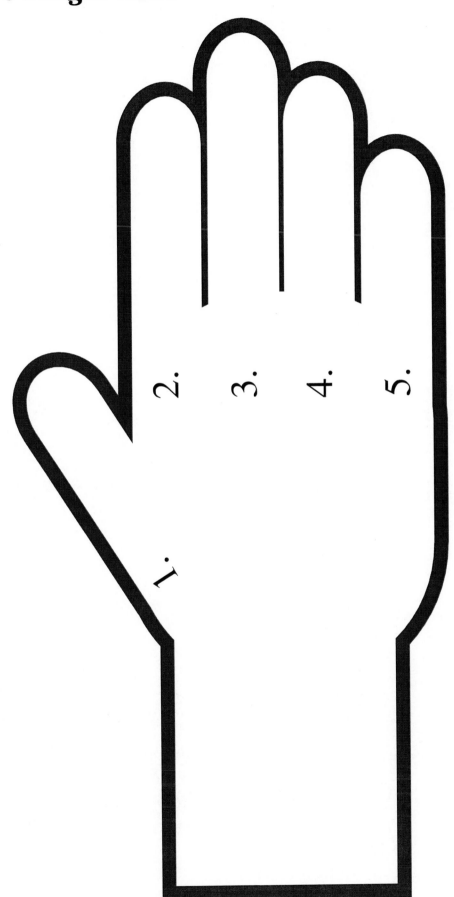

1.

2.

3.

4.

5.

Appendix C

Long Versus Short Vowel Sound

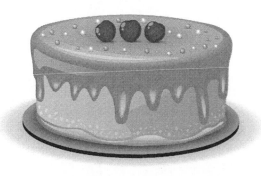

Oral Reading Record Form

Student: _____

Date: _____

Text: _____

Page	Oral Reading Record	What cue* was used?	What cue was not used?

*Mark cues as: V = visual (graphophonic); M = meaning (semantic); S = structure (syntactic)

Comprehension questions asked:

Notes about visual (graphophonic) cues:

Notes about meaning (semantic) cues:

Notes about structure (syntactic) cues:

Notes about self-corrections:

Appendix C

Sample Completed Oral Reading Record

Student: Carlos

Date: September 5

Text: *Titch*

Page	Oral Reading Record	What cue* was used?	What cue was not used?
1	✓ ✓ ∧ᵃ ✓ ∧ boy	M, M	V, V
2	✓ ✓ mmm ✓ ✓ b̄it̄ b̄iḡger	V	V, V
3	✓ ✓ ✓ ppp ᵀⁱᴳ ✓ ✓ little ✓	V	M
4	ppp ᵀⁱᴳ ✓ ✓ great ✓ lot blue big sc	V, M	M, M
5	✓ ✓ ✓ ✓		—
6	✓ ✓ has sc / had ✓ ✓ tri/tri-sick-le tricycle	V, V	M, M

*Mark cues as: V = visual (graphophonic); M = meaning (semantic); S = structure (syntactic)

Comprehension questions asked:

- Who is the littlest member of the family? (*Titch*)
  Student: √

- Why does Titch have a tricycle? (*He is little.*)
  Student: Because the other kids have all the big bikes.

- Why is Titch's tool so important? (*Because they can't plant the seed without it.*)
  Student: The older kids need it.

Notes about visual (graphophonic) cues:
predominant strategy to focus on letters

Notes about meaning (semantic) cues:
used for self-correction half the time

Notes about structure (syntactic) cues:
not used

Notes about self-corrections:
related to the meaning of the sentence, so appears to be self-monitoring for sense of story

Appendix C

Record of Analysis of Oral Reading

Student: _____

Date: _____

Text: _____

Student Read	Teacher Given	Substitution	Omission	Insertion	Repetition	Self-Correction	What cue was used? V = **visual** (graphophonic) M = **meaning** (semantic) S = **structure** (syntactic)
Totals							V = M = S =

Number of comprehension questions asked: % correct:

Use of visual (graphophonic) cues:

Use of meaning (semantic) cues:

Use of structure (syntactic) cues:

Self-corrections:

Sample Record of Analysis of Oral Reading

Student: Carlos
Date: September 5
Text: *Titch*

Student Read	Teacher Given	Substitution	Omission	Insertion	Repetition	Self-Correction	What cue was used? V = visual (graphophonic) M = meaning (semantic) S = structure (syntactic)
A				X			M
Boy		X		X			M
** (bit)		X					
** (bigger)	(Pete)						V
PPP		X					V
little	(Pete)		X		X	X	V
PPP		X			X	X	M
** (great)						X	S
lot							M
has							
tri-tri-sick-le							
Totals							V = 3 M = 4 S = 1

Number of comprehension questions asked: 3   % correct: 67%

Use of visual (graphophonic) cues:
some similarities between miscue and correct word—seems more reliant on visual cues

Use of meaning (semantic) cues:
some use of semantics to correct miscue

Use of structure (syntactic) cues:
only one example of hearing the syntactic error

Self-corrections:
self-corrections vary—meaning and syntax

Evaluation of Oral Reading

Accuracy	Level
95–99.5	Independent
90–94	Instructional
50–89	Frustration

(Adapted from Armbruster, Lehr, and Osborn 2001)

Accuracy

Divide total words read correctly by total words in the text, multiple by 100 = %

For example: Student correctly read 69 of 72 words (4 errors) = 69 ÷ 72 = .9583 x 100 = 95.8%
Level: independent

Self-Correction Ratio

Add self-corrections + errors, divide by self-corrections = 1: ___

For example: Student self-corrected 3 times and made 5 errors

$$\frac{3+5}{3} = 2.6 \text{ (round up to 3.0)}$$

Ratio is 1:3
1:3, 1:4, and 1:5 are good rates in that they show the student is attending to his/her own reading.

Class Oral Reading Record Form

Student Name	Notes on Visual Cue Use	Notes on Meaning Cue Use	Notes on Structure Cue Use	Reading Level	Additional Notes

Appendix C

Name: _____ Date: _____

Compare and Contrast Template

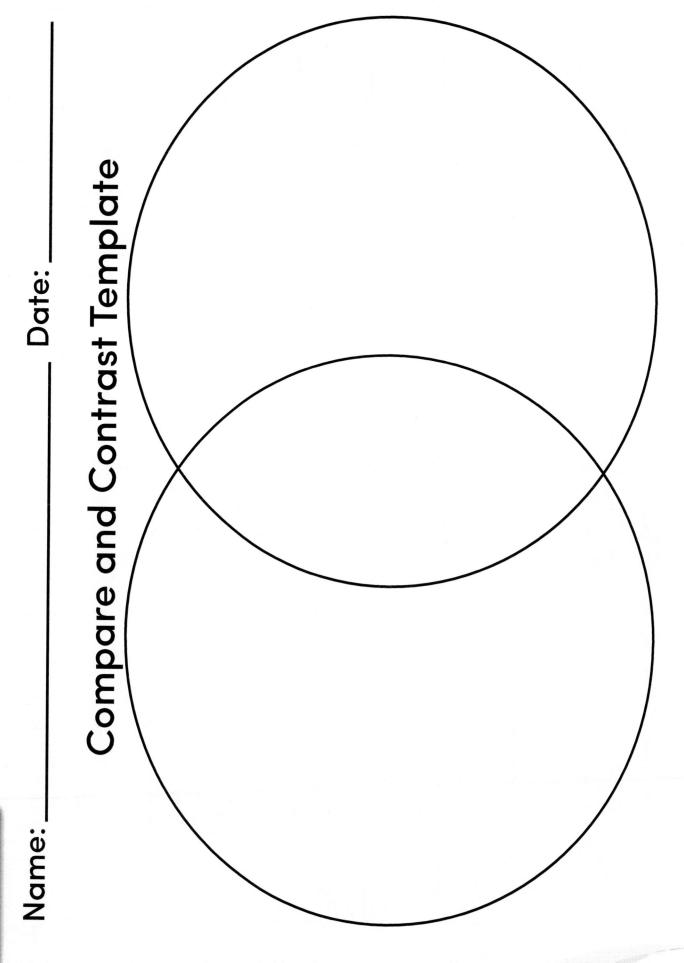

Vocabulary Boxes Chart

Words from

A	B	
C		
D	E	
F		
G	H	
I		
J	K	
L		
M	N	
O		
P	Q	
R		
S	T	
U		
V	W	
X		
Y	Z	

Appendix C

My Independent Reading Log

Name: _____ Date: _____

Fill in the chart for each self-selected book. Rate each book when you finish reading it:

★ = I finished this, but did not really like it   ★ ★ ★ = I loved this book

★ ★ = I liked this book   ★ ★ ★ ★ = I would highly recommend this book to others

Title and Author	Reason I Chose This Book	Date I Started Reading This Book	Date I Finished Reading This Book	How I Rate This Book

Shared Reading Lesson Plan Template

Name:	Date:

Title of text:

Strategy focus for lesson:

Before reading (prepare students to hear and participate in the text):

During reading (plans to guide students in shared experience):

After reading (extending the reading with independent practice):

Vocabulary discussion:

Assessment notes for group:

Assessment notes for individuals:

Lesson Plan Template for Meeting with Literature Circles

Students in group:
Book selected for session:
Check-in with group:
How is reading going?
Comprehension check about content read thus far:
How are students rotating jobs?
Oral reading of passages:
Mini-lesson:
Closure:
Notes about individual readers:

Literature Circle Reading Log

Name: _____

Book title and author: _____

Dates	My Job	Pages	Notes for Group Meetings

Words new to me as I read:

Literature Circle Self-Assessment Chart

Literature Circle Self-Assessment	Yes	No	Sometimes	Comments
I came prepared for our group meetings.				
I completed my assigned role for each meeting.				
I listened to other students during the group meetings.				
I set goals for myself as I read.				

Literature Circle Self-Assessment	Yes	No	Sometimes	Comments
I came prepared for our group meetings.				
I completed my assigned role for each meeting.				
I listened to other students during the group meetings.				
I set goals for myself as I read.				

Literature Circle Self-Assessment	Yes	No	Sometimes	Comments
I came prepared for our group meetings.				
I completed my assigned role for each meeting.				
I listened to other students during the group meetings.				
I set goals for myself as I read.				

Literature Circle Self-Assessment	Yes	No	Sometimes	Comments
I came prepared for our group meetings.				
I completed my assigned role for each meeting.				
I listened to other students during the group meetings.				
I set goals for myself as I read.				

Lesson Plan Template for Guided Reading

Students in reading group:
Book(s) selected for lesson:
Other materials needed:
Familiar book observational notes (including problem solving observed) during reading:
Familiar book skill focus:
New book observational notes (including problem solving observed) during reading:

In the Book
    Right there:
 	
    Think and search:

In My Head
    Author and me:
 	
    On my own:

New book skill focus:
Closure:
Notes about individual readers:

Appendix C

Status of the Class

Directions: Add a date in the column next to your name that indicates where you are in the writing process

Name	Starting New Project	Researching	Drafting/ Writing	Revising	Need Conference	Publishing

Computer Composing

Directions

1. Place your hands so your index to pinkie fingers rest on the middle row of keys (*a-s-d-f* and *j-k-l-;*). Your thumbs go on the space bar.

2. What do you notice about the keys under your pointer finger? (*bumps*) What letters are there? (*f, j*) Strike those keys.

3. Where are your pinkies (*a, ;*)? Strike those keys.

4. How could you make a capital letter? (*shift key*) Make the capital that begins your name. Type the rest of your name.

5. Strike all the keys your eight fingers are resting on from left to right (*asdfjkl;*).

6. Repeat, but this time hold down the *shift* key. (*ASDFJKL:*)

7. Strike all the keys above where your fingers are resting. (*qweruiop*)

8. Repeat, but this time use the *shift* key. (*QWERUIOP*)

9. Strike all the keys below where your fingers are resting. (*zxcvm,./*)

10. Repeat, but this time use the *shift* key. (*ZXCVM<>?*)

11. Type a sentence.

12. Print your work.

Grammar List

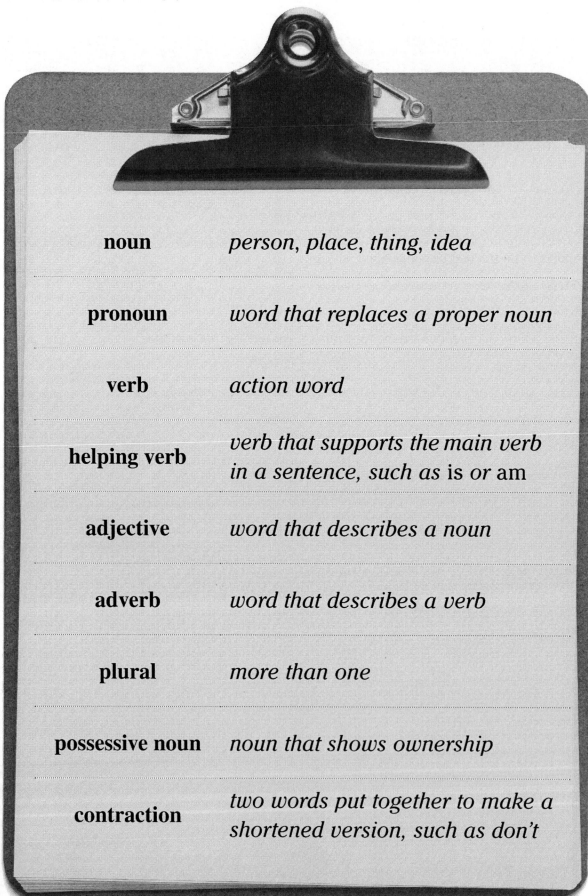

noun	*person, place, thing, idea*
pronoun	*word that replaces a proper noun*
verb	*action word*
helping verb	*verb that supports the main verb in a sentence, such as* is *or* am
adjective	*word that describes a noun*
adverb	*word that describes a verb*
plural	*more than one*
possessive noun	*noun that shows ownership*
contraction	*two words put together to make a shortened version, such as* don't

Name: _____ **Date:** _____

Paragraph Outline

1. Paragraph 1: Introduction.

2. Paragraph 2: One reason and some supporting details.

3. Paragraph 3: A second reason and some supporting details.

4. Paragraph 4: A third reason and some supporting details.

5. Paragraph 5: Summary or conclusion. Rephrase the main idea and three reasons.

Appendix C

Revision Marks Chart

Editing and Proofreading Marks

Editor's Mark	Meaning	Example
≡	capitalize	they fished in lake tahoe.
/	make it lowercase	Five $\cancel{S}$tudents missed the $\cancel{B}$us.
sp.	spelling mistake	The day was clowdy and cold. (sp.)
⊙	add a period	Tomorrow is a holiday⊙
✗	delete (remove)	One person knew the ~~the~~ answer.
∧	add a word	Six ∧ were in the litter. (pups)
∧ (comma)	add a comma	He planted peas∧ corn, and squash.
∪	reverse words or letters	An otter swam in the bed kelp.
∨	add an apostrophe	The childs bike was red.
∨ (quotes)	add quotation marks	Why can't I go? she cried.
#	make a space	He ate two red # apples.
◡	close the space	Her favorite game is soft ball.
¶	begin a new paragraph	to know. ¶ Next on the list

Compound Sentences

I like eating ice cream.	I don't like vegetables.	My sisters arrived on time.	The train was late.	I forgot my lunch.
I called Mom to bring me money.	I changed the light bulb.	The room was no longer dark.	I know a shortcut home.	The road was closed.
The boys went to the football game.	It was a miserable night to sit outside.	I will set the table.	My sister will pour the juice.	I love to read the comics.
My sister looks at the shopping ads.	We all got sick.	The measles were going around.	The electricity went out.	My computer shut down.
My watch quit working.	I was late for school.	The baby was crying.	The dog would not stop barking.	We went to the zoo.
We cannot go to the park.	It rained all day.	The baseball game was cancelled.	We went to the movies.	We saw all our classmates there.

Appendix C

Which Word Is Best?

Average	Outstanding!
ask	interrogate
rise	ascend
sweat	perspire
smell	odor
buy	purchase
answer	response

Appendix C

Early Literacy Skills Class Checklist

Directions: Use this checklist to note student need in each skill.

Student Name	Auditory Discrimination	Phonemic Awareness	Alphabet Knowledge	Book Concepts	Word Construction

B = basic understanding   L = limited understanding   P = proficient   N = no knowledge

Appendix C

Individual Record Sheet for Writing
Kindergarten through Grade 2

Student Name: _____

Note the date when a student attempts to incorporate the skill described and/or when the student appears to master the skill.

Skill	Attempts	Masters
Concept of Word		
Considering Audience		
Correct Formation of Letters		
Deciding on a Genre		
Deciding on a Topic		
Developing and Using a Personal Word Bank		
Differentiating Between Drawing and Writing		
Expressing Ideas		
Grammar		
Helping a Buddy Revise		
How to Revise		
Matching Sound to Print		
Publishing Final Copies		
Punctuation		
Recalling Sight Words		
Rereading Own Writing		
Use of Lines		
Using Classroom Resources		

Appendix C

My Writing Record Sheet

Grade 3 through Grade 5

Student Name: _____

Note the date when you tried this skill and describe what you wrote.

In the Evaluation column score yourself using these marks. You can change them whenever needed.

✗ = I don't have it quite yet!　　　✔ = I'm working on it!　　　★ = I've got this one!

Skill	Date/Description	Evaluation
Considering the Purpose and Potential Audience		
Deciding on a Genre		
Deciding on a Topic		
Developing and Using a Personal Word Bank		
Drafting Writing		
Expressing Ideas		
Finding the Apostrophe		
Grammar		
Helping a Friend Revise		
How to Revise		
How to Transition Ideas		
Incorporating Technology in Composing		
Publishing Final Copies		
Punctuation		
Recalling Sight Words		
Add a Word		
Self-Correcting Spelling		
Using Classroom Resources		

Individual Record Sheet for Writing
Grade 3 through Grade 5

Student Name: _____

Note the date when the student attempts to incorporate the skill described and/or when the student appears to master the skill.

Skill	Attempts	Masters
Considering Purpose and Potential Audience		
Deciding on a Genre		
Deciding on a Topic		
Developing and Using a Personal Word Bank		
Drafting Writing		
Expressing Ideas		
Finding the Apostrophe		
Grammar		
Helping a Friend Revise		
How to Revise		
How to Transition Ideas		
Incorporating Technology in Composing		
Publishing Final Copies		
Punctuation		
Recalling Sight Words		
Add a Word		
Self-Correcting Spelling		
Using Classroom Resources		

Individual Record Sheet for Writing

Grade 6 through Grade 8

Student Name: _____

Note the date when the student attempts to incorporate the skill described and/or when the student appears to master the skill.

Skill	Attempts	Masters
Considering Potential Audience		
Crafting Texts		
Crafting Text: Narrative		
Crafting Text: Explanatory		
Crafting Text: Poem		
Deciding on a Variety of Topics		
Deciding on a Genre		
Developing and Using a Personal Word Bank		
Grammar		
Helping a Classmate Revise		
How to Revise		
How to Transition Ideas		
Incorporating Technology in Composing		
Organizing by Paragraphs		
Proofreading for Possible Revisions		
Publishing Final Copies		
Punctuation		
Recalling Familiar Words		
Self-Correcting Spelling and Grammar		
Using Classroom Resources		
Using Correct Capitalization		
Using Correct Word Usage		
Vocabulary Choices		
Writing Compound Sentences		

Appendix C

My Writing Record Sheet
Grade 6 through Grade 8

Student Name: _____

Note the date when you tried this skill and describe what you wrote.

In the Evaluation column score yourself using these marks. You can change them whenever needed.

✗ = I don't have it quite yet!   ✔ = I'm working on it!   ★ = I've got this one!

Skill	Date/Description	Evaluation
Considering Potential Audience		
Crafting Texts		
Crafting Text: Narrative		
Crafting Text: Explanatory		
Crafting Text: Poem		
Deciding on a Variety of Topics		
Deciding on a Genre		
Developing and Using a Personal Word Bank		
Grammar		
Helping a Classmate Revise		
How to Revise		
How to Transition Ideas		
Incorporating Technology in Composing		
Organizing by Paragraphs		
Proofreading for Possible Revisions		
Publishing Final Copies		
Punctuation		
Recalling Familiar Words		
Self-Correcting Spelling and Grammar		
Using Classroom Resources		
Using Correct Capitalization		
Using Correct Word Usage		
Vocabulary Choices		
Writing Compound Sentences		

Mini-Lessons Class Checklist

Kindergarten through Grade 2

Directions: Record the date(s) the following skills are taught.

Skill	Date(s)
Concept of Word	
Considering Audience	
Correct Formation of Letters	
Deciding on a Genre	
Deciding on a Topic	
Developing and Using a Personal Word Bank	
Differentiating Between Drawing and Writing	
Expressing Ideas	
Grammar	
Helping a Buddy Revise	
How to Revise	
Matching Sound to Print	
Publishing Final Copies	
Punctuation	
Recalling Sight Words	
Rereading Own Writing	
Use of Lines	
Using Classroom Resources	

Mini-Lessons Class Checklist
Grade 3 through Grade 5

Directions: Record the date(s) the following skills are taught.

Skill	Date(s)
Considering Purpose and Potential Audience	
Deciding on a Genre	
Deciding on a Topic	
Developing and Using a Personal Word Bank	
Drafting Writing	
Expressing Ideas	
Finding the Apostrophe	
Grammar	
Helping a Friend Revise	
How to Revise	
How to Transition Ideas	
Incorporating Technology in Composing	
Publishing Final Copies	
Punctuation	
Recalling Sight Words	
Rereading Own Writing for Possible Revisions	
Self-Correcting Spelling	
Using Classroom Resources	

Appendix C

Mini-Lessons Class Checklist

Grade 6 through Grade 8

Directions: Record the date(s) the following skills are taught.

Skill	Date(s)
Considering Purpose and Potential Audience	
Deciding on a Genre	
Deciding on a Topic	
Developing and Using a Personal Word Bank	
Drafting Writing	
Expressing Ideas	
Finding the Apostrophe	
Grammar	
Helping a Friend Revise	
How to Revise	
How to Transition Ideas	
Incorporating Technology in Composing	
Publishing Final Copies	
Punctuation	
Recalling Sight Words	
Rereading Own Writing for Possible Revisions	
Self-Correcting Spelling	
Using Classroom Resources	

Appendix C

Lesson Plan for Writer's Workshop Mini-Lesson

Standard/Strategy

Materials

Instruction

Connection to previous mini-lesson or writing:

Discussion of application of mini-lesson:

Developmental Continuum Chart

Description of Development	Language	Spelling	Writing	Reading
Emergent (PreK-Mid 1) (Becomes aware of formal function) — *Alphabet →*	Babbling to sentences	Random scribbles (no direction)	Random scribbles	Develops phonemic awareness
	Monologue to Dialogue	Wavy marks (imitates cursive)	Pretends to write (left to right)	Pretends to read (non-directional, non-unit)
	Begins use of "adult-like" language	Letter-like production	Draws picture to tell story	Pretends to read (left to right)
	Random play with rhymes	Writes random letters of alphabet	Combines writing and drawing	Attention to printed letters
		Spells with initial consonant (k=cold, j=drip)	Names objects	Attention to written words
	Working vocabulary of 2,500–5,000 base meanings		Labels picture	Knows alphabet and letter sounds
	Uses imaginative talk/language		Inventory (I like, I love) egocentric	Recognizes some familiar words (names, signs)
Beginning (K-Mid 2)		Represents nearly all phonemes	↕	Accurately voice points in memorized text
	Sustained talk (complex sentences/"story language")	Consonant represents each syllable	Short, simple sentences	Says one syllable while pointing to each word (Twinkle, twinkle)
	Working vocabulary of 4,000–8,000 base meanings	Asks - "how is ____ spelled?"	Inventory + Description (I like, I love because...) Series of simple sentences Self and family/personal experience	Concept of Word (understands "word" is group of letters sounded by white space; now understands multiple syllables can make one word)
	Understands use of synonyms (big/large)	Represents vowel phoneme	↕	Segments words in sentences
	Understands use of antonyms (big/small)	More accurate with beginning consonant phonemes, ending consonant phonemes		Reads aloud, finger points
		Uses obvious strategies to attempt spellings (c=sea, u=you)	Writing stands alone to convey message	Sight vocabulary increases

Developmental Continuum Chart (cont.)

Description of Development	Language	Spelling	Writing	Reading
		Substitutes closest long vowel sound for short vowel (lag=leg)	Inventory + Description (I like, I love...) Topics: Family, school, friends. Considers audience	Comprehension at 80% or above
		Alphabetic, moves across word, phoneme by phoneme	Stronger evidence of punctuation, capitalization knowledge	Rereads familiar stories
Transitional (1–Mid 4)		Partial conventions based on reading experience	Description of personal interest (My dog barks at squirrels.)	Makes connections across reading experiences
	Use of complex language in both written and oral form	Uses vowel unit "chunks" to help in attempts	↕	Understands onset and rime aids in word reading (chunks)
Pattern	Vocabulary knowledge increases	Similar strategies used in spelling attempts and in reading	Uses more textual features (narrative/expository)	Word-by-word reading
	Working vocabulary of 6,700–12,200 base meanings	Omits silent letters and preconsonant nasals (mp, nt)	Writes with a variety of purposes and genres	Self-monitors/self-corrects based on one or more cues (semantic, orthographic, syntactic)
		Uses knowledge of other words to help attempts (payper=paper)	Greater word choice Logical order in composition (beginning, middle, end)	Phrase-by-phrase reading (some fluency)
		Sizeable sight vocabulary	Consistently organized, fluent writing	Automatic word recognition
		Can proofread own work for misspellings	Revises and edits on own	Variety of reading styles
		Correct knowledge of long vowel markers	Self-selects variety of topics and audiences	

Developmental Continuum Chart (cont.)

Description of Development	Language	Spelling	Writing	Reading
Intermediate and Advanced (3–adult)		Less errors at syllable juncture	Tries styles and genres	Reads faster silently
		Correctly doubles consonant before adding ending	Note taking/outlining	Self-monitors for comprehension
		Includes silent letters and preconsonant nasals (mp, nt)		
		Uses meaning layer to provide information		
		Syllables and affixes correct		
		Automaticity apparent		
	Eventually reaching working knowledge of 30,000–200,000+ words	Understanding of relationships between words/spellings due to meaning (sign/signature)		

Meaning →

Contents of the Digital Resources

Word Study

Page Number	Title	Filename
251	File Folder Pocket Instructions	folderpocket.pdf
252	BINGO Board	bingo.pdf
253	Blends and Digraphs List	blendlist.pdf
254	Basketball Hoops	hoops.pdf
255	Basketballs	basketballs.pdf
256	Who Belongs Together?	belongs.pdf
257	Who Belongs Together? Answer Key	belongans.pdf
258	Hop to It! Note Cards	hoptoit.pdf
259	The Magic of E	magice.pdf
260	Presto Wands	presto.pdf
261	Build a Word Sample List	buildword.pdf
262–263	Mix and Match Compound Pairs	mixcompound.pdf
264	Mix and Match Vocabulary	mixvocab.pdf
265	Compound Pairs	compoundpair.pdf
266	Top 100 High-Frequency Words	hfwords.pdf
267	Vowel House Template	vowelhouse.pdf
268	Vowel Alternations List	vowelalt.pdf
269	Circus Rings	circusring.pdf
270	Circus Animals	circusani.pdf
271	Circus Performers	circperform.pdf
272	Circus Words	circword.pdf
273–274	Quiet Letters Cards	quietlet.pdf
275	Football Jersey	jersey.pdf
276	Football Field	football.pdf
277	Automobiles	automobiles.pdf
278	Awesome Automobile Words	awesome.pdf
279	Double Consonant Cards	consonant.pdf
280	Meatballs Template	meatballs.pdf
281	VCV and VCCV Word Suggestions	vccv.pdf
282	Doubled or Dropped Word List	doubled.pdf
283	Arrow Template	arrow.pdf
284	Ant Template	anttemp.pdf
285–286	Pancake Compounds	pancake.pdf
287	Comparatives and Superlatives List	comparative.pdf
288	Pear Template	pear.pdf
289	Word Pairs	wordpairs.pdf
290	Top Hat Template	tophat.pdf
291	Hit or Miss Chart	hitmiss.pdf
292	Vocabulary Word Template	vocabtemp.pdf
293	Make-a-Word Cards	makeword.pdf
294	Word Cards	wordcard.pdf
295	Explanation Signs	explanation.pdf
296	Bases and Affixes	baseaffix.pdf
297	Greek and Latin Bases	greek.pdf
298–299	Word Hunt Cards	hunt.pdf
300	Synonyms and Antonyms	synant.pdf
301	Base Template	basetemp.pdf
302–303	Base Examples	baseexamp.pdf
download	What If?	whatif.pdf

Word Study *(cont.)*

Page Number	Title	Filename
download	All Together Now	alltogether.pdf
download	Monkeys in the Trees	monkeytree.pdf
download	Monkeys	monkeys.pdf
download	Under Construction	construction.pdf
download	Bulldozer	bulldozer.pdf
download	Caution Tape	cautiontape.pdf
download	Dirt Piles	dirtpiles.pdf
download	Go Team!	goteam.pdf
download	Footballs	footballs.pdf
download	Helmets	helmets.pdf
download	Digging In	digging.pdf
download	Excavators	excavator.pdf
download	Hey! Let's Play in the Hay!	hayplay.pdf
download	Haystacks	haystacks.pdf
download	Barns	barns.pdf
download	Hanging Out Together	hangingtogether.pdf
download	Dipthong Cards	dipthongcard.pdf
download	Letter Cards	lettercard.pdf
download	Shhhh! Fishing in Progress	fishprogress.pdf
download	Fish	fish.pdf
download	Letter Squares	lettersquare.pdf
download	Cube It	cubeit.pdf
download	Cube	cubetemp.pdf
download	Uh…How Is that Spelled?	uhspelled.pdf
download	How Is That Spelled? Signs	spelledsigns.pdf
download	Dear Deer	deardeer.pdf
download	Homophone Cards	homophonecard.pdf
download	Family Tree	familytree.pdf
download	Trees	treetemp.pdf
download	Greek and Latin Bases	greek.pdf
download	Play Ball!	playball.pdf
download	Baseball Mitts	mitttemp.pdf
download	Baseballs	battemp.pdf
download	Consonant Alternations List	consonantlist.pdf
download	Soak It Up!	soakup.pdf
download	Sponges	spongetemp.pdf
download	Meet the Relatives	meetrel.pdf
download	Robot Family	robotfam.pdf
download	Robot Words	robotword.pdf

Appendix D

Reading

Page Number	Title	Filename
304	Bookmark Template	bookmark.pdf
305	The Five Finger Rule	fivefinger.pdf
306	Long Versus Short Vowel Sound	longshort.pdf
307	Oral Reading Record Form	oralrecord.pdf
308	Sample Completed Oral Reading Record	oralsample.pdf
309	Record of Analysis of Oral Reading	recanalysis.pdf
310	Sample Record of Analysis of Oral Reading	sampleana.pdf
311	Class Oral Reading Record Form	classoral.pdf
312	Compare and Contrast Template	comparetemp.pdf
313	Vocabulary Boxes Chart	vocabbox.pdf
314	My Independent Reading Log	independent.pdf
315	Shared Reading Lesson Plan Template	shareread.pdf
316	Lesson Plan Template for Meeting with Literature Circles	lessonlit.pdf
317	Literature Circle Reading Log	litlog.pdf
318	Literature Circle Self-Assessment Chart	litself.pdf
319	Lesson Plan Template for Guided Reading	guidedread.pdf
download	Look Around the Room	lookroom.pdf
download	Rhyme with Text Words	rhymewords.pdf
download	Analyzing Images for Details.	analyzephoto.pdf
download	Concepts About Print	conprint.pdf
download	Circle the Pattern	circlepat.pdf
download	Retell the Story	retellstory.pdf
download	Create a Graphic Representation	graphicrep.pdf
download	Cloze Procedure	cloze.pdf
download	Identifying Author and Illustrator	authorillus.pdf
download	Connecting to Writing	connectwrite.pdf
download	Book-Based Art	bookart.pdf
download	Compare and Contrast	comparecontrast.pdf
download	Fluency and Expression	fluencyexpress.pdf
download	Summarizing	summarizing.pdf
download	5 Ws & How Questions	whow.pdf
download	Table of Contents, Glossary, and Index	tablecontents.pdf
download	Word Analysis	wordanalysis.pdf
download	Anticipation Guide	anticipation.pdf
download	Character Attributes	characattributes.pdf
download	Character Attributes Template	attributestemp.pdf
download	New Words	newwords.pdf
download	Ordering Story Events	storyevents.pdf
download	Major vs. Minor Details	majorminor.pdf
download	Personal Project	personalproject.pdf
download	Posing Questions	posingquest.pdf
download	Predicting What's Next	predicting.pdf

Appendix D

Writing

Page Number	Title	Filename
320	Status of the Class	status.pdf
321	Computer Composing	compcomp.pdf
322	Grammar List	grammar.pdf
323	Paragraph Outline	paraout.pdf
324	Revision Marks Chart	revision.pdf
325	Compound Sentences	compsent.pdf
326	Which Word Is Best?	whichword.pdf
327	Early Literacy Skills Class Checklist	earlylit.pdf
328	Individual Record Sheet for Writing (K–2)	writingk2.pdf
329	My Writing Record Sheet (3–5)	writereck2.pdf
330	Individual Record Sheet for Writing (3–5)	writing35.pdf
331	Individual Record Sheet for Writing (6–8)	writing68.pdf
332	My Writing Record Sheet (6–8)	writerec68.pdf
333	Mini-Lessons Class Checklist (K–2)	minik2.pdf
334	Mini-Lessons Class Checklist (3–5)	mini35.pdf
335	Mini-Lessons Class Checklist (6–8)	mini68.pdf
336	Lesson Plan for Writer's Workshop Mini-Lesson	workshop.pdf
337–339	The Developmental Continuum Chart	continuum.pdf
download	Considering Audience	considering.pdf
download	Correct Formation of Letters	correctform.pdf
download	Differences Between Genres (four-day lesson)	diffgenres.pdf
download	Drawing versus Writing	drawwrite.pdf
download	Helping a Buddy Edit	helpbuddy.pdf
download	Publishing	publishing.pdf
download	Deciding on a Genre (five-day lesson)	decidegenre.pdf
download	Developing and Using a Personal Word Bank	wordbank.pdf
download	Grammar Fundamentals	grammarfund.pdf
download	Grammar Fundamentals Cards	fundcards.pdf
download	Publishing Final Copies	pubfinal.pdf
download	Rereading Writing for Possible Revisions	rereading.pdf
download	Revisions Make the Difference	revdifference.pdf
download	Revision Marks Chart	revisionmarks.pdf
download	Crafting Texts: Informational	craftinform.pdf
download	Crafting Texts: Narrative	craftnarr.pdf
download	Crafting Texts: Poetry	craftpoetry.pdf
download	Cultivating a Personal Word Bank	cultivateword.pdf
download	Determining a Topic	determine.pdf
download	Homophones	homophones.pdf
download	Misused Word Cards	misusedword.pdf
download	Putting it all Together	puttogether.pdf
download	Recalling Familiar Words	familiarwords.pdf
download	15-by-15 Grid	grid.pdf
download	Transitions Make the Difference	transitionsdiff.pdf
download	Transition Categories	transitionscat.pdf
download	Using Correct Capitalization	correctcaps.pdf
download	Utilizing Classroom Resources	classroomres.pdf
download	Interesting Pictures	intpics.pdf
download	Correlation to the Standards	standards.pdf

Notes